LORIMER

LORIMER

His Gazetteer and Britain's Pursuit of Knowledge

ALAN DILLON

Medina Publishing

First published in 2024 by Medina Publishing Ltd
50 High Street
Cowes
Isle of Wight
PO31 7RR

www.medinapublishing.com

Printed and bound by Interak, Poland

ISBN (Hardback): 978-1-911487-84-5

CIP data: A catalogue record for this book is available at the British Library.

Contents

List of Illustrations

p.6: The newly-built political agency in Manamah, considered to be one of the best buildings in the Bahraini capital at the time. (Open government licence)

The political agency and residence in Muscat alongside the Sultan's palace. (Open government licence)

p.7: Bushire coastline, known locally by British officials and expatriates as 'the colony'. (Open government licence)

Political residency and RIMS *Comet*. The presence of both was a constant irritant with the Ottoman authorities. (Open government licence)

p.8: Bushire residency in Kuti, one of the town's four principal wards. (Open government licence)

Troops on parade at Rishehr garrison, Bushire. Many would later form part of Lorimer's funeral precession. (Open government licence)

North West Frontier
Province 1903
Chitral
Kashmir
Afghanistan
To Kabul
Malakand
Durand Line
Mardan
Hazara
Jamrud
Peshawar
Khyber
Kurram
Toru Sar
Kohat
Khushalgarh
Thal
Khwarra Plain
Northern Waziristan
Mianwali
Kabul Khel
Indus River
Miran Shah
Kaitu Valley
Punjab
Sheranni
Tori Khel
Tochi Valley
To Jhelum
Mohmit Khel
Bannu
Maizur
Nasran
Wanna
Southern Waziristan
Dera Ismail Khan
Shahpur
Biluchistan
10 0 20 40 60 80 100 120 Miles
To Lahore
10 0 50 100 150 200 Kilometres

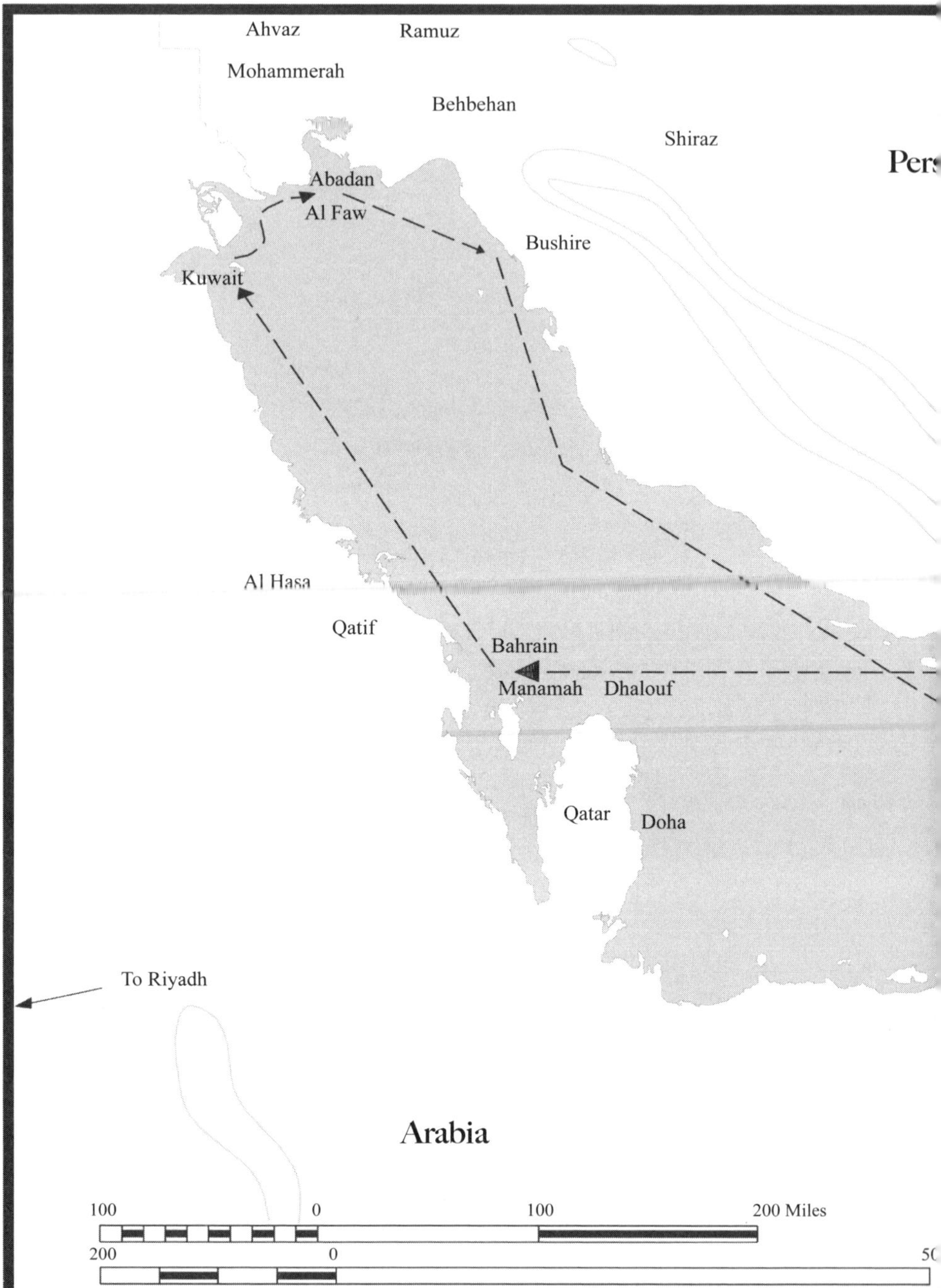
Ahvaz
Ramuz
Mohammerah
Behbehan
Shiraz
Pers
Abadan
Al Faw
Bushire
Kuwait
Al Hasa
Qatif
Bahrain
Manamah
Dhalouf
Qatar
Doha
To Riyadh
Arabia
100
0
100
200 Miles
200
0

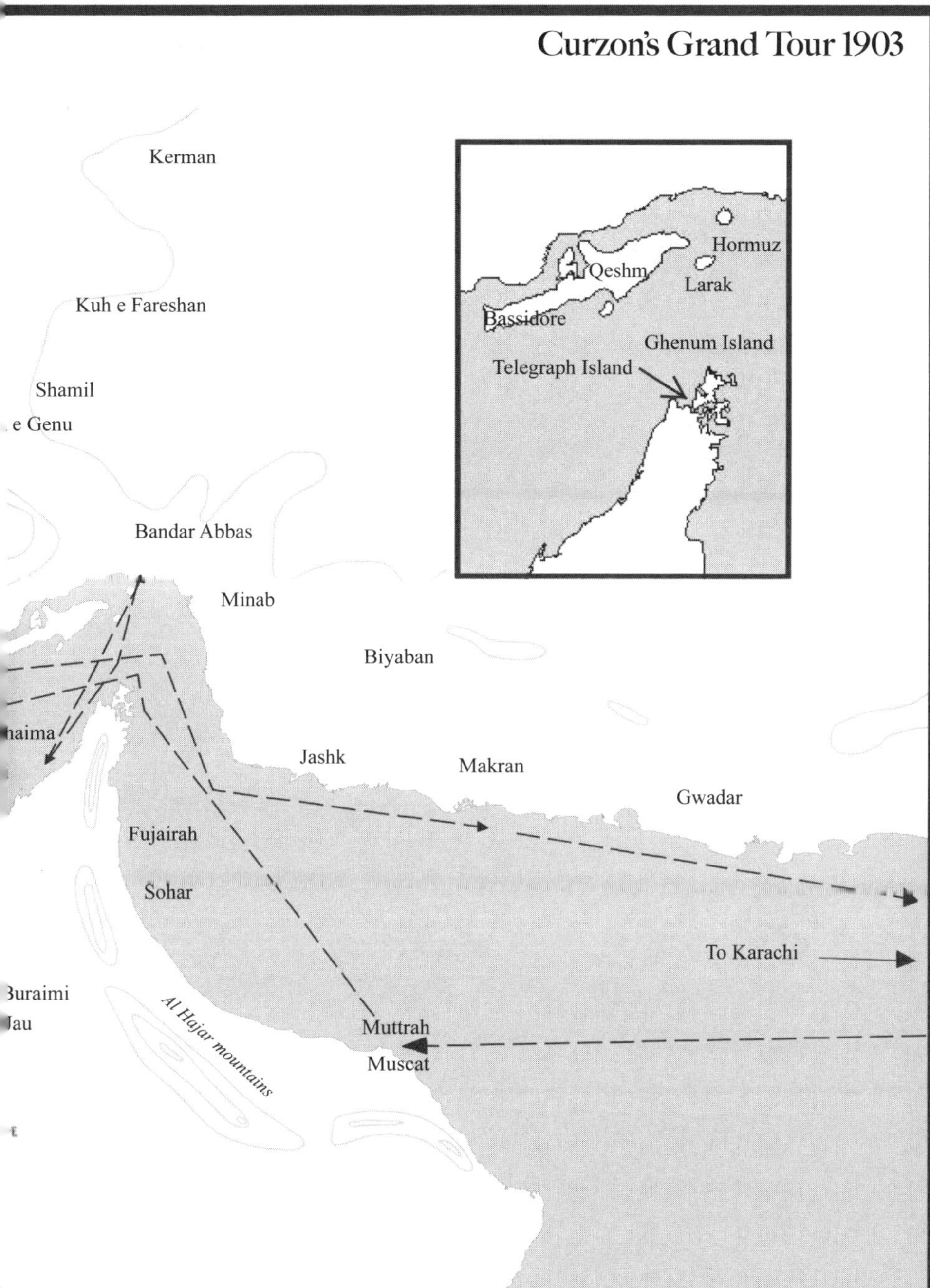

Curzon's Grand Tour 1903
Kerman
Kuh e Fareshan
Shamil
e Genu
Bandar Abbas
Minab
Biyaban
haima
Jashk
Makran
Gwadar
Fujairah
Sohar
To Karachi
Buraimi
Jau
Al Hajar mountains
Muttrah
Muscat
Hormuz
Qeshm
Larak
Bassidore
Ghenum Island
Telegraph Island

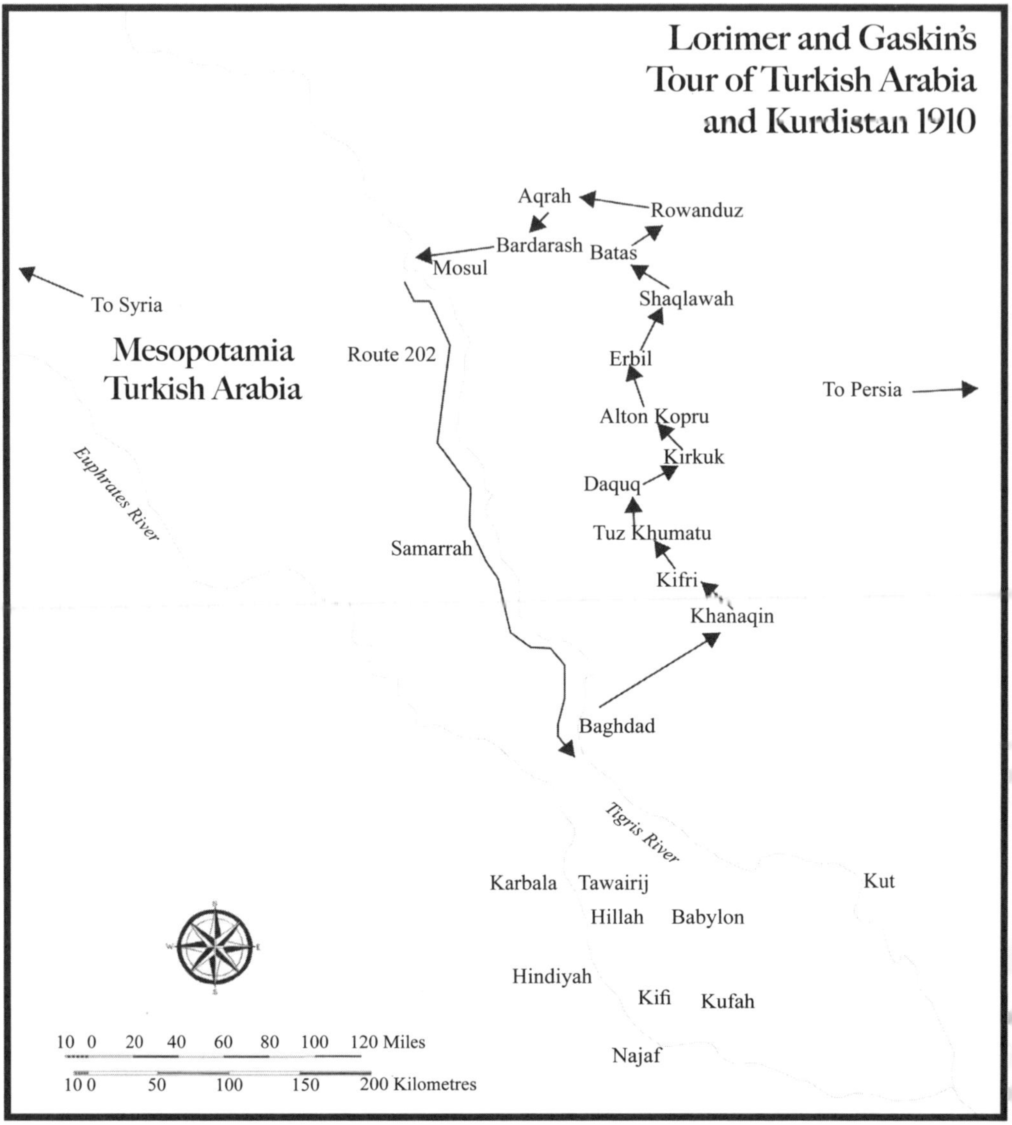
Lorimer and Gaskin's
Tour of Turkish Arabia
and Kurdistan 1910
Aqrah
Rowanduz
Bardarash
Batas
Mosul
To Syria
Shaqlawah
Mesopotamia
Turkish Arabia
Route 202
Erbil
To Persia
Alton Kopru
Kirkuk
Euphrates River
Daquq
Tuz Khumatu
Samarrah
Kifri
Khanaqin
Baghdad
Tigris River
Karbala
Tawairij
Kut
Hillah
Babylon
Hindiyah
Kifi
Kufah
Najaf
10 0 20 40 60 80 100 120 Miles
10 0 50 100 150 200 Kilometres

Author's Note

Stylistic Conventions

Within the spirit of the gazetteer, I should have complied with Lorimer's system of transliteration even though it has long fallen out from use. A full explanation of his approach can be found in Volume One, Part Two, Appendix S. Although I have mostly used his spelling, there are a few exceptions, when quoting directly or where there is a more familiar English version. I have also mostly omitted diacritical accents, something that Lorimer and others would have undoubtedly frowned upon. Names of places in India, Iraq, Iran, Pakistan and Turkey have been given as they were known before 1946. All errors are unintentional and are my own.

Acknowledgements

I would have been amiss if I did not thank my wife, Nichola for her patience (again), continued interest (feigned or otherwise) and full support (foolishly) after gifting me a notebook embossed with 'Book Two' on its front cover. I am not sure what else she expected me to do with it, other than do as the title suggested. I must also add my daughters, Bethany and Lauren, to this shortlist for either humouring me or having the knack of sourcing publications and academic papers when my own efforts failed me.

I am grateful to Peter Harrigan at Medina Publishing who, after I finished writing *Captain Shakespear*, asked if there was any unfinished business that I still felt needed to be shared. The unfinished business was the gazetteer and of course, Shakespear's friend, Lorimer.

I must also thank Lorimer's great-grandson, Sir John Gordon, and the wider Lorimer family for their full support and assistance in helping me tell the story. The bundle of correspondence was critical in providing much-needed colour and exposing the man rather than the monochrome official.

It would be more appropriate for me to give a Bravo Zulu (BZ) to Wakeel Tariq Jameay from the Royal Navy of Oman for his work in translating my scribbles into respectable maps.

Lastly, I am indebted to Professor Ali Ansari and Doctor Stuart Horsman for keeping me on the straight and narrow with their comments, observations and encouragement despite their own heavy workloads. Stuart's agreement to offer an editorial eye was particularly welcomed, an act he managed to achieve whilst carrying out his own research on another great regional warrior-scholar, Sir John Malcolm.

Foreword

I WAS NAMED AFTER MY GREAT-GRANDFATHER, John Gordon Lorimer, born some 48 years after his untimely death in Bushire, Persia. Within the Lorimer family, he had near-legendary status. In the family flat in Edinburgh, his library occupied pride of place. I remember his picture on the wall: his stern face gazing out at me, medals on chest, sword at side, pince-nez on nose. I was aware of some of his exploits and achievements, but I did not know the details.

It was my familial connection to the Middle East that probably led me to study Arabic and Islamic Studies at Cambridge University. There I discovered that JGL (as we called him) was recognised far beyond the family. On hearing my name for the first time, Dr Martin Hines, my supervisor in Arabic, asked "are you any relation to *the* JG Lorimer?" On being told that I was his great-grandson, Dr Hines replied; "Oh good. We expect great things of you!" However, I did not follow JGL into a diplomatic career, serving for nearly 40 years in the British Army instead. But I did unintentionally follow in JGL's footsteps, as I soldiered frequently in Pakistan and Afghanistan, Kuwait, Bahrain, Iraq and throughout the wider Middle East. To my regret, I never got the chance to visit Iran, but that remains an aspiration, particularly to Bushire, where JGL is buried.

In 2007, I was the Commander of the British Task Force in Helmand, Southern Afghanistan. During that long, hot summer of fighting, I used JGL's personal copy of his Waziri-Pushto dictionary and grammar to help me learn more about the culture and language of the local population. Ten years later, when spending increasingly more time in the Arabian Peninsula, I started to refer more and more to the gazetteer, as I researched many of the extraordinary places that I was visiting. Indeed, in 2018, on hearing of my appointment as the United Kingdom's Defence Senior Advisor Middle East, the King of Bahrain, His Majesty King Hamad bin 'Isa Al Khalifa, said "Of course, you should have that appointment: *maktoob* (it is written)". His Majesty clearly thought that JGL's extensive knowledge, renowned expertise and love of the region was in the Lorimer blood. I spent over three years in that role and sincerely hope I did not disappoint either His Majesty or JGL.

My favourite memory of seeing the gazetteer 'in action' comes from the United Arab Emirates. Using one of the genealogical family trees from an original version of the gazetteer held in the British Embassy in Abu Dhabi (still marked Secret), I helped an eminent sheikh locate his grandfather and other ancestors on the 100-year-old document. Tears rolled down the cheeks of this wonderful old gentleman as he saw the connections materialise and in print for the first time. He had never seen his ancient lineage portrayed in such a manner and he was almost overwhelmed by its significance to him and his sons and grandsons, who were also present.

I first met Alan Dillon in early 2019 when I was visiting Oman. He accompanied me to Musandam, Oman's most northern point, where we exchanged tales of JGL and his friend, fellow political officer Captain William Shakespear, both of whom had also passed through the rugged peninsula. Alan's portrait of JGL is a task that I thought I might tackle in retirement. I am hugely relieved that it was Alan who took on the challenge, because he has done a far better job than I would have. This book has all the hallmarks of patient and in-depth research, detailed and expert analysis underpinned by regional and historical knowledge. Alan tracks JGL from his childhood in the bosom of a most remarkable Scottish family – his parents and siblings were all exceptionally bright, well read, enquiring, multi-lingual and polymaths. Alan then leads us through JGL's early career in the Indian Civil Service on the North West frontier of the British empire; his role during Lord Curzon's cruise of the Gulf in 1903; and finally, his successive special duties that would ultimately result in the creation of the monumental gazetteer.

On behalf of the family, I cannot thank Alan enough. We are delighted to see JGL's life formally recorded for posterity. There is no doubt that he was a remarkable man, from a remarkable era.

Lieutenant General Sir John Gordon Lorimer KCB DSO MBE

Prologue

HMS *Cyclamen* was hardly a Dreadnaught or the pride of the Royal Navy's fleet. Displacing just a little over twelve hundred tons, she boasted a pitiful main armament in contrast to the warship behemoth, just two four-inch guns, one forward and one aft. *Cyclamen* and her sister *Arabis*-class ships might not have fared well in the open seas protecting the British empire's maritime trade routes, but they were ideal for instilling a sense of calm in warmer, shallower waters. In the early 1920s, the twin-funnelled sloop of war was one of several posted to the East Indies Station operating as part of the Royal Navy's Gulf Squadron. The squadron's primary mission was a longstanding one: to patrol the Gulf Sea, Gulf of Oman and the Arabian Sea to interdict stateless or unprotected dhows smuggling guns or slaves. In certain circumstances, it also served as an extension of the government of India's regional political residency network, reinforcing soft power with gunboat diplomacy through the threat, and sometimes use, of its hard power.

On 5 June 1923, *Cyclamen* slipped away from the Gulf Squadron's base in Henjam Island off the southern coast of Persia. A zigzag course was plotted that would take her to familiar waypoints, passing Khor al Sham, Sharjah, Abu Musa Island, Abu Dhabi and Zirku Island. Twelve days later, she held station off the coast of Manamah, Bahrain. She arrived at the island sheikhdom at a particularly turbulent time. Just a month before her arrival, Sheikh Hamad ibn Isa Al Khalifa had proclaimed himself as the island's *de facto* ruler, having assumed the position following the forced abdication of his father, Sheikh Isa. It was a move that was supported by the British government as the succession impacted little on its national and imperial interests, but would, it hoped, ensure long-term stability on the island.

But as with any sudden change in power, it was inevitable that there would be those who would look to test the strength of the new sheikh's suzerainty. It was also not unfamiliar to see such a challenge to come from an aggrieved relative or contender, although Sheikh Hamad's first internal trial was not to come from within the family. On 19 June, he ordered the arrest of Ahmed Al Dosairi, head of the powerful Dowasir tribe after his tribesmen had attacked some Baharinah pearl divers.[1] Disturbed by events, not least because the Dowasir had never recognised the ruling sheikh of Bahrain's rule, Major Clive Kirkpatrick Daly, the resident British political agent in Bahrain, immediately reported developments to his senior, Stuart George Knox, the acting political resident based in Bushire.[2] Daly's account also included a recommendation that should the Dowasir continue to seek trouble, a light bombardment of their settlement in Budaiyeh, courtesy of *Cyclamen*'s main guns, might be sufficient to discourage any further dissent.[3] If thought appropriate, given the Royal Navy's interference into what was essentially an internal dispute, Daly was confident that Hamad's approval in writing could be obtained before any punitive action was taken.[4] As the region's protector and security guarantor, Knox concurred with Daly's recommended use of British military force. But he was also clear that there was to be no immediate light bombardment or rounds fired overhead, as either action required explicit approval from the government of India, something that could not be secured at such short notice.[5]

Days later, after Daly and Knox's reports finally landed in Whitehall, Victor Cavendish, the Duke of Devonshire and secretary of state in the Colonial Office, challenged the government of India's regional representative's proposed use of force, demanding a more convincing argument to justify the potential course of action.[6] Cavendish's concern centred on the belief that the navy's intended target, Budaiyeh, was a variation of the spelling of Ras Al Bidya, which was little more than a 'low sandy promontory with tufts of grass'.[7] The latter was in fact over a hundred miles north-west in Al Hasa, territory under the control of Ibn Sa'ud, the legitimate 'ruler of Najd, El Hassa, Qatif and Jubail, and the towns and ports belonging to them…', territory which fell under Cavendish's ministerial remit.[8] It was left to the India Office to reply to its geographically challenged Colonial Office counterpart, simply done by referring the duke to 'pages 324, 391, and 395, of Volume II, of Lorimer's gazetteer of the Persian Gulf, from which it will be seen that Budaiyeh is situated on the North West of the island of Bahrein'.[9] The brief, almost condescending letter continued 'in these circumstances Viscount Peel [secretary of state for India] assumes that the Duke of Devonshire will see no objection to leaving the matter in the hands of the Political Resident at Bushire and the Government of India'.[10] Embarrassed by its apparent lack of regional knowledge, the duke's ministry ceded to the wisdom of the political resident and agent, subsequently giving 'no objection to such measures'.[11]

Cyclamen remained on duty in Bahrain until 4 July and in the wider vicinity until early January 1924, steaming north up the coastline to Basrah and south through the Strait of Hormuz to Muscat. It returned to Bahrain in late July, October and November as much as a visual reminder of Britain's expectation for calm on the island as it was to champion Sheikh Hamad. Despite the ship's ample supply of gunpowder and ammunition, *Cyclamen*'s captain would not be called upon that year to close up his gun crews to project the British empire's influence in the Gulf by force.

Introduction

DOES TRADE FOLLOW THE FLAG or does diplomacy flourish where commerce already exists? In the case of the British and their relationships with the Gulf Arabs, it could easily be perceived to be the latter. In 1646, the English or Honourable East India Company (EIC) was the first British entity to establish itself in the Arabian Peninsula. Its first trade agreement, signed with Imam Nasir bin Murshid Al Ya'rubi of Muscat, allowed the company to trade with his people in Sohar.[12] The coastal town was more of a waypoint than a main destination for commerce as the trading body did not establish a permanent presence in the Gulf until the early 1700s. Despite various attempts since the 1620s to maintain a factory, or to be exact, a warehouse in Bandar Abbas to trade Persian silk, wool and spices for English linen and tin, overseen by a factor or company agent, it was not until 1728 that an agency was firmly established in Basrah to facilitate trade into Mesopotamia. A residency in Bushire followed in 1763, a designation given to denote its primary role in overseeing all commerce in the Gulf, one that it would keep until its duties were reallocated in 1946 and its operations wound down.

By the turn of the nineteenth century, two more British agencies were founded to facilitate trade, Baghdad in 1766 and Muscat in 1800. In 1839, the EIC's next and last factor was despatched to oversee trade in Mosul. Further agencies were established in Persian Makran or Gwadur in 1863, Karbala in 1870 and Muhammerah (Arabistan) in 1890, but with different remits and responsibilities, functioning as political agencies under the government of India's authority rather than the now defunct EIC's. Alongside the agencies, the EIC also established trading posts, with local or 'native' agents rather than British factors representing their affairs. In 1829, both Sharjah and Bahrain were added to the trading network, with Bandar Lingeh following a year later. They too, would eventually come under the government of India's control. As the nineteenth century made way for its successor, in 1899, another local agent was established in Kuwait and a year later, a British agent finally returned to Bandar Abbas.

As early as the 1660s, the EIC's trading functions had already expanded to include political ones, securing the confidence of the local rulers and merchants, negotiating preferable tariffs and obtaining safety guarantees, both for their people and their merchandise. But it also found itself having to compete for trade and relationships against its adversaries, the Dutch *Vereenigde Oostindische Compagnie* as well as the *Compagnie Française pour le Commerce des Indes Orientales*, at times to the point of insolvency, at others, facing physical destruction by their cannon.

Enter the twentieth century, and having seemingly seen off its competitors, Britain was by far the most prominent trading power in the region. Its placement of agencies along the Persian coastline and caravan routes in the hinterland reflected the considerable commercial opportunities that the country offered, with primacy on political and diplomatic affairs in the hands of the British legation in Tehran. The smaller number of establishments along the Arabian Gulf coast and for the most part, the delegation of duties to local, rather than British agents, however, was indicative of the lack of commodities and opportunities that Arabia had to offer in comparison. Indeed, in the age before oil, the only global industry that Arabia had to offer was pearling. Whereas the exploration for oil in Arabistan in the early 1900s by the British D'Arcy Oil Company was given minimal coverage by Lorimer, pearling was subject to a seventy-four-page appendix and animated in one of only two maps attached to the gazetteer, showing the various pearl banks scattered along the Arabian and Persian coastlines.

Despite Britain's regional prominence, that did not automatically translate into the monopoly on trade or relations. With the safety of the seas ensured by the Royal Navy, land-side Britain's agents had to contend with the ever presence of the Ottoman Turks, the Dutch and the French, as well as the Russians, Austro-Hungarians, Americans, Belgians, Swedes and Norwegians, all of whom sought to establish their own permanent trade links. And as their commercial presence increased, their agents' remits also expanded to include consular and political duties as their own nationals followed the flow of commerce to set up small expatriate communities.

So, if the flag did follow trade to Arabia, could the same be said of colonial knowledge and imperial intelligence? Arguably not. At the turn of the twentieth century, very little was known of Arabia in Britain or in wider Europe outside the commercial transactions and political dynamics that dominated the Gulf littoral. Beyond the efforts of a few intrepid British officials who dared to travel outside the safety of their agencies, the vast desert interior was unknown, and with just a few exceptions, mostly untouched by academia and explorers. It was this deficit, alongside the perceived infringement on British interests and investment, why the government of India introduced its forward policy, looking beyond the narrow and immediate field of profit to understand more about Arabia and its interior, expanding its network of political officers to explore, establish and expand its relationships and appreciation of the communities that they lived within and beyond. With so much responsibility placed on so few hardy officials, it is surprising that so little is known about those who played a considerable role in the history of the region.

In 1991, Professor Paul Rich published *Creating the Arabian Gulf: The British Raj and the invasions of the Gulf.* It was a serious attempt to look beyond superficial accounts of the history of the British in the Gulf by focusing on the political officers who served there. He argued that rather than being products of the British Raj, manufactured and manipulated at their whim, the amirs, emirs, sheikhs, kings and sultans instead owed their being to a small number of British political agents who served in the region, who championed, endorsed, protected and ultimately reinforced their hosts' legitimacy. Such validations, in turn, provided a mandate for other foreign powers to recognise the various rulers, not least so they could attempt to align them with their own governments' regional ambitions. After Rich had carried out his extensive research on the cohort of political officers who had served in the Gulf, he observed the dearth of biographies of key officials, including Lewis Pelly and David Robert Ross, both of whom were political residents in Bushire in the mid- and late-nineteenth century. Distinction was also given to Gerald de Gaury, who served as the political agent in Kuwait in the late 1930s. Rich lastly made the case that more needed to be known about two other prominent political officers, the Lorimer brothers, the elder John Gordon and sibling David Lockhart Robertson.

Some decades after Rich's research, Dr James Onley's *The Arabian Frontier of the British Raj; Merchants, Rulers and the British in the Nineteenth-Century Gulf* offered a slightly different interpretation. Rather than the agents and residents from the government of India's Political Department being the master architects of the Gulf monarchies, he believed that it was the work of their predecessors, the local agents from long-established Arab, Persian and Indian merchant families who had laid the foundations of support to these monarchies. In many ways, both are right, but arguably, equal recognition must also be given to the *Gazetteer of the Persian Gulf* for the role that it too, would eventually play in shaping the modern Arabian Gulf and affirming legitimacy. And although both Rich and Onley answer the questions to who and when, we also need to understand the answers to why, what and how to fully appreciate the role of the British in the Gulf. Why was the gazetteer commissioned? What was motivation behind it, both at a personal and political level? And how was this information gathered and understood to become colonial knowledge and imperial intelligence? In attempting to answer these additional leading questions, I have also identified the motivations behind the various obstacles and frustrations that were introduced to hinder that pursuit.

Although synonymous with the Gulf, like every other political officer, Lorimer started his career in India, spending his first eleven years of Crown service at its northern frontier near Afghanistan. He only came to the attention of the viceroy, Lord Curzon, after he had challenged policy recommendations being devised by his political and military seniors, policies which would, he believed, destabilise rather than strengthen the border region. Lorimer's confidence, intelligence and foresight intrigued Curzon, who had his own ideas about shaking up the governance of India. It was not long before the outspoken official was brought closer to the viceroy and his key foreign policy adviser, Louis Dane, to become one of the viceroy's chosen few. The Arabian Gulf too, only really came to the attention of the government of India under Curzon's tenure after decades of insignificance. His persistence in wanting to both visit and to understand the Gulf was despite a longstanding reluctance in the British government and the Foreign Office in particular, to acknowledge Arabia's very presence, or at the very least, the people who lived therein.

Curzon's first visit to the Gulf in 1889 had been cursory. His return fourteen years later, with Lorimer part of his entourage, was the most visible and highest-ranking visit yet to have been carried out by the British empire. As well as a clear statement of Britain's intent in the region, Curzon's grand tour also served as the precursor for Lorimer's similarly grand creation, *The Gazetteer of the Persian Gulf*. Now over a century old, the gazetteer has passed through three phases of relevance. At the turn of the twentieth century, it was designed to inform through knowledge, how to protect India's western flank. By the century's mid-point, it would become a valued, almost critical source of knowledge when identifying the winners in the race for oil and would be a crucial one when settling international borders at the century's end.

And yet, despite the gazetteer's undeniable provenance, the lack of interest in revisiting Britain's imperialist motives in India and beyond in what was once Persia and the Arabian Gulf, has left considerable gaps in knowledge of both Lorimer and his legacy. His work is without parallel in regional academia, referenced extensively and at length by scholars and historians alike, but is himself little more than a footnote or a brief and at times, inaccurate pen portrait. I must admit being equally at fault for taking Lorimer and the gazetteer for granted when I was researching for my biographical account of another political officer, Captain William Henry Irvine Shakespear. It was only in the latter stages of my research that I felt compelled to agree with Rich that more needed to be known and understood about the Lorimer brothers.

I can only offer a modest portrayal, rather than a weighty biography, of the elder brother who arguably influenced the future of the Arabian Peninsula more than any other British or foreign official, both as a history-teller and history-maker. It is a portrait that was sketched following a clean and strong outline provided by the India Office, Foreign Office and Cabinet Office archives in London and fine detail courtesy of the National Archives of India. And while the numerous official minutes, reports, telegrams and correspondence both official and demi-official helped produce a bold monochrome, the few faint patches of colour that I have been able to add were only possible because of the personal correspondence that the Lorimer family kindly shared with me.

Chapter 1

Terra Incognita

Arrogant, egotistic and self-centred. If such denigrations of character are to be believed, then one could hardly have expected anything less from George Nathanial Curzon, The Lord Curzon of Kedleston, viceroy and governor general of India from 1899 to 1905 when he penned 'Remember what books I have read, in order to save you the trouble of reading them, and be thankful'.[13] The far from modest declaration, including the quotation from Voltaire in Curzon's 1892 *Persia and The Persian Question*, formed part of the introduction to his substantial two-volume travelogue recording his six-month passage through Persia several years earlier as a *Times* correspondent.[14] His work was, he claimed, his attempt to fill the many gaps in knowledge of the country he had recently observed. It also directly challenged the notion held by some politicians that the world was comprised of living and dead nations, with Persia among the latter grouping. It was a call to arms, a demand for Britain's foreign policy with Persia, among others, to be proactive, consistent and strategic.[15]

Partly political, historiographical, archaeological and topographical, Curzon claimed to have placed in one place the past, present and future of the relationship between Britain and Persia. He briefly strayed beyond Persia's boundaries, believing that no political account would be complete without considering the Gulf, 'a quarter of the globe of similar physical configuration that has had so romantic and varying a past, that contains more diverse nationalities and clashing interests…'.[16] To this end, a single chapter was allocated to the vast 'country' as Curzon saw it, beginning with an account of his short stopover in Muscat before he sailed north-west up the stunning coastline, rounding Musandam headland and through the Strait of Hormuz, skirting the Trucial Coast, Qatar and Bahrain along the way. His journey ended at Al Faw, a port town on the mouth of the Shatt al Arab River, the most northerly point of his cruise, having exhausted recording anything he deemed to have been of significance. His experience of this other country was at best superficial, seen mostly from the upper decks of a steam mail-ship rather than on horse back or on foot, one that engaged little if any with the rulers and the ruled, merchants, mercenaries and quacks who lived or plied a livelihood along the coastline and yet it was he claimed, an experience that had exposed him to the most 'quaint conglomerations of colour, race, language and religion'.[17]

His limited exposure was but a minor detail, doing little to stop him from dedicating much of a chapter on the landmass. It was compiled, he recalled, from his own direct observations and enquiries, complemented by the works of others as well as various classified official reports that he boasted had been made available specifically to him.[18] It was a sparse chapter considering the size of the Arabian Peninsula but was, he mused, where 'there were few, if any, authorities upon the Persian Gulf, per se' to draw from.[19] By dedicating seventy-eight pages to Arabia out of nearly seventeen hundred in total, Curzon considered himself to be part of that very small cohort of an informed elite, but the chapter was at odds with the rest of the book, seemingly ignorant of the two peoples, the Arabs and the Persians who, although only separated by a short stretch of sea, were far more than the quaint conglomeration of societies he presumed. Although brought together mostly by trade links between coastal towns and ports on opposing sides of the Gulf Sea, there were also immense and unreconcilable differences between their rulers, not least their respective interpretations of Islamic faith. The Arabs had also never forgotten Persia's hegemonic past and persistent claim to parts of the Gulf littoral and islands.

And so it was that in a time before modern transportation, aggressive exploration of oil and industrialisation, only a small number of western travellers, government officials, wanderer-scholars and pretenders dared to venture into or traverse the Arabian Peninsula. Many of those who had, either published their personal accounts or later recalled their experiences in various institutions, helping to inform Curzon's tome and adding dabs of colour to knowledge. This emerging enlightenment, however, was patchy and as sparse as the arid wildernesses that these notable pioneers claimed to have explored. Like palm trees that had taken root in an oasis, fertile pockets of knowledge quickly formed in the more accessible or hospitable tracts of Arabia with Jerusalem, Palestine and the Biblical north, Syria and Egypt, all easily reached from the Mediterranean Sea being well-trodden and comparatively well-chronicled. Personal accounts of Jeddah, accompanying the pilgrimages and Hajj, gained honestly by pious duty or incognito explorers, also educated scholars as well as those with curious or staunch theological minds alike. There was for the most part however, a vague and mostly inaccurate understanding of Arabia's seemingly uninhabitable and impenetrable interior and the peoples who struggled to live there.

Given the paucity of indigenous archives and accessibility where they existed – with just a few exceptions – most Arab accounts of similar journeys and experiences were discounted. Orientalism was a European, if not primarily a British, scholarly discipline; the study of the oriental east, Asia and the Middle East. But it was also a means to ensure intellectual primacy, to patronise and to dominate knowledge and understanding. Most of all it reinforced a self-sense of supremacy over the other by boasting a superior understanding of the languages, cultures and history than those who ruled – or were ruled – in such faraway places. The continuous and at times, conspicuous consumption of knowledge was after all, not an outcome of the British empire. Given the countless census and survey teams, special duties, sponsorship of expeditions and seemingly innocent archaeological missions sent out to record, map, measure and comprehend the unknown, knowledge was arguably an explicit condition of it. In India and beyond, the British also tried to understand and control their empire through cartography, legitimising and rationalising the very concept of power through science, metrics and mathematics, believing that it could be better governed if the territory was better understood.[20] In the words of German geographer, Albrecht Penck, if 'knowledge is power, geographical knowledge is world power'.[21]

For a British scholar of orientalism, nationality, social status and family wealth, education and religion were all factors that added weight and credibility to a traveller's account. Ethnocentricity ruled. Gender was for the most part, not even a consideration as exploration was primarily a manly pursuit despite the pioneering efforts of, for example, Lady Anne Blunt, Mabel Bent and Gertrude Bell, all of whom had also travelled deep into Arabia. Like their male contemporaries, all were skilled linguists who chronicled their accounts for wider readership. Blunt, along with her husband Wilfred, travelled extensively through northern Arabia in the 1870s, principally to purchase Arabian horses. Twenty years later, Bent and her husband Theodore, explored Arabia's southern extremities, passing through Yemen and Oman. Bell was arguably the most established and seasoned traveller, having spent most of her adult life from the early 1890s travelling through Persia and later the Middle East, either on her own or as part of archaeological expeditions, including one with a young T.E. Lawrence. Although both Blunt and Bell travelled into the peninsula's interior, neither made it any further south than Ha'il, a popular waypoint for the various caravan routes that carried trade and pilgrims across the peninsula's northern deserts.

During an age when the Royal Geographical Society (RGS), a preeminent institution founded in London in 1830 to advance geographical science, did not entertain female membership regardless of their family connections, ability or spirit, for many female explorers, their own contributions to the advancement of such knowledge were limited to writing up travel notes on behalf of their male companions or husbands. If they were lucky, they might receive a couple of lines of gratitude in a preface or introduction as a silent travelling partner. One of Lorimer's sisters was among them, having her own travelling exploits in support of a male explorer downplayed. As a companion of Sir Aurel Stein during his exploration of Inner Asia, she was briefly acknowledged but with some patronisation as his 'Recording Angel'.[22] Both Blunt and Bell were able to publish their journals in their own name. Bent in contrast, had to be content with seeing her experiences recorded under her husband's monicker.

Within imperial establishments, the word of a British traveller was typically paramount, not least because most had some form of quasi-official status, prestigious sponsorship or direct association to the state. They also had the monopoly. Of the ninety-one travelogues of Arabia published between 1800 and 1950, forty-eight were penned by a British hand. Far less in number, the works of Dutch (two), French (eighteen) and German (nine) orientalists were also consumed by British academics although sometimes read with a cynical eye given the author's potential patronage or questionable motivation.[23] Travelling in disguise added to the romance and adventure rather than discredit the authenticity of an account. Any potential act of blasphemy by travelling incognito into a restricted holy city was outweighed by the overwhelming Christian desire to understand foreign lands and potentially condemn the acts and practices of heathen or religious adversaries. Alongside the factual, descriptive and sometimes imaginative observations of intrepid voyages were countless embellishments, subjective judgements and downright fabrications. Heroic self-promotion, too, played its full part in influencing and contaminating intellectual and political minds.[24] While Curzon boasted to have read nearly three hundred books on Persia, a burden he deemed necessary for the benefit of others, he read far fewer on Arabia before he penned his brief observations on the peninsula because so few existed.

An English gentleman's words might have been preferred to a foreigner's within these same establishments, but that did not mean that they were automatically exempt from challenge or critique. Penck's observation was just as relevant at a personal level. One such suspect authority was the scholar, William Gifford Palgrave. In 1864, he delivered various contentious presentations to the RGS where he claimed to have spent nearly two months in Riyadh in the company of its emır, Faisal Al Sa'ud, leading some self-styled orientalists and seasoned desert travellers to question the accuracy and authenticity of his account. Questions of his potential sponsorship also sowed seeds of doubt, later validated when he was found to have been under Napoleon III's patronage. Not wishing to be seen to be ungentlemanly as the society was as much a men's dining club as it was a depository for knowledge, rather than call Palgrave out directly, it instead encouraged anyone with both the constitution and capability, to respond to some of their members' doubts. A call was also made to obtain the capital's exact position. Unclear itself of the accuracy of Palgrave's claims, the society also sought forgiveness by confessing that even with all of the means, scientific know-how and resources at its disposal, it was still far 'less acquainted with this huge peninsula than the ancients in the time of their great explorer Ptolemy', the great Ancient Greek geographer.[25]

Less than a year after the society's geographic gauntlet had been thrown down, it was picked up by the government of India's political resident in Bushire, 40-year-old Lieutenant-Colonel Lewis Pelly. Pelly boasted an eventful career since joining the EIC in 1841, having also served in the Indian province Sind and various parts of East Africa including Zanzibar. His arrival in Bushire in 1862 was precluded by being shipwrecked at Comora (an alternative name for Bandar Abbas), which seemed rather apt for a man who had a reputation for being 'frank, straightforward, ardent [and] fond of adventure … the more novel and hazardous the better'.[26] Accompanied by a man of modern science, the Indian Medical Service's (IMS) residency surgeon Dr William Colvill, Lieutenant Dawes (a volunteer from the Royal Indian Navy) and a small caravan of camels and hired local guides, Pelly trekked south from his start point in Kuwait to Riyadh making detailed notes along the way. After arriving at the desert capital, he enjoyed three audiences with Emir Faisal Al Sa'ud, where during the course of their deliberations, he established an understanding of the ways of life and informal form of governance of Najd that had hitherto, been unknown. He also established Riyadh's latitude and longitude, something Palgrave had not – or possibly could not have – produced, in the process fulfilling the society's particular request. The officials left the peninsula's shores having completed their quasi-official mission after following a caravan trail east to the coastal town of Al Uqayr in Al Hasa. On his return to Britain, Pelly presented his observations to the society, disproving elements of Palgrave's alleged desert wilderness adventure whilst honourably confirming others.[27] When Colvill later publicised his own observations of their short expedition in British newspapers, he was reprimanded by Pelly, who made it clear that the expedition's various findings were to be in his name alone.

Palgrave was not the first British traveller to pass through Riyadh. That honour fell to an EIC soldier, Captain George Sadlier, in 1818, who was despatched initially to Muscat and then to Qatif, a thriving port in Al Hasa, to try to build a coalition military action against the Sharjah and Ras Al Khayma-based Al Qawasim brigands. His subsequent published travelogue of a trek across Arabia in service of the company offered a glimpse of the unknown. In their own way, both Palgrave and

Pelly offered much more of an insight than Sadlier, notably through their respective mapping efforts. Whilst Pelly provided a generous amount of geographic detail and appreciation of the immediate terrain he had travelled through, Palgrave overwhelmed the reader with settlements and town-steads scattered far beyond his travelled route, many of which he could not have possibly seen or visited. His cartographical shortcomings also included a gross underestimation of the dominant features that severely restricted the ability to travel easily through the desert plains and rocky features, even with a trusted guide leading the way. And yet, if a cartographer had thought to overlay their illustrated routes, it would have provided the foundations of a credible map, but for those who doubted Palgrave's credentials and the accuracy of his observations, there was a hesitance to use his work. Had Palgrave ventured to challenge his critics, he would have found that very few had been to Arabia as he had, and even fewer had managed to travel as far as Ha'il or Al Jawf, never mind Riyadh, which was a few hundred miles further south.

With so little recorded about Central Arabia and the heart of Najd after Pelly's brief venture – and virtually nothing of the Empty Quarter to its south – seventy years later, Palgrave's work was still subject to challenge and criticism in the absence of any other accounts with renowned British Arabist, Harry St. John Philby, dedicating over forty pages in his 1922 travelogue to criticising Palgrave.[28] With no western traveller following either man's footsteps or corroborating their geographical fixes for at least another four decades, there was no way of telling in the meantime whose appreciation of the political, social and geographical nature of Najd was more accurate. A political decision later made by the Foreign Office to refuse any government business or travel into the interior because of its desire to maintain its close alliance with the Ottoman government who claimed Arabia as part of its caliphate even if it only maintained a physical presence along parts of the peninsula's coastline, only helped to further reduce the chances of building on what was already known or believed. The now illusive 1887 Gazetteer of Arabia, written by Major J.R. Povah, served as the only central point of reference to inform those within the British and Indian governments about the peninsula and its people.

In 1912, a young Danish explorer and keen botanist, Christian Raunkiaer, was the next to travel deep into the interior, partly to retrace Pelly's steps. At the beginning of the twentieth century, ninety per cent of the peninsula was still unexplored by western travellers, but with the Foreign Office expressing no desire to reduce this deficit and the RGS unable to motivate its members to travel there, it was left to its counterpart the Royal Danish Geographical Society to lead the way. Given the visible and prominent British presence in the Gulf, Raunkiaer naturally sought British assistance given their wealth of local knowledge. With both the British and Indian governments seeing only intrigue rather than innocent exploration, they refused to support the mission[29] and left Raunkiaer to his own devices.

So strong was the feeling in both capitals, London and Calcutta, that the political agents in Kuwait and Bahrain were reprimanded by the political resident in Bushire when word spread that they had allegedly helped the Dane. In Kuwait, the political agent felt wronged as he had only offered general observations to Raunkiaer on his planned route after he was confident that the traveller really was a botanist as claimed rather than a spy and an ill-prepared one at that.[30] The political agent in Bahrain had even more reason to feel aggrieved by his rebuke, as he had only come across the Dane after he had completed his exploration, having seen him arrive on the island in an extremely poor state of health.[31] In 1913, Raunkiaer wrote an account of his desert exploits which soon came to the attention of the RGS who observed that 'some of the ground had not been touched by Europeans for a considerable time… [and] was, in fact, to a small extent new'.[32] Any opportunity to invite Raunkiaer to expand on his published findings was lost in 1915 when aged twenty-five, he died of tuberculosis, possibly as a result of his expedition into Arabia's interior.

Beyond Raunkiaer's brave if amateurish effort, the peninsula and its interior continued to exist as a 'mostly known unknown' to British and other European orientalists alike. While the British could claim primacy of knowledge of Arabia's coastline through extensive maritime surveys and charting since the Royal Navy and Bombay Marine's earliest days of navigating the Gulf, deeper knowledge was needed to inform strategic reasoning. While Persia theoretically served as a buffer zone to protect India's south-western flank from other global powers just as Afghanistan did in the north, the peninsula and its harsh desert environment potentially offered additional strategic depth alongside other buffer states.[33] And even though Curzon claimed to have reduced the knowledge deficit with regards to Persia, as well as an appreciation of how best to cajole it to Britain's advantage, no one really knew if the townsfolk, tribes, bedouin and sheikhs within the peninsula's vast land would also be content to be part of any perceived extended defence. British notions of loyalty amongst the Gulf rulers to the Crown were ambiguous. Povah's gazetteer offered little. The lack of an established political agency network and over-reliance on local agents, likewise, provided nothing substantial. The government of India was, instead, reliant on orientalist publications, which were themselves, scant.

The General Clauses Act (X of 1897) was clear that native states immediately beyond the periphery of the British empire were not British territories or their inhabitants, British subjects. That did not stop Sir Courtenay Ilbert, distinguished British lawyer and legal counsel for viceroys from the 1870s onwards, from giving the view that, as a paramount power, sovereignty between the British government and the rulers of each state was something that should be shared in proportions appropriate to the state's history and importance to the empire. He was clear that the government's primary role should be to act as their security guarantor and protector against external aggressors. He also believed that the British government had an obligation to assume a general – albeit very limited – responsibility for ensuring safety and security within the state itself.[34]

Despite this informed opinion, as long as Britain's maritime trade was adequately protected and flowing freely, there was little reason to penetrate beyond the hinterland to explore the unknown. Nor was there – until the arrival of Curzon – the political or military desire to be exposed to either the potential threats or hostile environment that lay beyond the coastline. The British and Indian governments had therefore justifiably excused themselves from Ilbert's judgement. With so little of the peninsula of commercial interest to the British and their own subjects concentrated in just a few major coastal towns, they avoided taking on any formal responsibility of reducing this particular knowledge deficit.

They instead maintained a preference for non-interventionism unless absolutely necessary, even if that meant not knowing how much control and influence the Ottoman central government or the Sublime Porte, had in this part of its caliphate, or to what extent the presence of the French, Russians and regional-new comers the Germans had on influencing their surroundings.[35] Dutch, Austro-Hungarian, Belgian, Swedish and Norwegian interests also had to be taken into account, having established their own consulates alongside British ones.

Curzon, however, had other ideas. His tenure as viceroy spanned a period of monarchical transition from a stagnant Victorian foreign policy to a contemporary and revitalised Edwardian one. It was, he hoped, to be the re-establishment of Pax Britannica, regional peace ensured as much by knowledge as anything else, hoping to cast aside the painful memories and vulnerabilities of Britain's governance of its subjects in India that were initially exposed during the 1857 mutiny. His term of governorship also contended with the fears and the consequences of the gradual erosion of the Ottoman Caliphate's legitimacy in the Gulf, not that it had any meaningful presence in central or eastern Arabia beyond its loose administration of Al Hasa and foothold in Qatar. Heightened perceptions of French and Russian encroachment, and German exploitation of all three, also featured. Curzon's frustration with the way that the government of India had overseen domestic and foreign policy in India and beyond was evident when he tersely remarked that 'had a committee been assembled from the padded chambers of Bedlam, they could hardly have devised anything more extravagant in its madness or more mischievous in its operation [of governance]'.[36] With just two British political officers and a handful of local or 'native' agents operating in, and reporting on, developments on both sides of the Gulf Sea, and a scattering of British consuls and vice-consuls in the Foreign Office's Levant Consular Service serving in Baghdad, Basrah, Mosul and Jeddah, madness was accompanied by ignorance. Curzon looked to change the Foreign and the Indian Offices' desire to maintain the status quo in India and beyond. Arrogance, egotism and self-centrism to some, was seen as visionary, competitive and righteous to others who believed in a living rather than dead and declining British empire.

A more forward policy was needed to counter the various strategic threats, both real and perceived, not just in India but also in the Gulf. When Curzon presented his recommendations to Lord Hamilton, Secretary of State for India, and ministerial cohort Foreign Secretary Lord Lansdowne (who served as viceroy from 1888 to 1894), he was firmly rebuffed by both. He received the same response when he suggested a viceregal tour of the Gulf in 1901 as a necessary projection of power. Even Prime Minister Lord Salisbury, a believer in the living versus dead country concept, objected to Curzon's push. He was readily swayed by the view that expansionism in the Gulf at a time when the government was bogged down politically and militarily in southern Africa with the Boer War was inappropriate. As affluent as the empire was perceived to have been, the political and financial cost of such a change in policy was more than the government could afford, with Curzon told in clear terms that 'we must cut our coat according to our cloth.[37] It is obvious that our fighting power in the Persian Gulf must be confined to the sea coast. In the rest of Persia we could only fight at the cost of efforts which would swallow twice or thrice as much income tax as the Transvaal'.[38] Exasperated by their blinkered belief that retreat rather than resolve was the right course of action, Curzon wrote to Lord Percy, under-secretary of state in the Indian Office, declaring that 'when you hear a Foreign Minister say anywhere that all he wants is to defend the status quo, you may guess in 9 cases out of 10 that he has no policy at all'.[39] He was wrong in his assessment that a policy did not exist; it did, it was just that it endorsed an overarching policy of non-interference in 'Turkish Arabia', that is, Mesopotamia and most of Arabia. Despite the obvious pragmatism and rationality of not having two different foreign policies, in the face of the clear opposition from London, Curzon remained committed to his strategy of proactive outreach and power projection but for now, had to bide his time.

That time came in May 1903 when Salisbury's policy of 'splendid isolation' was retired and replaced with an approach that was consistent with Curzon's worldview.[40] With the war in southern Africa over, Britain's military and political wounds needed to heal. Engagement rather than withdrawal was the prescribed tonic. It was just what the viceroy needed to hear when in a debate in the House of Lords, Lansdowne declared that it was only due to

> British enterprise … expenditure of British lives and money, that the Persian Gulf [was] … open to the navigation of the world. It was our ships that cleared those waters of pirates; it was we who put down the slave trade; it was we who buoyed and beaconed those intricate waters.[41]

While acknowledging that even though no immediate threat had been detected, the pressure of competition in the Gulf was being felt, not least because of the relative freedom of maritime travel and trade being enjoyed at the expense of British blood, sweat and gold. The more that another power saw its commercial interests increase in the Gulf, Lansdowne opined, the more it could justify the need to deploy military forces to protect those interests. With primacy itself at risk, Lansdowne was compelled to state clearly that any move by a power to establish a military presence in the region would be considered 'a very grave menace to British interests, and we should certainly resist it with all of the means at our disposal'.[42]

That Lansdowne rather than Hamilton announced Britain's step-change in the region was striking. It also highlighted the complexity and absurdity of Britain's regional foreign policy. Relationships with the various sheikhdoms, sultanates and imamates established across the Gulf's eastern and southern littoral had for the most part, been within the India Office's geographic terms of reference since the ministry's inception in 1858. Administering and functioning on its behalf was the government of India in Calcutta, which assumed various personal ties and agreements originally established and negotiated by the EIC through its political agency networks. Arabia's western coastline and most southerly extremity in contrast, was the responsibility of the Colonial Office, another new entity which theoretically claimed primacy on relationships and transactions including in Aden, Yemen and Jeddah. And yet it was the Foreign Office as the senior partner in global affairs, which was now exercising its policy responsibility for a region that it had previously neglected. Justification for this interest and interference in the affairs of both the Indian and Colonial Offices was the overlap of the peripheries between the British and Ottoman empires in Arabia and Whitehall's continued desire to appease and uphold the Sublime Porte. Such details no longer mattered to Curzon; he could now push through an open door to get the support he needed for his forward policy.

Notwithstanding Salisbury and his secretaries of state's earlier policy fetters, the government of India had not in any case, been idle in the Gulf. In 1899, the government's Bushire-based political resident struck an agreement with the ruler of Kuwait, Sheikh Mubarak Al Sabah, which included an implicit security arrangement to protect the sheikhdom against Ottoman political aspirations and military threats. Curzon could hardly claim credit for initiating the dialogue, that honour fell to his predecessor Lord Elgin. There were also limits as to how much he could boast that it had been completed in line with his vision as the joint British-Kuwaiti covenant had been kept secret, not least to prevent the Sublime Porte from taking exception to one of their eminent subjects and one of their close ally's scheming against them if the agreement became known. To ensure that remained the case, Sheikh Mubarak was paid fifteen thousand rupees, courtesy of the residency's local treasury.[43] Five years later, Kuwait would find itself subject to further interest from the government of India through the establishment of a political agency, temporarily at first, with Stuart Knox the incumbent. Having served previously as the British consul in Basrah and briefly as first assistant in Bushire, Knox came with some knowledge of the sheikhdom. The Kuwait political agency was among the first of many new posts to be established, not least because of Curzon's frustration with the most 'spasmodic and unreliable' information that had typically been reported from the local agent there.[44] This lack of visibility or robust reporting meant that no-one really had any idea if Sheikh Mubarak was a British ally despite the pact between the two and substantial hush-money he had been gifted. This was not a problem unique to Kuwait. Local agents had originally served as commercial agents throughout the Gulf and beyond on behalf of the EIC and were typically selected from within well-established, wealthy and therefore influential merchant families whose responsibilities grew over time. The decline and ultimately deconstruction of the EIC left both a commercial and political void that needed filling with the increase of British economic, political and military interests. The local agent's ability to act as the government of India's eyes and ears and as a primary source of information soon deteriorated as a result.

The increased British presence served multiple purposes beyond addressing any exaggeration, rumour, inaccuracy or commercial self-interest apparent from local agent reporting. It was a tangible sign to the various emirs and sheikhs of their significance and value to the empire. But it also served as a couched warning to the same rulers that a closer eye would now be trained on any treaty breaches or illicit activities such as gun running or slave trading, both of which were outlawed by the British. When brought together, the totality of this concurrent activity signalled the empire's regional intent more generally as a deterrent to its competitors. Even if the ability to establish new relationships with indigenous communities, especially those deep in Arabia's interior, would be hampered by replacing or demoting local agents, a well-bred English gentleman political agent would immediately improve the quality and accuracy of reporting and ability to provide both credible quantitative and qualitative analysis regardless of the additional cost to central coffers. Indeed, many British agents were born in distant parts of the empire rather than in Great Britain and spoke many of the local languages used in and around the Arabian Peninsula. Their patriotism and absolute duty to the Crown also made them immune to foreign powers, which was not necessarily the case for their local counterparts. At pace, the government of India's Foreign Department's regional presence began to expand as a result of Lansdowne's speech and Curzon's policies. While some of the existing outposts were strengthened or upgraded with native representatives being replaced by British political agents, elsewhere new agencies were established. Bandar Abbas, Seistan, Shiraz, Isfahan, Tabriz, Muhammerah Arabistan (modern-day Khorramshahr), Ahvaz and Kermanshah all saw the raising of the Union flag atop new political agency buildings under full-blooded British stewardship.

Curzon was not the only one to note Whitehall's general policy paralysis in the years preceding Lansdowne's speech. The Fourth Estate was also questioning the British government's inertia. Henry Whigham, an accomplished war correspondent who had reported the Boer War on behalf of *The Morning Post* and *The Standard*, wrote to Major Percy Cox, the then political agent in Muscat in 1902, with much the same opinion. 'What we really need … is a little knowledge [but] I know from experience that the FO has a distinct distaste for acquiring geographical knowledge' he opined.[45] His thinking was shaped by observing that there were few detailed maps of southern Africa and a general lack of appreciation for demographic data, which severely hampered the British Army's early planning and campaigns against the Boer. Although not explicitly criticising Lansdowne, who had been secretary of state at the War Office at the time, he was arguably accountable for preventing the allocation of sufficient resources to ensure that his senior commanders in the field had up-to-date information. Why Whigham wrote to Cox is unknown but may have been because of doubts about the magnanimity of Lansdowne's resignation in November 1900 for failing to service the war effort and then his immediate appointment as Foreign Secretary after leaving the War Office. Whigham was not alone in criticising Britain's wider policy of non-interference. In 1904, Major Francis Maunsell, military attaché in Constantinople and leading military intelligence and topographical expert, complained that, when drafting a report on eastern Turkey, not a single officer from the Levant Consular Service was able to produce any sociological, topographical or geographical information of the people and region they were imbedded in. Although he blamed Foreign Office policy rather than the officials themselves, he could not help but feel disappointment that many did not seem to display any inclination, voluntarily or otherwise, to observe their immediate environment.[46]

Curzon's encouragement of the pursuit of knowledge served to correct this lethargy and ignorance, motivating a breed of 'warrior-scholars', political agents who typically joined the Indian Civil Service (ICS) with time served in either the British or Indian Armies, giving them the ability and constitution to employ their previous skillsets alongside their diplomatic ones, appreciating both the political and military application of newly acquired knowledge. As some ICS civilian political officers earned their spurs by accompanying military campaigns, the accolade was arguably, far from exclusive. The various government printing presses established in India ensured that ample opportunities also existed for personal accounts and quasi-academic works to be published and circulated afar.

The expansion of the regional political agent network, staffed by scholars, wanderers and warriors alike, was just the start of Curzon's projection of power. More audacious plans were to follow, some of which had been previously postponed following Whitehall's foreign policy entrenchment. Other initiatives would take shape over time as Curzon contemplated further on his vision. Two men were central to his aspirations in the Gulf. One was political agent and later resident Percy Cox, while the other was an equally seasoned political officer, John Gordon Lorimer.

Chapter 2

Competition Wallah

The salutation, *'mubarakin fi hal maulud al sa'aid'* was once a familiar greeting used by Iraqi migratory shepherd tribes in particular to welcome new-borns, or so British officials familiar with the region's tribes recorded.[47] Regardless of its provenance, it or its English translation, ('you are blessed to have this happy new-born baby'), would have been an equally apt proclamation to announce the birth of John Gordon Lorimer, born in Glasgow, Scotland on 30 June 1870. Known to all as Gordon rather than his Christian name, the first-born to Isabella Lockhart and the Reverend Robert Lorimer had a nomadic early childhood.[48] He and his parents moved from place to place within Scotland before finally settling at Lunburn Cottage in Mains and Strathmartine where his father filled the ministerial vacancy at the recently founded Few Church.[49] In 1881, in addition to The Reverend Robert, Isabella and a few household staff, Lorimer shared his childhood there with his sister Elizabeth Hilda Lockhart (more commonly known as Hilda) born in 1874 in Edinburgh and brother David Lockhart Robertson (known as Lock) who was born in the parish in 1876. Ten years later, Lunburn Cottage's occupancy had increased with Amelia Stuart, twins Florence (or Floss, Stein's 'Recording Angel') and Charles Stuart. William Laughton and Robert (sometimes known as Robin) Campbell added to the list of siblings, along with a larger domestic servant presence to ensure its smooth running.

The cottage was a house of learning, not least in foreign languages. At meal-times, the Reverend Robert often forbade the use of English at the table, either deliberately or not, against the spirit of The Reverend David Cannan who had encouraged the recent adoption of the English language by the parishioners in Mains and Strathmartine. In a gazette of Scottish parishes, he welcomed that

> a considerable improvement [had] taken place in the language of the people [of Mains and Strathmartine]

> within the last forty years. Many Scottish phrases are becoming obsolete; and a number of trades-people speak English with considerable propriety [50]

Rather than mimic his flock's recent linguistic and elocutional advances, a foreign language would be chosen in its stead in the cottage and all of the children expected to converse in it accordingly. Whether punishment was distributed to Lorimer or his siblings for failing to engage as they broke bread together is unknown, but the cast was set at a very early age as nearly all would prove their linguistic talents in adulthood. William would arguably be the most mischievous in how he would later use his aptitude for languages, again at odds with the Reverend Cannan, by playing an important role contributing to the Scottish National Dictionary to help keep the language alive. He also translated the New Testament into Scots, with the notable exception of the Temptation of Christ, where the Devil's narratives were left in English. This, perhaps, hinted of prejudice against those south of the border or at least was an implicit suggestion as to why all Englishmen had horns and tails.[51]

For the most part, Lorimer's education was private. This was to be expected as Mains and Strathmartine was a small rural parish served by just a couple of parochial schools offering a limited curriculum.[52] He had a physically active upbringing in the Scottish lowland as well as a religious and academic one.[53] When he applied to join the ICS, he made it known that he had been predominately privately educated but had also attended the Dundee Institution and High School, located just a few miles south of Lunburn Cottage. The school's student archives are selective and incomplete, having no record of his admission, suggesting that he spent just a short spell there. They do, however, record Lock's enrolment as a twelve-year-old in the same year that Lorimer submitted his ICS application. Mains and Straithmartine's 1881 census also fails to shed light on Lorimer's schooling beyond his status as a 'scholar', which suggests that rather than any administrative oversight of Lorimer's schooling, it may have been just a brief episode of his life to prove his inclusion in structured learning.

In 1889, Lorimer entered Edinburgh University as the first step towards public service overseas. Like so many Scotsmen before him, he saw his future beyond the country's shores, persuaded by the trappings of the ICS (or its predecessor the EIC). Motivation for his countrymen to head overseas was varied. Many sought to secure or recoup the family's fortunes, while others looked to either escape religious discrimination as Roman Catholics or to fulfil their own religious calling. Some sought knowledge or enlightenment, while a few indifferent to mammon or missionary, looked for the chance to prove their mettle in service of the Crown as a soldier, administrator or possibly both. There was also Henry Dundas' lingering legacy as a former president of the EIC's Board of Control, whose discriminatory recruitment policy from the late 1700s favoured the employment of fellow Scotsman above the English, Irish or Welsh to oversee the EIC's interests.[54] Given the prominence of Scottish surnames in both the EIC and government of India's archives, Lorimer was able to judge that most seemed to have come from fellow Lowland rather than Highland families.[55]

With no application form pinned to his ICS personal file, one can only guess what motivated Lorimer to apply. Isabella's birth and early childhood in Bareilly, India must have been of some influence, sharing her positive experiences rather than the horrors that Bareilly saw as the epicentre of the 1857 Indian uprising. Her place of birth, witness to the murder of many British and Anglo-Indian officials and their families, among them, her father David Robertson, a high court judge, certainly highlighted the dangers. The Free Church of Scotland's evangelical drive to establish itself beyond its immediate shores might have additionally been a factor. Lorimer might not have been destined to serve the church like his father, but he remained a religious man all of his life and would often lead a congregation into prayer when overseas in the absence of a minister.

If the ICS was an expected career choice, so too was his initial decision to go to Edinburgh University as one of nine ICS-approved academic establishments. Once a popular institution for preparing young gentleman for a life in foreign service, from the 1870s onwards, it no longer provided the bedrock upon which the ICS sat as a source of future residents, commissioners and governors. To observers at the time, its approach to teaching the Classics was seen to be a factor. The two 'great universities' of Oxford and Cambridge had seen a similar decline in supplying the Crown with manpower despite their teaching techniques being more acceptable to the public service commissioners. The other chosen universities of Dublin, Glasgow, St. Andrews, Aberdeen, University College London and King's College, London undoubtedly saw a similar decline in the number of their own alumni in Crown service in India as the century progressed.

The universities' apparent shortfalls as the primary source of future civil servants overseas were the cumulative effect of social changes and numerous reforms made to the ICS's recruitment policies, all introduced with a veneer of self-belief that it levelled the playing ground for Indian applicants by instilling a modicum of meritocracy. The introduction of a competitive system for recruitment in 1855 was the first attempt to improve the quality and diversity of ICS officials.[56] A maximum age limit of twenty-three was also introduced. Until then, 'gentlemen' destined for the 'Covenanted Civil Service' were almost exclusively chosen by virtue of who they knew or were related to, to ensure their successful nomination to the Board of Control (as opposed to the Un-covenanted or Subordinate Civil Service, which recruited within India to oversee menial and lower levels of administrative work). Entrance exams majoring on Classics and theology typically followed and although initially a formality, the self-proclaimed heirs of Alexander the Great were expected to demonstrate at least some level of competence on entry.

Rather than rely solely on the universities, many candidates also looked to crammer schools to increase their chances of success once the persuasive power of patronage and nepotism had been exhausted and failure in the eyes of the family, was a realistic possibility. For some, two years study at the Company's Haileybury College in Hertfordshire preceded their employment. Persian, Hindi, Hindustani (a form of Urdu), Bengali and Arabic were all taught at the college as were Classics, Ancient Greek and Latin even though the value of such languages in administering India's interior were questionable. Sanskrit was also taught and was the only language that students had to pass at examination even though that too, had limited utility once in service. Lieutenant-governor of Bengal, Sir George Campbell, observed that it was no 'more useful to an Indian magistrate than a knowledge of the tongue of ancient Germans would be to a modern commissioner of police' but he was stonewalled.[57] Once competent in Sanskrit, 'Haileybury men' of between eighteen and twenty years of age were sent to India and beyond, initially as writers or proconsuls to account, administer and later to govern. For others, such as Lorimer's maternal grandfather, it was to maintain law and order.

The EIC's poor handling of the India mutiny of 1857 changed everything. When the Government of India Act was passed in August 1858, the company was stripped of its powers and its responsibilities handed over to the governor-general, who by nomenclature would also carry the title, viceroy of India. He, in turn, was supported by a newly established government of India in Calcutta and made accountable to an equally new secretary of state, who sat in his grand ministry building, the India Office in Whitehall. The 1858 Act also required the wholesale transfer of recruitment to the public service commissioners who continued to have their own doubts about the quality and competence of the ICS, even with the competition system. This saw the closure of Haileybury as a place of learning with its equally grand establishment eventually put aside after its 1876 and final batch of candidates had completed their coveted education in December the following year. The responsibility for preparing the next generation of public servants would now be expected to be in the hands of more reputable and credible places of learning.

After reviewing the competition intakes, the commissioners reported discouragingly that very few applicants and appointees held bachelor's degrees from either Cambridge or Oxford, both of which were highly desirable under the new scheme. Others were found to have had no academic study at undergraduate level at all. Although neither were ultimately prerequisites, to address these latest concerns, in 1859 the commissioners announced that the maximum age limit for recruitment was to be reduced to twenty-two. This amendment was justified by their belief that by lowering the ceiling, recent university graduates might be more inclined or enticed to join the ICS as a time-limited opportunity and reducing the window for them to be lured by more lucrative employment elsewhere. Equally unconvincing was the commissioners' judgement that for those potentially looking at service in India but without sufficient knowledge, they could use their first year after graduation to obtain a rudimentary understanding of orientalism, another gesture that would in theory be advantageous to the great universities and their preferential prospectuses.

Still with little uptick in the perceived quality or diversity of candidate, the age limit was lowered to twenty-one just seven years later alongside the compulsory introduction of a two-year course in Indian subjects at a preferred university. For the most part, the entrance exams themselves remained untouched. In addition to Classics, Sanskrit and Arabic continued to be core subjects to help fulfil candidates' orientalist requirements, obligations that would not have bothered Lorimer given his aptitude for languages. But when they were perceived to favour Indian candidates, their relative value at final assessments were made less than those in Greek or Latin, both of which in turn, had their weighting increased. It was only after various representations from a few influential Indian voices that this unbalanced method of scoring was eventually rescinded. It was a positive start but when the lobbyists also suggested that the knowledge of other Indian vernacular languages should be tested given the diversity of the country, the commissioners were unmoved by their progressive arguments.

Both serving and retired 'Haileybury men' alike, scoffed at their successors and the criteria being used to recruit them, labelling them 'competition *wallahs'* in a derogatory rather than light-hearted tone to denote the origin of their recruitment. Had Isabella's father survived the Indian Mutiny, he may well have considered his grandson to be among them. In November 1864, *The Times* felt compelled to observe without basis, that the competition *wallahs* lacked both the physique and energy of their predecessors.[58] The author continued that they were deficient in character, incapable of impressing the native population they were expected to rule and lacked the social values and acumen more generally than those of the 'covenanted'.

Ten years later the *Edinburgh Review* carried a similarly critical article, giving a condescending opinion that men of undistinguished family and academic background were severely damaging the service's reputation. Men like Lorimer. If the gentry could not be persuaded to serve the Crown in India, it implored successful candidates to at least attempt to embrace aristocratic values and *esprit de corps* through compulsory attendance at one of the great universities. Without the social and academic enlightenment that only a great university could provide, the *Review* argued that the current approach was just 'not the way in which rulers of a nation should be prepared for their great duties … as much by the force of… the impalpable qualities which make up the English gentleman, as by mere ability and book learning'.[59]

Both articles were written anonymously but their authors' affiliations and social status were clear. *The Irish Times* in contrast, celebrated the open competition, which had at last teased the door ajar for more of its compatriots to join the ICS, but it was not blind to the institutional bigotry that still hampered fair recruitment. The 'success of Irishmen in the competition' it argued, gave 'Englishmen such a disgust against the system'.[60] Neither the *Review* nor *The Irish Times* ventured to consider what a Scottish gentleman might have thought of the new scheme, despite their high numbers in India. The thoughts of a Welsh gentleman were also unsought. In 1876, recruitment policy changed again with the maximum age of recruitment reduced to just nineteen. Acknowledging that university graduates would be ruled out of the competition by doing so, the commissioners required all applicants who passed the entrance exams to spend two years residence at a selected university just as the critics had suggested, exposing them to the desired academic and social sophistication. Reducing the age limit also attempted to reduce the number of applicants passing through the crammers.

With recruitment policy unchanged since then, in June 1889, Lorimer sat the open competition exams, the outcome of which would decide whether he could become an ICS Selected Candidate. There were various conditions to his application, among them having to prove that he was a natural-born subject of Her Majesty, between seventeen and nineteen years of age, without disease, constitutional affection or bodily infirmity which might otherwise deem him unfit for public service. As well as proving that he was of good moral character, he was also required to pay upfront, a five pounds application fee. Although he did not excel, he came third overall, easily securing his candidacy and proving his aptitude to pass whatever tests the commissioners put his way.

Despite the family's embrace of foreign languages, he achieved just 57 and 58 percent respectively for French and German whilst scoring 78 percent in English composition. His Latin was a respectable 65 percent but he struggled with his maths, history and political economy papers, scoring 54, 41 and just 27 percent in turn, his score in the latter just enough to prove to the commissioners that he was not a 'mere smatterer' trying to secure easy credit wherever he could.[61] A pass, however good or bad, came with an annual allowance of three hundred pounds, to help fund his studies for the next two years until he was expected to sit his final exams. In the autumn of 1889, not long after Lorimer had begun his study at Edinburgh, the rules changed again, returning the maximum age for recruitment to twenty-three in a bid to broaden the scope of potential candidates. The commissioners' latest hope was that any undergraduate or recent graduate attracted to the ICS would be able to walk straight into an examination room and compete on equal terms with any other fellow who had been specially prepared at one of the detested crammer schools.[62]

To them, it was still unfathomable why so few properly educated gentlemen bothered to sit the papers and even more unacceptable that the crammers continued to be the main source of their applicants. This followed another review, which found that in the last ten years, the number of applicants seldom exceeded two hundred for the forty-five vacancies or so that were typically on offer each year.[63] Despite these favourable statistics, this increase in age catchment may have influenced Lorimer's decision to change universities. Notwithstanding having already won several academic awards, Edinburgh University had been unable to satisfy him that his study there would be sufficient to pass or exceed the ICS's minimum requirements. That October, he headed south and was matriculated as a scholar in Christ Church College, Oxford University, not that the move would have automatically improved his chances of success as even with the benefit of the commissioners' bias, Oxford's percentage of new ICS recruits remained consistently low.[64] Its competitor, Cambridge, had also only seen a slight increase in recent years. To their alumni, the Indian jewel had lost its allure.[65]

Not privy to the poor application numbers or the odds in his favour, Lorimer also enrolled at Wren and Gurney's crammer school in Powis Square, London to improve his chances of passing the final entrance exams. Walter Wren and Henry Palin Gurney's enterprise was one of the most successful of the crammer schools scattered around London and the major university cities, preparing young impressionable gentlemen for Crown Service examinations.[66] Entry into the Royal Military College, the Home, Colonial and Foreign Office Service, the ICS and even the Chinese Customs Service were all possibilities under their tutorage. It was a very profitable enterprise as their services did not come cheap, but their results spoke for themselves. In August 1888, Wren and Gurney paid for a column in *The Times* where they boasted at being consistently responsible for preparing over half of the ICS's successful candidates. A second-to-none preparatory education was advertised, using publications such as Knight's *Practical Guide*, Euclid's *Essential elements of plane geometry*, Smith's *Wealth of Nations* and Mill's *Principles of Political Economy* as primary teaching aids. By providing 'careful supervision, efficient teaching, individual attention, and ample opportunities for necessary exercise in gymnastics and football', the crammer almost guaranteed success.[67]

It was a boast that few would-be mercenaries, missionaries or misfits could resist and better still, it was a fraction of the cost of undergraduate study. Given Lorimer's religious upbringing, he must have been thrown by some of his crammer contemporaries whose lifestyles and aspirations differed considerably from his own. One former student felt sufficiently short-changed by the constant distraction in Powis Square that he bemoaned a 'blackguard lot [of] fellows such as hang around [Wren and Gurney's] crammer's [that] would about prevent ever getting an education at all'.[68] Students at nearby Scoones' crammer school in Garrick Street must have felt similarly distracted from their studies, given the lure of the infamous gentlemen's Garrick Club next door.

While postings in the ICS were now mostly dictated by the government of India's operational needs and associated financial costs, the same could not be said of those within the Colonial Service where crammer ne'er-do-wells and university alumni alike, still used patronage or attempted to court the secretary of state for the colonies' assistant private secretary who was responsible for allocating appointments overseas. The desk diary of one assistant private secretary was full of character assassinations and pithy observations from a 'flashily overdressed fool [with] doubts about sobriety… [an] uncouth man brought by a charming

Colonel father' and a 'handsome idiot in a fur coat, [with a] tiny laugh after each word...' all of whom attempted unsuccessfully to persuade him to post them overseas.[69] One chancer who recalled his time at Powis Square with his potential Colonial Service appointer in the hope that it might improve his chances, also failed to be posted. Their shared crammer alma mater counted for little after the applicant demonstrated a considerable lack of tact, commenting that his peer seemed to have an easy life; a comment that was not taken in the manner of jest that it was probably offered.

In the first two weeks of June 1891, now aged twenty, Lorimer and one hundred and fifty-four other candidates finally had the chance to compete for the forty-nine ICS vacancies that year. Over the course of the fortnight, he sat numerous written and oral exams on total law, the history and geography of India, political economy and agricultural chemistry as well as on Hindustani, Hindi, Arabic and Persian.[70] With a one in three chance of being appointed, these were very favourable odds, especially in light of his 1889 overall ranking. Had he sat the entrance exams two years later, still within the upper age limit, his chances would have increased to one in two, such was the lack of desire to serve in India.[71]

Deficient of the prestigious social background that his employers continued to yearn for, even though sons of the clergy typically represented the highest percentage of new recruits, Lorimer looked for any chance to improve his chances of impressing his assessors.[72] The opportunity came when he was presented both Arabic and Persian language exam papers. Believing that a practical demonstration of academic oriental prowess in the absence of a degree could work to his favour, he completed both sets of papers despite only being obliged to answer in one of the oriental languages. Evidently immune to the social distractions of Powis Square and with an appetite for risk, the duplication in effort was ultimately worthwhile even if statistically, his chances of success were already high.

Lorimer's final results proved without doubt his academic capability and compatibility with the ICS, ranking the highest scoring candidate overall, getting 2,727 out of a possible 3,500 marks on offer or 78 percent. For achieving the highest scores in foreign languages (84 percent in Hindustani, 76 percent in Hindi and 82 percent in Persian), he was awarded handsome prize purses of forty pounds, fifteen pounds and twenty-five pounds respectively.[73] He also scored a remarkable 82 percent in political economy, by far his weakest subject in 1889, coming sixth in his cohort. Both Oxford and Wren and Gurney's could notionally claim credit for his success, but if credit was due, it was Lorimer and his father's to be had, given the early introduction of foreign languages within the family household. As no-one had registered to sit the Arabic exam, no scores were recorded or financial award allocated to the best candidate when the results were announced.[74] It was only in late September when the public service commissioners recognised their marking error that they decided to make reparations for their oversight. Aware that Lorimer had already departed Scotland's shores and therefore not in a position to accept the additional bounty, they wrote to The Reverend Robert, asking if he could accept on Lorimer's behalf, the additional prize award of twenty-five pounds for achieving the highest – albeit the only score in Arabic, to be told light-heartedly in reply, that he could not as he would be answerable to his son if he did.[75]

After being informed that he was about to become a probationer in service of the Crown in India, on 26 August 1891, the India Office invited Lorimer to visit its Legal Department to enter into an obligatory covenant; a contract that would confirm his appointment, competition placing and posting; in Lorimer's case to the North-West Province under the presidency of Fort William in Bengal, with Oudh or Punjab as potential alternative placements.[76] The contract also obliged him to work towards a better government of India as set out in its 1855 Act. It was just as well that Lorimer had done well pocketing prize money, as the covenant also came with a mandatory one-pound stamp duty that had to be paid in advance.

Only after the covenant had been signed and the fee paid, would his sailing orders be released. As Lorimer was unexpectedly visiting London briefly in early September, he tried at short notice to arrange an appointment to sign his contract.[77] Unsuccessful in his task, he asked instead for the legal advisers to forward the document for signature and took matters into his own hands by making his own travel arrangements rather than rely on the government, initially bound for St. Petersburg to continue his studies of Russian. Once finished, he would later make his way to Trieste, Italy and finally to Bombay, departing in early November courtesy of the Austrian Lloyd steamer, *Imperator*.[78] A little over two weeks after his visit to London, he felt emboldened to write to the undersecretary of state for India setting out his personal ambition for employment in the service

> ...It is my earnest wish to be set apart sooner or later for political employment. With a view to qualifying for the work I have given special attention to Persian (as shown by the published results of the final examinations) and I have also studied Arabic. I am at present on the point of starting for St. Petersburg where I intend to carry on the study of Russian which I have begun. If my request should be favourably considered, but it should not be possible or not in accordance with usage to set one at once to learn the duties of the political department I would respectfully beg that I might in the meantime be assigned to the Punjab. If there is any opening for a newly arrived civil servant in the protectorate of Biluchistan it might perhaps afford still better opportunities of gaining knowledge and experience of the kind required...[79]

As the highest-ranking candidate, Lorimer was in theory permitted to choose the presidency to which he wanted to be appointed, subject of course to the government of India's operational needs, but there is little to suggest that the letter had any influence over Sir John Eldon Gorst, to whom it was addressed. On 23 November 1891, he arrived in Bombay as one of seventeen new ICS appointees to join the North-West Province as an assistant commissioner third grade, a grade given to all new joiners.[80] For the next two years he would still be known as a probationer, required to sit further administrative exams to prove his competence as well as a practical one to prove his ability to 'perform journeys on horseback'.[81] Failure in this last test of skill above others, would have resulted in immediate dismissal such was the expectation of the government for its officials to be mobile. His first nine months were spent in Gurdaspur, a district in the Lahore Division of Punjab, just as he had hoped to be posted.[82] There, he served an informal apprenticeship under a commissioner and his deputy who, in turn, took their direction on how best to administer 1,889 square miles of territory from a lieutenant governor, who spent most of his time in the more comfortable surroundings of Lahore.

To broaden his employability, in the following August, Lorimer was finally relocated to the mountainous frontier, to Peshawar to take on the responsibilities of a revenue officer as an assistant collector. Peshawar shared the border alongside other government outposts in Hazara, Kohat, Bannu (also known as Mianwali) and Dera Ismail Khan, administering law and order as well as tax calculation and collection in the surrounding settled areas. These outposts also took on more mundane and humdrum responsibilities, from the provision of education to public works construction, not exactly what Lorimer had originally signed up for. This part of the frontier was also served by a number of political agencies, scattered around North and South Waziristan, Khyber, Kurram and Malakand. These were far more testing assignments, where, for young officials like Lorimer seeking adventure and a challenge, the focus was more on gaining an intimate understanding of the tribes and acquiring influence rather than accounting and administrating.[83]

The substantial British presence in this part of the frontier reflected its strategic importance on the periphery of a buffer zone. Here, Indo-Afghan interests were intertwined, not least because of two weathered routes that carried trade between both countries. The same routes also had a history of leading the way for invading armies, something the British feared the Russians must have also been aware of even though the probability of Russia ever conquering India from the British was negligible. Hostility, both between the various tribes found there, but also with occupying forces, had always disturbed the peace. Earlier efforts by the Sikhs to stabilise the region had been unsuccessful. Its annexation by the British in 1849 just provided another outlet for tribal violence while the laying down of the Durand Line in 1893 to formalise the border between the two countries just compounded the unrest. Joining the district just as the camping season was coming to a close, Lorimer had little chance to prove his equestrian skills or to enjoy the field work that made revenue collecting a bit more interesting. Despite his desire to be a political officer, he risked being shaped into a bookkeeper when his immediate senior, the financial commissioner, noted that he had made an 'extremely promising' start as a tax collector.[84] It was not helped when the commissioner also remarked that Lorimer had demonstrated a 'marked zeal and energy in all his work'.[85] Seven months later, Lorimer was transferred again, this time to Kohat and away from revenue adjustment and collection. It was another short posting, just three months in length but gave him the time and space to pass the government of India's language exams in Pashtu and Persian, achieving a higher standard grade in both.

In July 1893, having just turned twenty-three, Lorimer was relocated once more to the government post in Bannu, again as assistant commissioner. The constant movement, detachment and distance between the desk-bound officials and the operational officers in the periphery did little to keep the working relationship a positive one. Transience also had an unsettling effect on the junior frontier officials as they never seemed to stay in one place for too long before they were shuffled around at a whim on orders from Lahore. This was also the case for Lorimer, who soon found himself bound for Hazara, just a month after finding his feet in Bannu, to take up the position as district judge. Again, it was to be another brief encounter, just two months in duration, where again he was noted for his zeal and intelligence by his immediate seniors.[86] As elsewhere at the frontier, the cases he judged there were predominately known in Urdu as '*zar*, *zamin* or *zan*' (money, land or women) giving him a privileged insight into local customs and formalities.[87] In the absence of being able to travel safely and freely in the tribal areas, such interactions with accusers and the accused proved to be an invaluable source of information.

After a short period of study leave, the ephemeral nature of employment at the frontier continued to feature heavily in Lorimer's life when, in November 1893, he returned to Peshawar to assume the position of settlement officer. In the following May, a second term in Bannu beckoned where, as assistant commissioner, he was again commended for his energy, commitment and ability. The additional observation that with increased experience he would make a first-class officer would be a regular comment of his overall performance in his early years of service. From early December 1894 to the middle of June 1895, Lorimer was relocated to Lahore, to serve as the officiating undersecretary to the government of Punjab.[88] Despite his enthusiasm, his time away from the frontier was not a good one, with the chief secretary observing that despite being a hard-working officer, Lorimer had been a disappointment in the temporary role, 'showing no grasp of subjects and no power of writing…'.[89] The criticism continued as he also considered that the junior official had too many irons in the fire, possibly distracting him from his core work.

But it was not all negative commentary as the chief secretary also confirmed what the lowland Scot already knew, that he had all the makings of a good frontier settlement officer. A month as deputy commissioner and district magistrate in Jhelum immediately followed, which was a welcomed relief following his horrid time in Lahore. In mid-July, he was moved on again, to Karnal in the Delhi Division where for two months, he took temporary charge of the district as deputy commissioner. It was just what he needed to positively project his competence, which were once again seen as areas of strength by his seniors. But the feedback was not all positive as his time in Karnal also exposed his perceived lack of experience. In his personal file, a reference to some undisclosed indiscretions in a couple of issues that were in hindsight, better left alone, was added. Despite this unhelpful observation, he was still considered to have the makings of 'an exceptionally good officer when he acquires more experience'.[90]

Back in Peshawar, general administration duties once again dominated his daily workload, although his routine got slightly more interesting when the Chitral relief expedition passed through his jurisdiction on its way to liberate the beleaguered fort. After a fifteen-thousand-strong military column, supported by thirty thousand pack animals and over nine thousand civilian followers, made camp and stripped his district clean of firewood and fodder, Lorimer and his compatriot, a forestry officer by the name of Haughton, were left to assess the impact of the expedition's destructive wake and the steps that needed to be taken to preserve the remaining woodland and plains. It was a familiar brief with a familiar co-worker, as it was the second time that they had worked together in Peshawar, having already jointly submitted a report to the government on the maintenance of forestry blocks and grazing land in the Khwarra plain. In September 1895, Lorimer looked once again to enhance his linguistic skills, taking two months leave to prepare for his Persian language exam, passing it with a higher proficiency grade which came with a two-thousand-rupee award. A brief return to Lahore in early November followed, but it was made palatable as Lorimer spent most of his time there on leave, rather than being back under the lieutenant governor's gaze.

Refreshed, in January 1896, Lorimer returned to Peshawar, this time for almost a year as assistant settlement officer, inspecting public works during which time he was promoted to assistant commissioner second grade. Whilst there, he also sat his Arabic exam, again to a higher proficiency and which again came with an additional allowance.[91] Life remained good when an opportunity to travel arose after he was given a mission to ride south-east with a small survey team to a prominent feature called Jalala Sar. Once there, he was to plot a seven-mile bearing to Toru Sar. Governed by compass and line of sight, the team scrambled up and down from point to point, mapping the terrain through the ravines and rocky high ground, none of it easily passable. By the end of September, Lorimer had completed his mission, establishing a curved line between the two points, in doing so, making his first contribution to statehood, demarcating a boundary that continues to exist, separating the Federal Administered Tribal Area from Khyber Pakhtunkha province in modern-day Pakistan.

Chapter 3

The Very Model of a Modern Waziri Political

In January 1897, impermanency continued to dominate Lorimer's life as he moved on once more, from Peshawar in the mountains to Shahpur in the agricultural plains, situated in the neighbouring Rawalpindi Division. For the two months that he was there to officiate as deputy commissioner, he was again noted for being keen, determined and 'quite [a] fit for the charge of a troublesome district' and yet despite having served in India for over six years, was still considered to be in the need of more experience.[92] One particular comment that, at times, he was too quick to come to a judgement, perhaps misinterpreted the ability to think and act on his feet.[93] A brief return to Peshawar followed as assistant commissioner where, again, he struggled to shake off the lingering perception that 'he need[ed] more knowledge of procedure and of [the] rules issued …[to guide] judicial officers'.[94] It is unclear if the sessions judge offered the comment that reflected a personal dislike, was an informed opinion of a professional shortcoming or was a standard observation given to all young temporary magistrates just passing through, as the divisional judge countersigning Lorimer's performance remarked that he had not carried out any civil judicial work at all during his brief tenure. It was fortunate that Lorimer was able to escape this echo-chamber of criticism when in May, he was relocated once more, to a new posting in Mardan, a fertile plain between Peshawar and Malakand.

The chance to put the negative commentaries aside and to prove he was both knowledgeable and experienced came in July 1897, when he packed his field gear and headed back to Bannu. He had received instructions to join a small cadre of political officers to be attached to the Tochi Field Force. After forming up a few weeks earlier over a hundred miles away near Khushalgarh, soldiers, cannons and caravans were now marching with purpose south-west to the troubled part of the frontier. The field force was the latest of four major military expeditions to be sent to the border region that year, to reaffirm British rule in the settled districts or to remind the tribes of their treaty obligations in the autonomous areas.[95] Its mission was to punish the Darwesh Khel, a Waziri Pashtun tribe by raising their Drepilai settlement to the ground and destroying their tribal fortifications in Maizar and Sheranni.[96] It was a familiar assignment, as such campaigns were a regular occurrence along the frontier, with sixty-two British military incursions mobilised from the region's annexation in 1849 to the end of the nineteenth century.

The punitive action this time followed a major tribal encounter involving Herbert Gee, the district's deputy commissioner and his three-hundred-strong military escort as they laagered briefly in Maizer, near the village of Drepilai.[97] As they settled in for a spot of breakfast having been lulled into a false sense of security by the local tribal chiefs, or *maliks*, volleys of gunfire from the village violently disrupted their morning routine. With only limited cover available outside the village walls, many British and native soldiers were struck down by bullets as their commanders attempted to appraise the situation. As an official rather than a military man, Gee watched on helplessly as the number of fatalities begun to creep up and officers fell. His escort soon returned fire, but an immediate counterattack against the aggressors, estimated to be over a thousand strong, was ruled out because of the limited supply of ammunition. Lacking options, the decision was made to withdraw. Gee, for so long a spectator, was finally able to contribute by evacuating a wounded British captain who was tethered to his pony's saddle, although the casualty bled out before Gee and his mount reached safety. The attackers' flanking actions were only beaten when substantial reinforcements skirmished their way back to the village and laid down overwhelming fire. Although over a hundred assailants were killed by the end of the melee, the government demanded that the 'premeditated and treacherous act of fanaticism' required further prosecution.[98]

The role of the political officers in such missions was to provide local knowledge to the military commanders. They also assumed overall political responsibility as the local government representatives although this often caused friction, particularly if they were civilian administrators with little or no military experience. As linguists, they had the additional unenviable task of meeting the elders within whose territory the deployed forces now dominated to either deliver ultimatums in their tribal councils, or *jirga*s, or to collect admissions of guilt and financial forfeits for their various misdemeanours. It was an extremely dangerous duty as neither could be handled through a third party or local intermediary. It also required tact and sensitivity, ruling out the military commanders who seldom had the linguistic or diplomatic skills required in such situations. Despite concerns in some quarters about his perceived lack of experience, Lorimer was still a person in demand. A specific request from the commissioner in a neighbouring district for him to take over the administration in Chitral in August, was turned down as Lorimer was considered to be of too much value to the Tochi Field Force. This was evident when it fell to Lorimer to take temporary charge within days of joining the expedition when Gee, who had been assigned as the mission's chief political officer, was struck down with fever and incapacitated. For ten days Lorimer provided political counsel to Major-General Corrie-Bird, the expedition's commanding officer.[99] Once relieved of this additional responsibility following the arrival of a more senior official to replace Gee, Lorimer received instructions to join the field force's First Brigade camped in the Miranshah garrison, some 30 miles west of Bannu.[100] Among its ranks were fellow Scots, the Argyll and Sutherland Highlanders, as well as a diverse grouping of religious and ethnic native regiments including Punjabi infantry and cavalry, Bengali sappers and a Peshawari mountain gun battery.

There, he remained in support of the brigade's commanding officer Brigadier-General Egerton until 28 October, when he received new orders. He was to accompany Corrie-Bird's senior military intelligence officer, Major Kemball, and his subordinate, Lieutenant Pirrie, a survey officer, for a two-week reconnaissance and survey of the villages of Mohmit Khel, Tori Khel and Kabul Khel. With just a small column of local cavalry, infantry and two field guns to provide a semblance of force protection, the detachment rode and marched for four days into the tribal hinterland before setting up camp at the mouth of Kaitu Valley. Once established, they spent another four days, surveying and reconnoitring their environs. Standard reporting procedures required that both the route in and out were sketched on a two-inch scale. A six-inch scale was afforded to separate sketches of the surveyed ground so that the detail of their surroundings could be better appreciated. Black ink was used throughout as the field service manuals forbade any creativity such as additional colour, shade or stumping to determine prominent features and relief. The British and Indian regiments had no intention of being found wanting for maps or lacking local knowledge unlike their army counterparts in southern Africa. While Kemball commanded, Pirrie surveyed and sketched his surroundings to required specifications. Lorimer helped Pirrie where he could or otherwise observed and engaged any passing locals, picking up morsels of intelligence that might add to the overall picture. All three were kept busy as none of the ground had been mapped before, ultimately contributing to the 920 square miles in total that was surveyed and the triangulation of 800 miles during the seven-month expedition.

In his eventual operational report, Kemball observed that 'for gazetteering, some knowledge of the local vernacular is practically indispensable as well as some previous training in the work', recognising Lorimer's specific contribution.[101] Brief but explicit gratitude was also expressed to Lorimer and his civilian political cohorts for their wider contribution to the mission in the field force's official account. Corrie-Bird, too, saw fit to submit a personal commendation to the government of India in recognition of Lorimer's particular services during the campaign, appreciating the work of 'a most capable and efficient officer'.[102]

Despite its size and composition, the field force was constantly vulnerable to harassing attacks resulting in fatalities and casualties. The altitude and local climate also plagued morale as men and pack-animal alike, struggled to acclimatise to the monthly changes. Temperatures in excess of 110 degrees Fahrenheit in July, soon dropped by over 70 degrees in November. In addition to the extreme fluctuations in weather, the heat, heavy rains and subsequent cold dry snaps, also brought with them heat stroke, malaria, diarrhoea and pneumonia. A few soldiers based in Bannu even managed to find the time to be struck down with venereal disease. As a veteran of the frontier, Lorimer in his quasi-official khaki suit, bowtie and standard-issue pith helmet, initially proved himself to be more than hardy to the changes in weather. The native regiments also seemed well suited to the climate, although the same could not be said of Lorimer's countrymen in the highlander regiment whose kilts soon became hot and heavy with sweat or rain as they marched, incubating an inevitable change of constitution in their stomachs. Eventually, Lorimer too, would succumb to fever.

Any non-medical suffering within the expedition came to an end in early January 1898 when relative calm returned to the sector. By June, the field force had been given permission to disband having succeeded in its objectives allowing the regiments to return to their garrisons scattered throughout Punjab. Although Lorimer's civilian status prevented him from being a fully fledged 'warrior scholar', he was able to reflect on his first experience of gazetteering alongside the military. He now had a valuable first-hand understanding of their operational requirements as much as the government of India's political and social ones: confirming or correcting routes, their compatibility with infantry, cavalry, artillery and caravans, obtaining descriptions of settlements and weapons to hand, as well as livestock and grazing, to inform navigation and encampment selections. For his part in the campaign, Lorimer was awarded the recently struck 1895 India Medal, a red and green vertically striped ribboned affair with a clasp inscribed with 'Punjab Frontier, 1897–98'.

Once the dust had settled in Tochi, despite being under no obligation to do so, Lorimer provided his own analysis on the administration of the valley since the expedition's punitive actions took place. His frank appraisal caught the eye of Louis Dane, chief secretary to the Punjab government. Dane in turn, wrote to the Foreign Department noting that the 'Tochi Report is so interesting and gives such a good account of the extremely useful work done quietly and unassumingly by Mr Lorimer that the Lieutenant-Governor thinks the Government of India would like to peruse it *in extenso*...'.[103] Plaudits continued with the conclusion that 'the progress and improvement made in the Tochi are largely due to Mr Lorimer's firmness and tact and ... political abilities which are exceptionally good...'.[104] As recommended by Dane, Lorimer's report was forwarded to Hugh Barnes, foreign secretary to the viceroy with a covering note observing that 'Mr Lorimer is evidently a good officer. He works on the right lines and is not afraid of acting on his own responsibility'.[105] The viceroy's reply was short but to the point, 'I entirely agree'.[106]

Following his spell in Tochi, Lorimer was back in his saddle, now headed for the Khyber agency for another temporary duty. Whilst in the agency, he offered another appraisal, this time on Peshawar's district commander, General Elles, and the government of India's Military Department's plan to introduce three new military posts along the Afridi tribal range, which they believed would reduce raiding and attacks in the area. Lorimer was frank in his report, questioning the rationality when the raiders would simply avoid carrying out illegal activities within the immediate vicinity of the outposts. He was, instead, of the view that the Afridi tribe should be given more responsibility for policing their homeland, with incentives for maintaining the peace and being held to account if the rate of criminality and raiding did not drop. He also shared his doubts about the proposed command structure, in particular that the outposts should take their orders from the local military commander rather than from the political officer who was the overall administrator and justice of the peace for the district. His counterview slowly worked its way up through the Punjab government and ultimately to the government of India where it was brought to Curzon's attention. The viceroy agreed with Lorimer's reasoning and commissioned a report acknowledging him for insisting on the principle of tribal responsibility. Curzon went further to demand that Lorimer's observation should become policy, although the question of command remained unanswered, stalled by the Military Department's reluctance to give such powers to civilians, even those who had served closely alongside the army on operations.[107]

Having now come to the attention of the viceroy, from Khyber, Lorimer received instructions to join the Foreign Department, spending time in Fort William in Calcutta and Simla as an assistant secretary.[108] As well as a respite from the physical challenges, political tensions and hardships at the frontier, the new role also gave him the chance to finish writing the *Customary law of the Main Tribes in the Peshawar District (1899)*, which was promptly submitted to the Lahore-based *Civil and Military Gazette Press* for publication, in the process extinguishing one of the many synonymic irons that he had in the fire. More an aide memoire than a book, Lorimer recorded the challenges and intricacies he had faced while administrating the district which could not be found in any official book of procedures.[109]

It took shape by asking one hundred and twenty-eight questions to hundreds of prominent Muslim and Hindu figures in Peshawar and the neighbouring settlements in Charsadda, Mardan, Nawshera, Pabbi and Lala Kala. Acknowledging the limitations to its accuracy, he hoped it could at least help prepare future judicial officers known colloquially as *munsiffs* and judges destined to serve justice in the frontier.[110] It was a modest observation as when the exercise was repeated thirty years later, none of the Muslim communities agreed to be questioned, arguing that they only followed *Sharia* not ancient tribal customs. No judgement was made on whether their disengagement was a sign of increased religious conservatism at the frontier, greater resentment of British interference or that Lorimer's successors had been unable to replicate his intimism and trust with the local tribal communities. A secondary survey of the same Hindu communities, however, resulted in just three amendments to his original guide.

Life remained mostly unchanged in Peshawar beyond attempts by the British to force their model of peace and governance upon its people. But as the twentieth century loomed, irreversible change would be thrust upon them by their current overlords. When Curzon became viceroy and governor-general in January 1899, he immediately looked to impose wholesale reforms on the governance of India. The perceived mishandling of the affairs in the frontier and independence of the Punjab government in particular, were high on the list of priority issues that he wanted to address. The more he probed to understand the extent of the problem at the frontier, the more he relished the thought of the lieutenant-governor of Punjab, Sir William Mackworth-Young, 'squirm[ing] a little at the apparition of a youthful Viceroy who asks questions, hazards doubts and is not content to leave [him] alone'.[111] Such conflict fed Curzon's ego, as he firmly believed that failure did not lie with the Pathan tribes and their resentment of British rule but with officials who were responsible for their governance. He considered many of his staffers to be unqualified, inadequately trained and incapable of developing deep knowledge of the region, not helped as they never seemed to spend long periods in any particular posting.

In many ways Curzon's view echoed *The Edinburgh Review*'s 1874 article, although it was more a criticism of the various lieutenant-governors and their desk-bound officials in Lahore and other provincial capitals, administering from distance rather than their compatriots, the political agents and commissioners who were trying to maintain the peace at the frontier in various states of hardship. This criticism also reflected his opinion of the ICS more generally, a derogatory view that had been handed down to him by his viceregal predecessors as well as from other high quarters. Queen Victoria the Empress of India, despite having never visited her Asian realm, had expressed her 'dislike of the [Indian] Civil Service… [a view that was] fostered not only by her entourage, but by the [wider] Royal Family'.[112] The Prince Regent no doubt helped foster her aversion of the ICS, having come back from his visit to India in 1875–76 with the strong view that the competition system was a failure.[113]

There might have been some kernels of truth in Curzon's accusations, but he failed to appreciate some of the reasons why so many officers did not want to serve at, or beyond, the periphery of the British empire. Many found themselves out of pocket and having to constantly argue for, or justify, their allowances. For others, some of the outposts were extremely unhealthy or dangerous and no place for a wife or a family, and few if any, were a place where a cad from Wren and Gurney's could continue to ride their luck. He may not have been sympathetic about their personal circumstances, but when consulting Mackworth-Young and his frontier officers about the overarching problems at hand, Curzon was quick to note the mutual distrust between the Punjab government and its men in the field. In a letter to Lord Hamilton, the secretary of state for India (and former viceroy), he took pleasure in the 'unanimous pronouncement of the leading officials of the Punjab government against their own system'.[114] In part Curzon considered, these failings could be remedied by a form of gerrymandering: establishing a new frontier province that would mostly contain the Pathan tribes, overseen by a chief commissioner in place of a lieutenant-governor, one who would be based in Peshawar as Curzon's representative, ultimately centralising power in Calcutta (or its fair-weather equal, Simla) rather than in Lahore. Another of Curzon's remedies was for the political officers to be recast, no longer working for the Punjab government but to be amalgamated into the Indian Political Service (IPS), working domestically in the Home or Political Departments or overseas as part of the Foreign Department.

Once Curzon's mind was set, he could not be dissuaded by senior officials most resistant to his 'Frontier Scheme'. Known for his combative instinct, he enjoyed sparring with them intellectually as they harrumphed against his plans, countering each argument they put forward for maintaining the status quo.[115] Hamilton, theoretically Curzon's superior in Whitehall, was also unable to land any successful blows despite his own belief that the existing model of governance at the frontier should be left as it was. By September 1900, Curzon had convinced the council, first individually and then collectively, to support his ambitions to establish the North-West Frontier Province and to restructure the regional government. The only remaining dissenter was Mackworth-Young, who Curzon had initially avoided and then ignored.[116] In January 1901, Hamilton admitted defeat and so, with Whitehall's reluctant approval, the restructuring began.

As men and boundaries moved in line with Curzon's wishes, he saw the opportunity to reduce some of the more mundane jobs currently being done by equally mundane civil servants by replacing them with well-educated Pathans. He also enquired whether the '*Maliki* System' could be introduced more widely throughout the province to maintain law and order. This novel approach was first introduced in Baluchistan around 1890 by Robert Sandeman, currently deputy commissioner of Dera Ismail Khan. Rather than try to persevere with the unsuccessful policy of direct rule, Sandeman introduced patronage, supporting suppliant *maliks* rather than tribal elders known as 'white-beards' or 'mashers' to maintain stability.[117] So far, Lorimer had been supportive in general of Curzon's vision and had been vocal about making the tribes more responsible for the security in their areas, but this latest initiative forced him to break ranks. Drawing from his long immersion in Peshawar, he wrote that 'with reference to the future management of the tribe... the Government of India ... [should] observe that the best method of dealing with the Pathans of Waziristan ... [remains] a matter for experiment'.[118] His use of the scientific term would later resonate in policy papers to flag the potential dangers of a shift in thinking in such a volatile tribal laboratory. Although Sandeman's model was lauded in Parliament over three and a half thousand miles away, on the ground, Lorimer's concern about introducing untested governance policies was an informed and respected interjection.[119] William Merk, commissioner of Derajat, which encompassed Punjab, Khyber and Baluchistan, agreed with Lorimer's doubts and considered the system to be impractical because of the way that some of the Waziri tribes governed themselves. Rather than just pay allowances to selected *maliks*, both believed that wealth should instead be given to the entire tribe with the caveat that they would also be held accountable collectively for any offences, regardless of the guilty tribal section or individual.

Whatever personal reservations Lorimer might have had more generally about the viceroy's view on the wider ICS, he was just the type of officer that Curzon believed should shape the North-West Frontier Province, who considered the region to be 'the nursery of the new school of political officers who would revive the memories and credit of bygone days'.[120] Lorimer's metamorphosis from a provincial political agent to a fully fledged 'political' would also bring him closer to the viceroy as a member of the IPS. It was the only part of the ICS that Curzon genuinely respected where the 'qualities of tact and flexibility, of moral fibre and gentlemanly bearing … are an instinct rather than an acquisition'.[121] One can only guess whether these were values adopted by those who had passed through Haileybury or the various scoundrels who fell out of the crammers. It also contradicted the belief that officials should have ideally graduated from one of the great universities (Curzon, a former Balliol scholar, was a strong supporter of this academic preference) but there was no doubting that Lorimer had the right personal qualities. He was now gaining a reputation beyond Lahore, as Curzon and his advisors in Calcutta became more aware of his activities and informed judgements.

While the viceroy sketched out his ideas for a forward policy along the frontier, Lorimer remained nearby to advise on affairs in the tribal areas. When his time in the department came to an end, he took a period of leave before an expectant return to the frontier. Not long after, Watson Cunningham, Curzon's foreign secretary, passed on the viceroy's gratitude, feeling that the Scot had worked 'with great industry and ability'.[122] In an unusually modest tone, Curzon's reflections continued that he had profited a good deal from Lorimer's experience of Waziristan and hoped one day, to be able to help the official in his future career in the IPS.[123] Lorimer's star was finally on the rise.

It was of some relief to the government of India when in November 1900, Lorimer was initially sent back to Calcutta at the end of his furlough despite Curzon's promise to post him to Baluchistan, as his experience was required once again to support another military expedition. His first expeditionary foray in Tochi was fronted with danger, equally at risk of being struck down by disease as he was by a bullet from a modern rifle, a long-barrelled *jezail* musket or with a blade of Damascus steel. He was expecting much more of the same this time as his latest special duty assignment was to support the military action as a blockade officer, a workload that would have to be managed whilst also serving as the deputy commissioner in Miranshah.[124]

The sanctions began in late 1899 when the Nasran border police station was attacked by Mahsud tribesmen, the outcome of which was the murder of two local soldiers and the spiriting away of eight Snyder rifles and ammunition. When Merk was unable to collect appropriate reparations from the tribe for their actions, an ultimatum was given. As the chiefs gathered together sitting on their haunches at the *jirga*, he announced in Pashtu that tribal allowances were to be stopped and a blockade established if penance and reparations were not received within fifteen days. The *malik*s deliberated his concerns but were either unwilling or unable to comply. At the end of the period of grace, they requested an additional two months to consider the terms. Sensing that this was a stalling action, Merk had little choice but to use his plenipotentiary powers. A blockade was proclaimed to commence on the first of December.

Signals were sent to the nearby garrisons and two columns of soldiers were quickly stood to, with orders to reinforce the existing troop strongholds and to picket a cordon around the whole of the Mahsud's traditional areas. Unable to travel, trade or raid, the Mahsud were soon forced to reconsider their options. After initially negotiating and agreeing terms for monthly repayments until the fine was paid off, another *jirga* was called when villages in neighbouring districts continued to be raided and cordon patrols harangued. Again, Merk was forced to warn the tribal elders that there would be reprisals if the attacks continued.

From afar, Lorimer initially followed the blockade with some detachment as things slowly unfolded. Rather than help coordinate a military action against the tribal aggressors, his time was spent skirmishing against the Waziristan Militia Committee. Comprised of Egerton (now a general and Chief of Punjab Command), senior representatives from the Military Department and Mackworth-Young, Lorimer tried to persuade its members into withdrawing all regular troops from North Waziristan. Before making a final decision, he called for some consideration to be given to keeping some regular troops in the district in addition to the local militia as too much expectation was being put upon the latter. It was his opinion that 'the Khyber Rifles have been overdone and the same thing seems likely to happen in North Waziristan, which is a more precarious place. Local militia, it should be remembered, are [still] only an experiment…'.[125]

It was not a dissenting view on the reliance of auxiliary forces as he had always understood that 'one of the objects of the militia scheme was to enable the government to hold exposed and dangerous posts, which must occasionally suffer, without loss to valuable regular troops or detriment to the army'.[126] Lorimer's concern was that if the scheme failed, control of North Waziristan risked being lost in the absence of a British military presence. Continuing with his counterattack, it was hard for him to see how the government's current policy of maintaining control over the tribes, its commitment to provide security so that revenues could be collected safely, ability to stop tribal raids into Afghanistan whilst also encouraging safe cross-border trade, could be achieved if there were no British military forces on hand to support the political officers. Remembering the problems faced in Khyber and the friction between the political officers and local commanders over primacy, Lorimer also felt obliged to revisit 'this thorny question [that has been] passed over in silence … but is one which requires to be definitely settled'.[127] Challenging the military commander and the committee further, he concluded by stressing that concentrating regular forces in posts far away from the frontier could only be seen by the tribes and the Russians as a sign of political if not military weakness. There was 'even a danger of "concentration" being used as an empty catch word and of action being taken under its authority without due regard to results'.[128]

In March 1900, Lorimer had the opportunity to accompany Curzon on his visit to the frontier, joining the viceroy, Mackworth-Young and Merk in Dera Ismail Khan as they met in committee to discuss the issue. Mackworth-Young remained in strong agreement with Egerton that withdrawing regular troops was the preference. Sympathetic to Lorimer and his fellow officer's views, but equally aware of the financial issues that worried the committee, Curzon compromised by agreeing that two battalions of militia should be raised from the local tribes to be commanded by British officers, while posts of no tactical value were to be abandoned.[129] He also demanded that new watchtowers should be built and agreed with the gathered committee members that the militia should take over from the regulars completely, but only if the experiment proved to be a success. Curzon also grasped Lorimer's thorny issue of overall command by deciding that the military commander should be subordinate to the political officer, regardless of any comparative length of service except in matters of drill, discipline and internal administration. Instructions to the Military Department ensured that the new directive was taken forward immediately.[130]

Family and official business intertwined several months later, when Lorimer wrote a letter of support for his brother Lock, seconding his sibling's request to transfer from the Punjab Frontier Force's Queen's Own Corps of Guides to the Khyber Rifles.[131] This was despite his personal reservations about the government's overreliance on the auxiliaries to plug security gaps. Lock had followed his elder brother overseas by joining the Indian Army in August 1896. Arriving in-country in mid-November, he remained unattached in Punjab Command until late December the following year when he joined the 8th Rajput Bengal Infantry as a wing officer.[132] In September 1898, Lock transferred to the guides, a highly mobile and deployable elite force that combined infantry companies with cavalry squadrons that had relieved Chitral in 1895 and participated in the 1897 Tochi campaign. He remained with the guides until he joined the Khyber Rifles, a move made easier by having the endorsement of a former political officer stationed at the frontier.

Although the Military Department had made clear its desire to reduce costs by decreasing the number of British military personnel serving at the border, a view that Curzon was sympathetic towards, the viceroy's immediate concern was the high rate of officer resignations within the frontier militias. If such acts continued unabated, it could have forced a decision to withdraw them altogether if too few remained committed before the concept could be fully tested.[133] Lock's request for transfer was immediately approved, a decision that was made easy given the source of the recommendation and retention pressures. On 28 December 1900, the younger Lorimer was posted as the quartermaster to the 2nd Battalion, Khyber Rifles based in Jamrud, one of only four British officers in charge of the 1,224 native soldiers who made up the local reactionary force.[134] Five days later, he was given the additional position as adjutant.

On New Year's Eve 1901, Lock would again call on his older brother to put pen to paper to support his application to 'seek political employment in the hope of getting a place in the new province…'.[135] This request followed a similar letter of endorsement which had been written in October by Captain G Roos-Keppel, the current political officer in Khyber who considered Lock to be 'an officer of exceptional ability … [with] a good manner with natives, … very hard working and an excellent linguist…'.[136] Like his brother, Lock had also sat and passed to a higher standard, exams in Urdu, Pashtu and Persian. He eventually joined the IPS in March 1903, but it would be on his own merit rather than any influence that his brother or his counterparts might have had, performing admirably whilst on special duty to help deliver the Coronation Delhi Durbar that had taken place earlier that year. His efforts compelled Dane to report to Curzon that Lock had been 'full of tact and resource, and had about the hardest work of any of the attaches'.[137] When in the same round of correspondence, the question was asked about whether he should be brought on as a probationer given his excellent fit as a 'political', Curzon agreed.[138]

In August 1901, Curzon unwittingly tested Lorimer's resilience when he was given the responsibility as the Wannu political officer in South Waziristan in addition to being the deputy commissioner in Miranshah and continuing his special duty as blockade officer. The viceroy had demanded a change in campaign strategy from one of passive policing to aggressive retaliation. Military mobilisation immediately followed with the formation of four columns, to be posted in Datta Khel, Jandola, Sarwakei and Wannu respectively to persuade the Mahsud through force to reconsider their position. The change in approach was immediate, with the official account recording that on 25 November 1901

> No.3 Column, consisting of 1,000 rifles of the 1st Punjab Infantry, 35th Sikhs, and 29th Punjab Infantry, under Colonel Macleod of the last-named regiment, left Sarwakei early on the 25th and reached the Shahur Tangi without opposition. Two days were spent in destroying all of the defences in the neighbourhood; after which the force returned to Sarwakei with seven prisoners and 500 head of cattle.[139]

Lorimer's despatch five days later of the same action as the patrol's accompanying political officer suggests that it was slightly more eventful than reported. Attached to the main force, along with a small party of local guides and Mahsud spies, he headed off towards the nearby villages just before dawn of the first day, making best use of the darkness. Such a large body would normally be conspicuous, but they were able to maintain the element of surprise by detaining a local leader who was responsible for warning the settlements of any approaching military patrols.[140] Many villages were levelled with explosives and caves full of grain were destroyed, leaving the tribal fighters and their families without shelter or food. Watchtowers manned by Mahsud snipers deterred some approaching patrols from attacking their villages when commanders assessed that they could not 'be entered without loss disproportionate to the object to be gained'.[141] Other settlements that had previously provided information to Lorimer were also spared from the column's wrath. It was a heavy-handed affair, but things were only considered to have got out of control when some of the villages were looted by soldiers from the 35th Sikhs and 29th Punjabs. As the patrol headed back to Sarwakei two days later with prisoners and confiscated livestock in tow, Mahsud fighters harassed the retirement with rifle fire but Lorimer was not alone in judging that the column's success must have been depressing for the tribesmen who had not been able to fight back in strength to prove their resolve.

Far from being an isolated event, the Mahsud found themselves subject to a series of major military actions as the four columns of Indian infantry, cavalry and mountain guns attacked strongholds and lookouts scattered across their territory. Lorimer assessed the Waziri tribe could call on a little over twelve hundred modern Martini-Henry and Snyder rifles while many more carried traditional *jezails*.[142] Despite this great imbalance in firepower, the fighters tried to give as good as they got with thirty-two British and Indian soldiers shot dead by Mahsud sharpshooters and a hundred and fourteen more wounded. A political officer was also among the fallen, killed during a skirmish at a village watchtower. The native regiments in turn claimed one hundred and twenty-six tribesmen dead and two hundred and fifty fighters wounded, with another two hundred taken prisoner. Between artillery and gun cotton, gunners, sappers and pioneers claimed the destruction of sixty-four watchtowers and the levelling of over a hundred and fifty villages, while the infantry repatriated in excess of eight thousand head of livestock as compensation.

Unable to sustain any further assaults against their homes and defences, in January 1902, the Mahsud invited Merk and his political officers to a *jirga* to negotiate a cessation of hostilities. Trusting their word and content that the government's original conditions would be met, Merk lifted the blockade in early March. Stability was again temporarily restored. As the campaign came to an end so did Lorimer's assignment as a blockade officer but not before Merk had reflected on his subordinate's role, confessing that Lorimer had carried out the brunt of the campaign's executive work, working admirably, indefatigably and zealously, showing remarkable qualifications for the role 'often under great exposure and failing health', all of which added to 'an already deservedly high reputation'.[143] Intra-political conflict within which, Lorimer had been a prominent figure, had also been resolved when Curzon's reforms reached a conclusion with a new jurisdiction, the North West Frontier Province, officially founded on the new King Emperor's birthday on 9 November 1901. In typical British fashion, its foundation was formally celebrated the following April by a *durbar* in Peshawar.

In between his routine and considerable blockade responsibilities, Lorimer found time to withdraw another notional iron from the fire when he completed and secured the publication of his second book, *Grammar and Vocabulary of Waziri Pashto*. His latest work was an opportunity to prove again, his selfless service to the Crown as well as his academic proficiency and remarkable knowledge of the tribal region despite the absence of a great university degree. It was a substantial piece of work, written to help British officers serving in Bannu and Peshawar, to better understand the differences in Pashtu vernacular used in the respective settlements despite them being just eighty miles apart. The nuance, he proposed in his introductory note, was hardly less than the challenges faced by a broad Scot and an English Cockney if they tried to converse. The comparison was probably informed more from his time at Wren and Gurney's rather than at Edinburgh or Oxford. The tome also provided a brief history of Waziristan, drawn predominantly from his time in both districts, demonstrating an incomparable depth of knowledge and ethos that Curzon yearned for from his officials. When concluding his work, Lorimer offered a candid view of the people he had tried his best to govern:

> If the reader closes these pages having gained a distinct impression of the race, free-born and murderous, hot-headed and light-hearted, self-respecting but vain, which peoples the hills of Waziristan, and of the gross Satyr-like spadesmen whose abode is in the main valley, then the present slight sketch has been penned to some purpose. Furthermore, if the reader quits the subject with relief, his feelings will only resemble those with which the writer relinquished political charge of the Tochi after a two years' residence there, and the cause will probably be the same – involuntary abhorrence of human types which deviate in such an extreme degree from what Europeans are accustomed to consider the human standard.[144]

Although written for local consumption, copies were also sent to the India Office in London with a covering letter from Curzon to Hamilton, welcoming its publication, which he believed would be of considerable use to both military and civil officers employed in the region. Recognising the effort of over two and a half years of Lorimer's personal time and nearly 800 rupees of his own money in preparing the book, Curzon also proposed the granting of an honorarium of 2,000 rupees for his selfless commitment, one which Hamilton was content to endorse.[145]

In addition to his financial award, at the end of the latest hostilities Lorimer also received the 'Waziristan' clasp to add to his India Medal. Another fitting tribute to his dedication was the recognition in that year's coronation honours for his wider contribution to political affairs.[146] He was made a Companion of the Order of the Indian Empire (CIE) and presented with a gold and red enamelled lotus flower medal mounted with a dark-blue ribbon. It was one of just thirteen CIEs to be bestowed that June. In the same gazette, Percy Cox in Muscat was awarded the same honour. Despite being fellow 'politicals', their paths had yet to cross, but they would soon meet beyond the empire's frontier. Despite his impending bestowage, on 19 June 1902, Lorimer headed off on leave, a week before his CIE was announced with plans to enjoy a very generous combination of one year and ten months statutory furlough, plus another two months privilege and special blockade leave.[147]

His departure from the newly founded province would mean missing Curzon's celebratory Peshawar *durbar*. Rather than head straight back to Scotland, Lorimer decided instead, to continue to broaden his horizons by sailing to British East Africa (Kenya) via Aden where by his own admission, he had the loneliest of birthdays.[148] Whilst there, he chanced his arm by sitting the government's Swahili exams given the various linguistic influences of Arabic, Persian, French and others. It was a gamble worth taking although he only received a pass, the minimum language requirement to be one of the Colonial Service's assistant district officers. Buoyed by his result nonetheless, he even considered becoming a superintendent in the Indian Immigration Service in East Africa if ever a temporary posting became available. With such postings outside the government of India's influence, success would require approaching the Colonial Office and its hypercritical assistant private secretary. As he continued his travels during his leave, he would later have doubts about working in the African continent, with his experiences of Djibouti, Zanzibar and Uganda in particular, all changing his mind. Although ultimately dissuaded from a future in Africa, while in Somaliland, Lorimer still had a thirst for service and military action when he tried 'to get on the Somali show … [to join] the scrimmage they had there up-country'.[149] It was a boy's-own reference to Lieutenant-Colonel Eric Swayne, commissioner of British Somaliland and commander of an ongoing military campaign against Muhammad Ahmad bin Abdullah, the self-proclaimed Mahdi of Sudan and his followers. The British knew him by another name, the 'Mad Mullah'. Lorimer was unsuccessful as the force had already set off before he could make his case to be added to Swayne's order of battle. Disappointed, he later 'came away disgusted from Berbera, and [hoped] it was not [my] curse that [eventually] brought misfortune on the expedition'.[150] What curse Lorimer believed he was under given his recent successful exploits at the Indian frontier is unknown.

By November he had made his way to Cairo, setting himself up at the Turf Club where he looked to improve his conversational and classical understanding of Arabic. As he whiled away the days taking in the local language and culture, he took time to reflect on his time there. In a letter to Alfred Grant, secretary to the chief commissioner in the North-West Frontier Province, he considered Cairo to be

> a wee bit disappointing: very much like Paris with the better class wearing fezes instead of hats and the workmen blue night gowns instead of blue blouses. The smells are those of Calcutta without any modification of colour or shape. The climate seems delightful however, and there are always the Pyramids and the Citadel.[151]

Despite his disappointment in his surroundings, Lorimer spent the winter in Cairo to avoid a much colder one in Straithmartine, but it was soon time to pack his belongings and look to return home. After securing safe passage from Alexandria, he set off to return to Lunburn Cottage. With more than a year of furlough remaining, Lorimer still had plenty of time to decompress from the constant pressures and threats he had faced on a regular basis at the Indian frontier. But whether the government of India could afford to be without one of its rising stars for so long, or Lorimer could survive such a period of inactivity, remained to be seen.

Chapter 4

Curzon's Grand Tour

Despite Whitehall's reservations about Curzon's forward policy ambitions, political free rein had been given when it came to handling India's domestic affairs. British ministers only pulled back hard when he looked westward with intent at Persia and the various friendly sheikhdoms scattered along the Arabian coast. Hamilton may have lost the argument for retaining the status quo in the North-West Frontier Province but was more successful in curtailing the viceroy's initial ambitions to tour the region in 1901. Even Curzon had to concede that neither the British nor Indian governments could afford a diplomatic or military spat with the Turks in the Gulf when British, Colonial and Indian troops were consumed fighting the Boer.

Hamilton's embargo and Salisbury's clear objection, however, only temporarily curbed the viceroy's expeditionary enthusiasm. Since his earlier travels to Persia, Curzon maintained that he would impeach any British minister guilty of surrendering even a quota of Britain's supremacy in the Gulf to the Russians.[152] Such claims might have been hyperbole, but in spring 1903 he pulled the reins for some political slack when news filtered through that the Russian and French warships *Boyarin* and *Infernet* had been seen cruising through the Gulf together. Their short stopovers and political outreach in Muscat, Bandar Abbas, Bushire, Lingeh and Kuwait, were seen as a deliberate attempt to encroach on British interests. The Germans too, with their Drive to the East or *Drang nach Osten* policy and their emperor, King Willhelm II's closeness to the Sublime Porte was also of increasing concern, not least as he had also claimed to be the protector of the Muslim world. The March 1903 signature of the Baghdad Railway Convention also gifted the Germans the opportunity to establish strong footholds in Baghdad, Basrah and beyond with their associated rights and concessions, potentially at Britain's expense.

One positive development was that the war in southern Africa no longer weighed heavily on the empire's consciousness or purse. At the end of May the previous year, Britain's deeply flawed military campaign had finally succeeded in forcing the Boers to come to terms. Peace might have prevailed, but the empire now needed to repair its reputation as a global power or risk questions being asked about the end of the war being the start of its demise. Curzon's reins were about to be loosened, although unexpectedly by the Foreign, rather than the India Office. On 5 May, a new policy was announced in the House of Lords when Lansdowne declared that

> there is no doubt that in the Gulf, as in other parts of Persia, we are feeling very keenly the competition of other Powers. That, I am afraid, is our fate not only in Persian waters; nor can we expect, because we have beer, in the development of commerce throughout the world, the pioneers of that form of civilisation, that we shall always be able to maintain the position of superiority which we at first enjoyed.[153]

The announcement meant little to Lorimer back in Scotland as he whiled away his days on leave, but in Calcutta, Lansdowne's change in policy direction was just what the viceroy was hoping for. Only he could answer the secretary of state for foreign affairs' call. But Curzon not only wanted beer; he demanded the brewery. Deciding against seeking permission from the India Office to tour the peninsula, he only informed Hamilton in mid-September of his intent after most of the planning had been done. With the various Gulf rulers now preparing for his arrival, to cancel the visit at such a late stage risked unnecessary reputational damage.

Curzon's November and December 1903 cruise would have all of the pomp, circumstance and kowtowing to meet the expectations of a young, dynamic but also self-absorbed viceroy. It would also have the prerequisite political and military clout to counter unwelcomed Russian, French or any other foreign intrusions. Gun salutes, originally introduced into India by the EIC as a respectful salutation to the rulers in the princely states, would additionally feature. The visit's official purpose was to inspect 'the [political agencies] maintained there, of visiting the Arab Shaikhs in treaty relations with the British Government, and of testifying to the paramount political and commercial ascendency exercised by Great Britain in Persian waters'.[154] A secondary objective was later introduced, to reconnoitre potential locations for British naval bases and stations should Curzon's forward policy gather considerable momentum and support within wider political and military circles. In reality, it was a performance to deceive in the absence of any other major policy announcements, ultimately about style rather than substance, the 'politics of pageantry' designed to massage Curzon's ego, to test his theories about Britain's regional prominence and to seek some answers to his '*Persian Question*'.[155]

He would have much preferred to have travelled alone but understood by including the Foreign Office's minister to the Tehran legation, Sir Arthur Hardinge, a joint Foreign Office and government of India excursion also reduced the likelihood of Hamilton turning his belated request down. Curzon could also not ignore that Persia was ultimately in the Foreign Office's domain, despite the government of India's presence in the south of the country, through its political and consular outposts. As it was, Sir Arthur's participation proved to be unimposing although his dealings with his Persian interlocutors did little to impress Curzon who was already aware of the Persian government's general manner of 'vis inertia'.[156] Rear-Admiral Atkinson-Willes, commander of the East India Squadron based in Ceylon, whose ships patrolled the Gulf and guaranteed Britain's security obligations as set out in the long-established General Treaty was also begrudgingly invited to participate in the grand tour. His inclusion, however, was not without moments of friction.[157]

Curzon needed the rear-admiral to participate, having agreed with advice given by Colonel Charles Kemball, the political resident in Bushire, and Major Cox in Muscat on the optics of having an imposing physical presence.[158] To help persuade the senior naval officer to increase the size of his escort, the offer was made to use the cruise as cover to support the Royal Navy's outstanding operational requirement to survey both the Persian and Arabian coastlines. Even after Atkinson-Willes agreed to join Curzon and committed ships to enhance the tour, there continued to be a clash of personalities between the Admiralty and War Office's regional representative, and Curzon and Dane, now the government of India's secretary of the Foreign Department and Curzon's chief aide.

This became evident when Atkinson-Willes corrected Dane's intended newspaper entry that would announce the forthcoming viceregal maritime excursion. Curzon would not be 'escorted by the East India Squadron' as the foreign secretary had drafted, but would instead be 'accompanied' by his ships as only the sovereign, King Edward VII, not his viceroy, could order such an escort.[159] The next day, he could not resist reminding Dane and the viceroy that the revised draft gazette, which declared that he would be accompanying the viceroy, was also incorrect, as he had received no such orders from the Admiralty to do so.[160] Knowing that without a substantial naval presence, Curzon's tour would look precarious and weak, Atkinson-Willes flexed his muscles further by demanding to know who would be paying for the coal needed to fuel the warships' boilers as no orders from the British government had been received to support the tour. Left with little choice, Curzon's accountants in Calcutta reluctantly agreed to fund the Royal Navy's running costs for the cruise. They also tried to have the last word by reminding the rear-admiral that although the government of India would cover all costs, *Pomone* was already being subsidised by their central coffers, but it was hardly a killer blow. It might have been Curzon's cruise, but they were definitely Atkinson-Willes's ships.

After the release of a factually correct newspaper announcement and to the sound of a thirty-one-gun salute, the mandatory number for a viceroy, late in the afternoon of 16 November, the white-hulled troopship RIMS *Hardinge* slipped Karachi harbour with the viceroy and his wife, Lady Mary Curzon, on-board. A small entourage, including Dane and Lorimer, recently returned from Scotland, accompanied them. Waiting outside the harbour entrance was HMS *Argonaut*, a *Diadem*-class, eleven-thousand-tonne, first-class cruiser. *Argonaut* was a visually impressive four-funnelled armoured battleship with heavy guns bristling fore and aft with many more at various points along its waist. It was a fortuitous addition to Curzon's assorted flotilla having just come off station in China with orders to return to England. Despite *Argonaut*'s prominence, HMS *Hyacinth*, a cruiser of just over five thousand tonnes, was to lead the Royal Naval complement for the cruise. On board the flagship was Atkinson-Willes. Smaller cruisers, the HMS *Fox* and HMS *Pomone*, also loitered nearby as they waited to join *Hardinge* on its voyage. All were dressed with flags from their masts, adding splashes of colour to break up the battleship-grey of their hulls and superstructures. Their bands played rousing tunes as Royal Marine guards manned the decks at attention, adding to the acoustic and visual aesthetics. Gun-crews also stood ready, all firing their own thirty-one-gun salutes as *Hardinge* passed them by, acknowledging the high-ranking human cargo that it carried. Little did the various gun-crew chiefs know that a considerable amount of gunpowder was going to be spent over the next few weeks as they followed the protocol for gun salute diplomacy. Once the ships had steered into formation, they set a course south-west to cross the Gulf of Oman.

On the morning of 18 November, Curzon's flotilla approached the still waters of Muscat harbour where RIMS *Lawrence* with political resident Kemball on-board sat at anchor. Nearby was HMS *Lapwing*, a *Redbreast*-class gunboat from the Gulf squadron that had also received orders from Atkinson-Willes to join the inbound flotilla. *Lapwing* would additionally serve as the flotilla's lackey, tasked to collect telegrams and mail from various telegraphic outposts and political agencies for the viceroy to read throughout his tour. As the designated flagship, *Hyacinth* was the first to enter the bay, where it was greeted by a twenty-one-gun salute from Mirani fort, one of two formidable citadels that overlooked the natural harbour.[161] *Hyacinth* dutifully returned each shot with one of its own. A further thirty-one guns were fired when *Hardinge* and its considerable maritime escort joined *Hyacinth*, signalling the viceroy's arrival. Cox initially suggested that the viceroy should also bring his bodyguard to likewise impress the Gulf rulers and general public of his status but was turned down by Dane. As a compromise, Curzon agreed that *Argonaut*'s detachment of Royal Marines could, instead, provide a ceremonial guard where appropriate.[162]

Waiting shore-side was the ruler of Muscat, Sultan Faisal bin Turki Al Busa'idi's older half-brother, Sayyid Mohammed, and Faisal's eldest son, Sayyid Taimur, both of whom were familiar figures to the political agency. The EIC initially managed relations with Muscat in 1763, through its residency in Bushire. This changed in 1800, when a treaty agreed that 'an Englishman of respectability, on the part of the Honourable Company, shall always reside at the port of Muscat…'.[163] It was one of the first agency outposts to be established and with just a few absences, the EIC and its successor, the government of India, remained true to its treaty obligations. The same could not always be said of the various Al Busa'idi sultans, who had, at times, paid lip service to their treaty commitments. With French complicity, they had even allowed Omani dhows to fly the Tricolour as they smuggled guns and slaves from Africa to Arabia and India, a ploy that prevented them from being boarded by patrolling Royal Navy ships. Despite these occasional differences, the bilateral relationship was for the most part, a positive one.

Once the crescendo of gunfire had stopped, the uncle and nephew were rowed out from the palace to *Hardinge*. Once on-board, Mohammed began formalities as the sultan's representative, by welcoming the viceroy to Muscat. After expressing his brother's honour and desire to celebrate Curzon's auspicious arrival, both royal representatives returned to shore as thirteen more gunshots fired in salutation. No sooner had they landed then the sultan headed out to *Hardinge*. But rather than head straight out to see the viceroy, he was first given a boat tour of the numerous anchored warships. Just four years earlier, Sultan Faisal had seen another sizeable British naval force in Muscat Bay and had been similarly invited on-board the flagship. That time, rather than receive a friendly welcome, the sultan had been given an ultimatum to rescind a recent coaling station concession to the French or watch HMS *Eclipse*'s guns open up on his capital.[164] It was a not-so-subtle, but ultimately successful, use of British diplomatic hard-power. Now, however, was a time for gunpowder rather than gunboat diplomacy and accompanied reassuringly by Cox, the sultan was ushered on-board and led to the quarter-deck where a tented area decked with golden-embroidered carpets had been arranged for his encounter with the waiting viceroy. After a brief conversation with Curzon who accepted the recent invitation and offer of hospitality, the sultan returned to his palace to the sound of twenty-one shots from *Fox*'s guns.

Gunpowder smoke hung in the air again just after noon when further audible salutes shattered the peace to mark the French and American consuls' arrival on *Hardinge* to pay their own respects to the viceroy, followed shortly after by another thirty-one guns as Curzon finally disembarked and headed to shore. Greeting him landside was three hundred yards of coloured bunting, hung from the sultan's palace to the British political agency while various flags flew from the two forts that in a previous age, had been substantial deterrents against any would-be belligerents. After lunch with Cox and a short address to local British Indian merchants who had assembled there, Curzon was taken to the palace to return the sultan's courtesy. Waiting for him at the entrance in unbearable heat was Sultan Faisal, *Argonaut*'s music band and thirty Royal Marines as a guard of honour. That the band and guard were present at the palace was not a forgone conclusion given another clash of wills between Curzon and Atkinson-Willes. When the viceroy was asked if the rear-admiral should land ahead of him in Muscat and in doing so, receive his own gun salute, his reply was that 'It is not the Admiral's visit but the Viceroy's and I can see no reason why there should be Admiral's visits or salutes at all'.[165] A simple withdrawal of Atkinson-Willes's sailors and Royal Marines would have amply expressed his feelings on the matter.

With the meeting at the palace just another formality, Curzon and the sultan filled their time together with rounds of pleasantries and awkward small talk, disturbed only briefly by Mohammad, who made a scene by wishing to make his own claim to the throne if the sultan ever abdicated. Cox would later record it as little more than an 'ebullition of wounded pride' from an elder brother whose own claim as sovereign was weak, but it signalled that all was not well in Muscat.[166] As Curzon returned to his floating palace, he saw the addition of HMS *Sphinx* at anchor in the bay, which had just carried Sir Arthur down from Tehran via Bushire to join the ceremonies. That evening, Lorimer joined Cox, Atkinson-Willes, Kemball and Sir Arthur at a dinner and reception on-board *Hardinge*, hosted by Curzon and Mary. Along the shoreline, lamps had been strung up, replacing the colourful bunting that had hung limp in the heat of the day. As Curzon and his guests enjoyed the slight sea breeze, the evening was finished with fireworks set off from both forts.

The visit culminated the following morning with a high-level court, or *durbar*, on-board *Argonaut* whose quarter-deck had now been decorated in tentage, carpets and assorted embroidered regalia. Its signalling guns were first primed and fired when the rear-admiral arrived on-board from *Hardinge* to participate in the day's proceedings. A second salvo greeted the sultan when he and his entourage of prominent sheikhs presented themselves alongside. A third volley was then ordered to welcome the arrival of Curzon. Considerably more formal than the previous day's events, the *durbar* was officially declared open and after an age of formal greetings and ingratiation, the sultan's address was finally read aloud in Arabic in front of the esteemed audience by a trusted sheikh, Rashid bin Ozaiz, the governor, or *wali*, of the lush and cultivated governorate of Samail, fifty miles inland of the capital. After it was translated into English by Cox, the viceroy rose and gave his own address, which was translated into Arabic by Khan Bahadur Abdur Rahim Hakim, an uncovenanted attaché working in the Foreign Department in Calcutta.

Before the day's regal proceedings were closed, Curzon briefly disappeared to return to the tented setting minutes later wearing the robes of a grand master of the Order of the Indian Empire. In his new garb, he invested Sultan Faisal with the Knight Grand Commander of the Indian Empire, the highest order of chivalry that could be afforded. It had not been a forgone conclusion that the sultan would get the grandest honour, or indeed any award at all given his constant threating to abdicate and receptiveness to French approaches. Ceremonies complete, the gun-crews closed up once again to fire appropriate salutations to mark the departure of the various guests and dignitaries as they headed for the shore or to their respective ships. Curzon and Sultan Faisal were the last to depart, heading for *Hardinge* where along with Cox, Kemball and Dane, they sat together for an informal but more serious discussion. There, Sultan Faisal was dissuaded from entertaining any further thoughts about abdicating or foreign power flirtation, especially now that he was a Knight Grand Commander. With the bestowage weighing heavier than it should have on the sultan's shoulders, he bade Curzon farewell and left to reflect on the visit from the sanctuary of his palace. To the now familiar sound of gunfire, *Hardinge* and its escorts departed Muscat while on the beach in front of the political agency, dancers in 'grotesque costumes and quaint disguises' frolicked around until darkness fell, all in honour of the viceroy.[167] Lorimer missed most of the tour's opening act, having stayed on *Hardinge* throughout the *durbar* and audiences, but the stage had been set for the rest of Curzon's travelling theatre of imperial magnificence.

The next day was spent under Curzon and Atkinson-Willes's joint-direction, surveying potential bases in the coves and inlets that feathered Musandam Peninsula, a rocky headland that dominated the southern shores of the Strait of Hormuz. After reconnoitring Ghanam Island at length given its suitability, that night the flotilla laid up at anchor out of sight near Telegraph Island tucked inside Elphinstone Inlet, one of many that cut into the peninsula. After a short but slightly rough transit the following morning, the ships arrived at the Trucial State of Sharjah, the programme's next destination. Unlike Muscat, the opportunity to have the imposing presence that Cox desired was lost as shallow water prevented the flotilla from getting close to the coastline. A gun-salute to announce Curzon's arrival was also ruled out, not because the ships were more than five miles offshore and therefore out of earshot of Sharjah's ruler and residents, but because the Gulf ruler lacked any cannon of his own to reciprocate. It was a suboptimal start to proceedings, not made any better by strong winds and a heavy swell that started to dampen the day's affairs, despite Kemball's optimistic forecast during the initial planning that there would be fine weather in November. Although they had enjoyed bright and pleasant weather so far, an impromptu foul-weather programme would be required to ensure that Curzon was not left completely disappointed.

The Trucial States was a term given to a loose federation of principalities or emirates comprised of Abu Dhabi, Ajman, Dubai, Fujairah, Ras Al Khaimah, Sharjah and Umm Al Quwain that were brought together in a series of treaties with the EIC. Since the mid-1820s, Bombay Marine and subsequently Royal Navy ships provided a security guarantee to prevent piracy and criminality off their coasts. It also deterred any potential aspirations to conquer neighbouring sheikhdoms and emirates. With Curzon's ships so far out at sea, the trucial emirs were persuaded, if not forced, to embark RIMS *Patrick Stewart*, a shallow draught cable-laying ship. *Patrick Stewart* had been commandeered at short notice from the Indian Telegraph Service with orders to take them to *Argonaut* for the second *durbar*. The unforgiving north-westerly swell ensured that all were violently sea-sick during their transit, making Lorimer question their lineage from sea-farers, pirates and buccaneers.[168] Finally on-board, if initially jaded from their journey, the rulers were led to the quarter-deck, which was again adorned in exquisite soft furnishings and regalia. The gun-crews stood idly by and only began their ceremonial duties when Curzon, accompanied by Atkinson-Willes, managed to cross-deck from *Hardinge*, despite the choppy seas.

After introductions and repeated courtesies from the assembled Trucial Chiefs, 'all elderly or middle-aged men, …[looking] dignified [with an] independent air and manly' appearance, Curzon delivered his next address to his guests. This time, the translation was provided by John Gaskin, the assistant political officer in Bahrain, who had accompanied the sheikhs on their perilous albeit short transfer on-board *Patrick Stewart*. The assembly was a brief affair and must have been bewildering to the rulers and their entourages, as there was no expectation or opportunity for them to give an address of their own, before or in response to Curzon's speech. Here, Britain firmly believed that its prominence was not in dispute, requiring just a single local agent in Sharjah to represent the government. The Trucial Coast, like the Imamate of Oman, was accredited to the political agent in Muscat, who oversaw matters of strategic importance, admittedly, from a distance. It was a strange arrangement as nearby Musandam Peninsula, although part of the sultan of Muscat's domain, was managed by the political agency in Bandar Abbas. With no government of India orders of chivalry on offer to prolong the ceremony, the sheikhs were instead presented with a variety of gifts, all of which had been organised and manifested by Lorimer before they were sent on their way. An early suggestion that sealskin coats might be suitable gifts was turned down although bizarrely because of cost rather than their impracticality.[169] That anyone thought a sheikh might need a waterproof winter coat underlined again the lack of knowledge of local conditions. Common-sense ultimately prevailed with more appropriate, attractive and useful alternatives purchased instead.

The bounty was plentiful with Sheikh Maktoum of Dubai and Sheikh Saqar of Sharjah both presented with mounted gold swords, gold hunting watches and Martini-Henry rifles. Without ammunition, the rifles were useless, a common form of control used by both the British and the Turks in Arabia when gifting weapons to tribes and factions. Fortunately, both were also given five hundred rounds. Their eldest accompanying sons also received a rifle with two hundred rounds each. Sheikh Zayed, the ruler of Abu Dhabi, and his eldest son received the same gifts as their counterparts although the father also received a pair of binoculars given his status as the most eminent figure within the trucial federation. Sheikhs Abdulaziz of Ajman and Ahmad of Umm Al Quwain, in contrast, had to make do with just a watch and a rifle but no ammunition, a subtle but noticeable sign of their weaker standing within the group. Although not a Trucial State, Sheikh Saif, the Emir of Hamriyeh, which neighboured Sharjah, received similar gifts despite not being an invitee. His absence at the *durbar* was because of his emirate's continued independence from the British, but if he considered his absence an insult, he could not ignore the fact that he had fared better than other coastal sheikhs and emirs who were also not treaty signatories, not that there was any appetite on the British side to increase the number of trucial sheikhdoms.[170] As *Patrick Stewart*'s boat tenders bobbed below *Argonaut*'s waist, its gun-crews closed up again, signifying the end of the proceedings. While five shots signalled the sheikh of Abu Dhabi's departure, just three followed the others as they disembarked and headed back to the eventual safety of land. Once the tenders had returned, the squadron pulled anchors and turned into the buffering sea with a course set for Persian shores.

The squadron arrived at the Persian port town of Bandar Abbas the following morning, a place Lorimer would later record, was notorious for its heat and general unhealthiness.[171] Although the local British-Indian community had called for an agency presence since 1877, it was only in early 1901, when the government of India finally posted a British officer there, temporarily at first, before regularising the position with a political agent a year later. Curzon's decision not to go ashore was likely because the first British political officer incumbent, Lieutenant William Shakespear, was still months away from commandeering the agency building. To greet the arriving flotilla instead was HMS *Sphinx*, which had steamed off ahead of the convoy. At anchor with *Sphinx* was the Persian gunboat *Persepolis*, which had received its own orders to sail to the port. An obligatory thirty-one-gun salute shattered the silence, this time from *Persepolis* to mark Curzon's arrival. This was reciprocated by twenty-one returns from *Sphinx*'s guns, to salute the Persian delegation, led by Shah Qajar of Persia's representative, Salar i Mu'azzam, governor of the Gulf Ports, who waited ashore. As guns fired, he headed out to *Argonaut* on the assumption that as the biggest ship in the flotilla, that was where the viceroy was most likely to be found. On being redirected to *Hardinge*, standard pleasantries were eventually exchanged before Mu'azzam delivered a personal message to Curzon on behalf of the shah. All seemed well as Sir Arthur and Dane headed shoreside with the shah's deputy, their departure marked by another salvo of cannon fire. Curzon, who was far too senior to attend their meeting stayed on-board, receiving instead, a small delegation of British-Indian traders, who expressed their gratitude for his presence in volumes, having finally been given their own vice-consul, receiving a stirring address in return. With most of his superiors and peers ashore, Lorimer at last had the chance to see first-hand his viceroy at work. What he made of the government's gun-salute protocolar, something that he had not been exposed to before despite its Indian origin, is not known, but he would count and record every salvo and rebuttal diligently in the gazetteer.

The next couple of days were spent sounding the nearby islands of Hormuz, and Qishm as well as Bassidore's coastline before the ships set course for Lingeh, the next port of call. The flotilla, now additionally boosted by *Persepolis*, arrived late in the evening on 24 November, to be welcomed by a spectacularly illuminated coastline in the absence of a gun salute. That night, Curzon entertained Mu'azzam where they toasted their respective sovereigns' good health. Curzon was also lauded by his Persian dinner guest for being such a distinguished representative of the British empire, generous words that were repaid with a gold repeater watch. With just a local agent representing the political network, no official commitments were scheduled in Curzon's itinerary for the next morning and with just a short official call shoreside organised for Sir Arthur, that afternoon the armada made its way back across to the Arabian coastline, to Bahrain, arriving at the archipelago the following morning.

Bahrain's inclusion in Curzon's tour was obvious given the prominence of its pearling industry in serving European fashion houses and Britain's security obligations. In 1861, the island assumed the same security guarantees from the British as the Trucial States. Nineteen years later, an 'Exclusive Agreement' was signed, later succeeded in 1892, making Bahrain a British protectorate. Despite its enhanced status, until Gaskin, Bahraini sheikhs were served by local Bahraini agents. Like Curzon's brief visit to the Trucial Coast, Bahrain too proved to be a challenge for the squadron. Its shallow waters meant that most of the flotilla were unable to impress the local inhabitants by their size and presence. Only the smaller ships, *Pomone*, *Sphinx* and *Lawrence*, were able to accompany *Hardinge* to the island's shallow inner anchorage. After counting off his gun salute, Curzon stood by on *Hardinge* to welcome Bahrain's heir apparent, Sheikh Hamad bin Isa Al Khalifa on board, followed shortly after by his father, Sheikh Isa, who was accompanied by Gaskin. It was an informal audience in an informal setting, with the viceroy and his entourage in 'undress uniform' rather than their full regalia. Despite this, Curzon's desired personal impact was still achieved as the sheikh kept his sandals on throughout the audience. Arab custom would normally see guests barefooted in such settings as a mark of courtesy and respect but was explained away by Lorimer as just an unfortunate oversight, down to the sheikh's nervousness in the presence of the viceroy.[172] Before leaving, the Bahraini ruler and his three accompanying sons received a wealth of gifts to mark their loyalty, including a mounted gold sword, three gold watches, three Martini-Henrys and fourteen hundred rounds of ammunition. The sheikh was also gifted a set of binoculars as an acknowledgement of his status, as was his five-gun salutation as he was seen off *Hardinge*.

Later that afternoon, Curzon and his delegation accepted Sheikh Isa's invitation to visit the urban area of Manamah on Bahrain's main island, to join him at Gaskin's political agency. It was achieved but with some difficulty. The party took two hours to get to the agency building, having first been man-handled ashore from *Hardinge*'s launch and piggy-backed a considerable distance across the beach. The return journey was only slightly easier, taking ninety minutes for the delegation to get to their boats, but was itself marred by another slip of custom when the sheikh left before they had all departed, something that could have easily been interpreted as a mark of disrespect. The following morning, the sheikh and heir apparent returned to *Hardinge* for a brief discussion with the viceroy about Britain's commitment to the small island. It also gave Sheikh Isa the chance to apologise to Kemball for his accidental protocol slights. Once they had departed with the assurances they sought and potential embarrassments waved aside, *Hardinge* and its small escort navigated carefully through the shallow waters to join the rest of the squadron. Fully mustered, they set sail for Kuwait, the northernmost point of the cruise. Like Bahrain, it was an obvious port of call to make but during the initial planning stage, it had initially been omitted from Curzon's suggested itinerary. Once confirmed that it was an oversight rather than a deliberate omission, it was quickly corrected by Dane.

Hardinge was one of the last ships to make it to Kuwait Bay on 28 November. By the time it had dropped its anchor, most of its escorts were already hanging off theirs in the inner anchorage. No sooner had Curzon received his requisite gun salute, than an eager Sheikh Mubarak Al Sabah was shuttled out by his boatmen and clambering on-board, asking when he could expect to meet the viceroy. Four and a half hours later at his allotted time, he returned to *Hardinge* with his eldest son, Jabir, to make his acquaintance. Although the cruise was just twelve days in, there were signs that ceremonial fatigue was beginning to creep in. Rather than be received in full regalia, father and son were met by Curzon in the same semi-formal fashion as was the case with the sheikh of Bahrain. They also received the same assortment of gifts, although unlike his sheikhdom counterparts down the coast, Sheikh Mubarak was energetic and spritely rather than overawed by events. He was, the viceroy observed, the most 'masculine and vigorous personality' that he had encountered during his tour.[173] On being presented with a golden sword, rather than show humility and graciousness on receiving his token of friendship, the sheikh jokingly also asked for a belt so he could carry it on his side, as he now considered himself to be 'one of [Curzon's] soldiers'.[174] Having reinvigorated the energy of his hosts with his joviality, he left *Hardinge* as five gunshots echoed overhead, leaving behind him, an invitation to his host to become his guest ashore the following day.

Accepting his hospitality, Curzon landed ashore the next morning. Given the lack of ceremony and dignity that had awaited him shoreside in Bahrain, he was surprised to find himself subject to a level of pomp and circumstance that more than matched any expectation. Customary cannon-fire to mark his arrival was followed by a ride in

> a carriage with the Sheikh (the only vehicle in the place), surrounded by a galloping and shouting cavalcade of Arab horsemen and camelmen, between lines of thousands of the inhabitants, and groups of women uttering shrill cries, [making it] one of the most picturesque incidents of the tour.[175]

Yet another thirty-one guns announced Curzon's arrival at the sheikh's palace, from where the Turkish flag normally flew given Kuwait's spurious inclusion in the Caliphate. That day however, the flagpole was bare. Curzon could also not fail to notice the portraits of King Edward VII and his wife, as well as one of Queen Victoria, mounted on the walls in Sheikh Mubarak's reception room. The sheikh returned to *Hardinge* for a final audience with Curzon later that afternoon, where he declared that all connections and loyalty to Turkey had been renounced. All recent approaches by the French and Russians during their port visit had also been refused. In return, he asked if the British would bestow a title or honour upon him to venerate his declared allegiance to the empire. It was an unexpected question. Unlike Sultan Faisal, who had Cox as his chivalric champion, there was not yet a political agent in Kuwait to argue for a similar award on the sheikh's behalf. Curzon could only reply as any diplomat would, that he would consider the request. After a short tour of the British warships that dominated Kuwait's coastline, Sheikh Mubarak had to make do with just another five-gun salute, returning to his palace empty-handed, but at least fully appraised of the extent of Britain's maritime military prowess. There, he and his subjects watched the ships as they set off for their next port of call over the horizon, Bushire.

While the flotilla remained on-course, *Lawrence* and *Sphinx* peeled away to appraise Babiyan and Warbah Islands, contributing to the tour's secondary goal. As Ottoman military bases were established on Babiyan and elsewhere on the river banks, both ships lowered their ensigns from their mastheads so that courtesies could not be returned if any of the outposts saluted them. It was a churlish but ultimately successful ploy, as they rejoined *Hardinge* and its escorts without diplomatic incident. On the morning of 2 December, their next anchorage at Bushire came into view.

So far, Curzon had seen the very best of what could be achieved in such a small period of time. He expected much more of the same in Bushire as the location of his political resident. Bushire was one of the EIC's earliest establishments in the Gulf, having first placed a representative there in 1763. Subsequent events in this Persian port town, however, were about to spoil any perception that the British were firmly placed and had any influence there. The comedy of errors began when the shah's initial designated representative for the Persian segment of the visit, the governor of Fars Province, claimed to be unable to meet Curzon in Bandar Abbas because of the lack of time he had been given to travel there. He then assessed that he could make the journey but only if he was given a large armed escort and paid five thousand pounds by the government of India to cover expenses.[176] Under no obligation to pay for the official's physical protection so that he could travel in his own country, the governor's request was politely turned down by Kemball, who pointed out that the local garrison could provide all of the protection the Persian envoy required. Mu'azzam would instead meet Curzon alone in Bandar Abbas as the sole Persian representative.

Matters got more complicated when the Persian government, which had been initially receptive to Curzon's plans, demanded that he be afforded official residences, one each in Bandar Abbas and Bushire for the duration of his stay. As Curzon had no intention of coming ashore in the former, it was agreed that no residence would be needed. Open to the possibility of staying shoreside in Bushire, several properties were identified by the Persian authorities as potential temporary residences for their guest. When all were found to be sub-standard, Kemball looked for a compromise. Rather than be accommodated ashore in Bushire, he offered that the viceroy might instead remain accommodated on-board and look to receive the governor of Fars at Bushire's government house. Rather than resolve the diplomatic impasse, matters deteriorated further. In response to Kemball's suggestion, Persian propriety as well as semantic mischievousness demanded that if the viceroy was not going to have an official albeit temporary residence in Bushire, he, rather than the shah's deputation, should be the one to be received.

Once the visiting principal became aware of the inadequate level of etiquette that was going to be afforded to him and the Persian government's attitude more generally, a telegram was immediately sent to Tehran. Evelyn Grant-Duff, Tehran's *charge d'affaires* in Sir Arthur's absence, was instructed to inform the Persian government that 'Lord Curzon must respectfully decline to land at Bushehr'.[177] An official reception that was due to take place that evening ashore would also have to be postponed. The Persian government's response was just as immediate, suggesting that it must be possible to find a suitable residence for the viceroy so that the visit could go ahead. This frustrated Curzon further, who considered the latest suggestion to be an insult to his dignity. It was simply not possible for the British viceroy to be seen bowing to the shah's demands. With no last minute resolution, a small reception was instead held that evening on board *Hardinge* for local British residents. Remarkably, all key Persian officials who had also been invited on-board either fell ill or made themselves unobtainable, making it a very small affair. With little to gain by remaining offshore, Curzon's squadron departed the following evening to the low rumbling sound of their steam engines rather than a gun salute crescendo. Kemball and Sir Arthur stayed behind to pick up the pieces and to deal with the consequences.

These soon became clear as during the unsuccessful stopover, Curzon, the Admiralty and the Persian government had also been unable to compromise on the number of gun salutes that should be afforded to both the viceroy and the governor of Fars. This time, it was the Persians who took offence, resulting in a political demarche to Lansdowne, complaining that 'the very discourteous action of the Viceroy, ... [was] extremely injurious to the relations of the two Governments'.[178] Kemball would later try to downplay the incident, reporting it as little more than a hitch in arrangements rather than a substantial diplomatic spat, a view not shared by Lorimer, who felt that the episode had 'marred' the programme.[179] Curzon too, must have considered Bushire a disappointing end to his imperial *tour de force*, given the warmest of welcomes he had received just a couple of days earlier in Kuwait and the overwhelming sense of British – and personal – supremacy that he had felt more generally throughout the visit. The Gulf Arab rulers might have been delighted by Curzon's presence, the same could not be said of the Persians. Rather than assurances, they saw nothing more than another foreign power's attempt to interfere with their sovereignty.

With Bushire scheduled as the final destination for the visit, the various ships that made up Curzon's small fleet of pageantry returned to their normal duties, either remaining in local waters to keep the peace, back to Great Britain or returning to Ceylon. *Persepolis*, a pretty but barely operational cruiser, was also dismissed and left to its own devices. Only *Fox* stayed with *Hardinge* as it slowly made its way south-east, stopping briefly at Jashk to exchange telegrams and then to Makran after navigating through the Strait of Hormuz. Despite being outside of the political network's constituency, an impromptu *durbar* was still organised on-board *Hardinge* for the tribal chiefs of western and southern Baluchistan, given Curzon's far greater geographical responsibility. On 7 December, *Hardinge* finally disembarked the viceroy, Lorimer and the rest of the viceregal party back in Karachi, but not before *Fox* fired its cannons a final time to announce the principal's return.

Reflecting on the viceroy's vision after he had decided to tour the Gulf, Dane wrote out that it would be 'a great departure, and will excite much interest and concern … [in] upholding British prestige in these parts'.[180] In his own letter to William St John Brodwick, Hamilton's successor in the India Office, Curzon too was convinced that his visit would leave 'upon the rulers and peoples of the Gulf a powerful and lasting impression of the incontestable predominance of British interests in those regions, and of the resolute intention of the British and Indian Governments to maintain them'.[181] Lorimer was equally intoxicated by the viceroy's vision. As Curzon's dedicated scribe to record the grand excursion, he was similarly convinced that it was an 'effectual demonstration of British power and influence … without precedent in the history of the Gulf … and an event without parallel in local annals…'.[182]

Given Curzon's combative nature, reports that the maritime procession had been a cause of concern for the Ottoman authorities in Mesopotamia, one of Britain's regional competitors, would have been well received. Mohammed Mohsin, the local agent at the British vice consulate in Karbala, wrote to his superior, Colonel Lindsay Newmarch, the political resident in Baghdad (who also served the Foreign Office as its consul general), saying that the visit had been followed by the Turks with 'perplexing anxiety'.[183] The bazaars were also alive with rumours that the viceroy and his men o' war had brought four million Indian rupees to pay for a fort to be built in Kuwait. This had left the Turks wondering if Curzon's tour was just the start of British encroachment into the Caliphate. It also increased their fear of the immediate vulnerability of Basrah to British temptation or threat.

Bushire aside, by Curzon's own admission, the visit was a success. The planning to make it so, however, had been fraught and challenging. A regional tour of such ambition would typically take months to arrange but just two were given for it to be organised. It was not made easier by the fact that Curzon made clear from the outset that it was then or never. As the government of India's most senior representative in the region, Kemball was expected to coordinate with the burden falling to Cox and Gaskin to persuade and prepare their respective hosts in the name of the viceroy. Kemball, however, was for the most part absent, possibly explaining the shortcomings in Bushire. The absence of senior British representation in Bandar Abbas, Sharjah, Lingeh and Kuwait only added to the political agents' workload as they had to organise remotely from Muscat and Bahrain respectively. Oversights were, therefore, inevitable.

As it proved throughout the tour, time and tide waited for no man – or viceroy. Such was the pressure to ensure Curzon's grand tour remained on schedule, that the running aground of *Sphinx* near Kuwait as it surveyed approaches to Kadhamah, normally a serious disciplinary offence in the Royal Navy, was overlooked, much to the captain's relief. Had Curzon not been on-board at the time, Atkinson-Willes might not have been so forgiving. Curzon's only window of opportunity also meant having to conduct the visit during Ramadan when the ruling sheikhs and emirs were fasting and in a fatigued state during daylight hours. This may have explained Sheikh Isa's minor *faux pas*. It could have easily been interpreted as a mark of disrespect for their religion. In the absence of any major policy announcements to their benefit, most would have much preferred to have spent their daytime reflecting on the month's religious meaning or resting in their tents rather than being preoccupied by superficial ceremony and circumstance in a mock-up canvased tent, or *majlis*, not that it seemed to deter Sheikh Mubarak.

Nor was the tour inclusive. There was a question by Gaskin if Sheikh Ahmed bin Muhammed Al Thani, the ruler of Qatar, could also be part of the programme. Known to have desired British treaty protections rather than remain the only Gulf sheikhdom under Ottoman rule, the plan was to encourage him to visit Bahrain when the viceroy was passing through so a discreet meeting could be arranged. If news broke of the dalliance resulting in a complaint by the Ottoman or even the British governments, the viceroy could counter in good faith, arguing that it had taken place by happenstance. By the time the sheikh received a letter from Kemball suggesting an opportune audience, it was in any case, too late. Curzon was also under strict orders not to engage with Sheikh Mubarak's protégé, Sheikh Abdulaziz ibn Abdul Rahman Al Sa'ud, or simply Ibn Sa'ud as he became known in the West, the ruler of the Najd. Ibn Sa'ud had recaptured Riyadh in early 1902 and sovereignty of much of the interior in the process. He too was attempting to court the British to obtain a security guarantor from them as his Kuwaiti mentor had done in 1899 (achieved while Ibn Sa'ud was living in exile with his family in Kuwait). His latest attempt to persuade the British was in March, shortly after he had been approached in Kuwait by Russian officials from *Boyarin*, who offered him guns and money in return for friendship. Kemball had initially doubted Ibn Sa'ud's claim, believing that the approach had been made up in an attempt to influence British thinking. Lorimer would later confirm through an independent source that the Russians had indeed looked to entice Ibn Sa'ud.[184] The lack of time again to organise a covert conference rather than abiding by any Foreign Office edict ensured that Ibn Sa'ud did not feature in Curzon's agenda. That did not prevent the viceroy from briefly considering deputising a political officer to the Najd to find out what was going on in the interior, identifying Lorimer as one of five potential officials who he believed would be suitable for the task. Already on special duty and pleading exceptional personal circumstances, Lorimer successfully persuaded his principal not to be given the role.[185] It would take another eleven years before the position was finally filled, albeit briefly.

Lacking a gazetteer, the viceroy's staff and political officers were forced to draw heavily from their contemporary understanding of their political constituencies. Knowledge was also bolstered by former Edinburgh-born ICS administrator, Charles Umpherston Aitchison's *Collection of Treaties, Engagements and Sanads*. Curzon's *Persia and the Persian Question* might have also been a source of information, even though quoting from it directly risked the viceroy challenging and correcting any 'imperfect information or erroneous hypotheses' that his politicals might have made. Such poor appreciation of the region not only highlighted the need to update and proliferate imperial knowledge; it also reinforced Curzon's desire to increase the number of political agencies in the Gulf, manned by British officials rather than local agents to ensure that forward momentum and primacy was maintained.[186]

The fledgling relationship between Lorimer and his fellow political agent and Companion of the Indian Empire, Cox, did not get off to the best of starts, a situation not helped by Dane. When Curzon reduced the size of his entourage to keep costs to a minimum, Lorimer survived the viceroy's cut. Cox only became aware of Lorimer's inclusion on the cruise when he and Kemball were told by Dane that 'we shall have Mr. Lorimer with us as interpreter in case Major Cox is weak in translating publicly'.[187] Although not a deliberate criticism of Cox's linguistic ability, it could have easily been received as such. Both could also have been forgiven for taking offence for considering that rather than use a familiar face from within the Gulf network, Curzon had deliberately chosen Lorimer as an outsider to be his voice in the Gulf when speaking to the Arab rulers. Not only was Lorimer expected to translate Curzon's English address in Muscat, but there was the intent to use his expertise at all of the *durbar*s, something that Gaskin too, was unaware of. When Lorimer pointed out that Gulf Arabic was very different to Egyptian Arabic he had just been immersed in and tested on, Curzon could have easily struck him from the ship's manifest. The viceroy instead, looked to employ him to translate his various addresses so they could be handed over to the Arab dignitaries after they had been delivered verbally. As there is no deviation in formal written Arabic, this was something that Lorimer was able to do, although he still employed the assistance of two local agents with an understanding of Gulf and Persian Arabic to check his work.[188] But Lorimer's observation about the different forms of Arabic was well made, later resulting in the amendment to the Military Department's interpretation test, giving more weight to colloquial rather than classical Arabic.

As it was, neither Cox nor Lorimer were called upon to interpret at the Muscat *durbar*. While Cox accompanied Curzon during his personal audience with Sultan Faisal to interpret on behalf of the two principals, Lorimer took on the temporary role as foreign secretary in Dane's stead, issuing telegrams, ensuring that timings were strictly adhered to and overseeing protocol whilst his superior stayed close to the viceroy. Such delegation of responsibilities ensured that both men's reputation remained intact. Just two months after the grand tour, Cox replaced Kemball as political resident in Bushire, tasked to deliver Curzon's forward policy by strengthening the regional political presence. This expanding network would also eventually serve Lorimer, who in turn had received his own orders to deliver Curzon's emerging policy: a gazetteering special duty. This forced the two men to put aside any lingering differences that Dane's clumsy correspondence and planning might have forced upon them.

CHAPTER 5

A Rather Particular Special Duty

IN EARLY 1903, Curzon's imposing demonstration of soft and hard power in the Gulf was just one proposed course of action among many starting to take form inside his head. At the same time, Lorimer too, was equally consumed with his own thoughts, having finally arrived back in Scotland from Egypt to continue his furlough. He made the most of his recent social immersion in Cairo by taking the army's Arabic interpretation exam in London, unaware of what Curzon would soon have planned for him. Scoring 644 out of a possible 800, he passed it comfortably to qualify as an interpreter. In late summer, he started to think about his return to India, most likely to Simla in the Himalayas if he had no posting or position to go back to. It was not the worst of possibilities as the mountain retreat was the government's seasonal capital where viceroys, rank and file relocated to every year when the heat of Calcutta became unbearable.

Having had a productive furlough both overseas and in Scotland, Lorimer's personal funds were running low. Pressure was on for him to regain paid employment within the IPS and the allowances that went with it, particularly since his personal circumstances had changed. At some point during the late spring, he was introduced to a fellow Scot, twenty-six-year-old Marian Agnes Maclean. Born in Edinburgh in January 1876 to Mary and George, Marian like Lorimer was more commonly known by another name; hers was Nesta. Their courtship was short, just a few months before they married on 8 October at St Andrew's Church in Edinburgh. Unable to conduct his son's wedding, the Reverend Robert instead, read Lorimer's banns uncontested at the Free Church. They had little time to celebrate with their families and friends as within days of their marriage, they were packed and setting sail for India.

Having left as an official from the Political Department's North-West Frontier Province cadre, Lorimer was expecting an eventual return to the same tribal areas. It was a fair assumption to make as an alumnus of

Curzon's metaphorical nursery. In mid-August, as Lorimer and Nesta were still getting to know each other and considering life in India, early discussions were underway within the Foreign Department about the viceroy's revitalised aspirations to visit the Gulf. As the department plotted and planned Curzon's tour, Elliott Colvin, the political resident in Kashmir, submitted a request to Dane, seeking Lorimer's services.[189] Colvin's settlement commissioner was suffering from ill-health and had expressed no desire to extend his position beyond May 1904. Learning that the frontier's prodigal son would soon be back from furlough, Colvin wanted him to join the mission to cast an experienced eye over the settlement mapping that had been carried out so far and to hopefully see the task through to completion. Expecting the assignment request to be just a formality, he had already written to Lorimer in Strathmartine, enquiring about his interest. A monthly salary of eighteen hundred rupees a month, with another three hundred rupees in expenses, had also been offered to entice Lorimer. Although it did not include any potential additional language allowance or the opportunity to use his Arabic, it was a decent salary nonetheless. And with Lorimer about to be a married man, settlement work in Kashmir would not put him in too much of harm's way. Unsure what alternatives might lie in store, Lorimer welcomed the opportunity to return to the familiar border setting and agreed to start on his return in the autumn. All that was needed now was Dane's endorsement. Curzon's foreign secretary, however, was distracted. At the same time that Colvin's letter had been received, he had also been passed a letter from Curzon with the tightest of deadlines, listing the various locations he wanted his viceregal tour to include.

Long before Curzon returned to India as viceroy, his contribution to regional knowledge had, arguably, already been defined. As a young explorer and correspondent, he had always exercised his right to travel overseas. Although it was painful to admit, as the head of the government of India, it was no longer in his gift to continue with his own leisurely pursuit of geographical enlightenment. His travel was now governed by risk-averse foreign policies. Instead, he endorsed or encouraged others to continue the pursuit, or at least those who fell favourably under his eye.[190] Despite Lorimer being out of the viceroy's sight for over a year, he was surprised to find that he still counted as one of Curzon's chosen few. He was also still in favour with Dane, not least as the foreign secretary considered him to be a protégé of sorts, believing that he had made Lorimer into a competent and reputable political officer when the Scot had served under him in Peshawar.[191] Dane may have also seen a little of himself in Lorimer as a fellow man of the frontier and as another ICS competition *wallah* without a university degree. Shortly after Dane had drafted Curzon's letters of commission, one to Kemball in Bushire to prepare for his arrival in the Gulf and another to Atkinson-Willes in Ceylon to prepare the ships, Colvin received a reply to his. His application for Lorimer was refused as the viceroy felt that to 'employ him for two or three years upon this, would be a sacrifice … for which [an] even more important use might be found elsewhere'.[192] 'Might be', in fact, meant 'has been', as Curzon and Dane had already been working on a set of cursory instructions for Lorimer about his imminent employment.

By late October, Lorimer knew that his immediate future would not be a return to the frontier, but would instead, involve another period of special duty. Curzon required someone who was competent, capable, inquisitive and intelligent, someone who would understand and appreciate the value of what he was about to commission. Having proved himself on all counts in India and authored several intellectual publications, Lorimer was the only person that Curzon had in mind who could take on the challenge. On 6 November 1903, he received formal instructions from Curzon to create a geographical and political handbook of the Gulf for use by political officers and officials.[193] As a means to carry out this endeavour, he was to conduct 'in geographical order the circuit of the Gulf [to] indicate the status, government and interests in each port or district as it is encountered, finally drawing together the several threads, and weaving them, if possible, into a succinct and intelligible whole'.[194] This circuit would, in turn, capture, codify and contextualise in one place, a unique 'book of reference in which the history of every political question or relationship affecting this region can be traced from the beginning…'.[195]

On receiving his orders, the Foreign Department had also made clear that Lorimer's particular terms of reference would be different to most special duties as would the conditions he would be working in, with the expectation that he would be required to spend most of his time away from India. It was acknowledged that the special duty was also likely to hinder his immediate financial and promotion prospects as well as being a 'particularly uncomfortable prospect for a newly married man'.[196] It was an unattractive caveat, but Lorimer could hardly turn down his viceroy's request. Unsure what else the special duty would entail, Lorimer and his new bride tried to make plans as best they could on their voyage to India. On 7 November, after a brief stopover in Aden, Lorimer and Nesta finally landed at Bombay, where he immediately began to prepare papers for his special duty. They were given little time to settle as new orders required him to travel another 600 miles up the coastline to Karachi. They arrived there on 14 November. Two days later, special duty called, obliging Lorimer to leave his wife in a strange foreign port while he joined Curzon and Dane on *Hardinge*.

Having never served in the Gulf, Curzon's tour had given Lorimer only the briefest of insights into the region. Even the landscape was unfamiliar, not that he had any opportunity to get ashore to engage with the people, or to travel inland to appreciate the geography that lay beyond the coastline. To help him take forward his immediate task, Lorimer was given the services of an assistant who collated a small collection of archived papers.[197] He also accompanied Lorimer on *Hardinge*, but rather than use the time and additional resource to read, reconnoitre and report on the region, both found themselves mostly carrying out Dane's duties, fulfilling very few of their own.[198] As soon as the ship returned to port, Lorimer excused himself from the viceroy's touring party and set off for Bombay to scour through the government's records and archives. From there, he headed to Agra, a town 130 miles south of Delhi, where Nesta had found some accommodation, to settle in and to await further orders.[199]

His hopes for a small respite were dashed when he was immediately directed back to Karachi, where he continued to search through dog-eared reports, maps and charts. As frustrating as it was to be temporarily separated from Nesta, Lorimer had little choice but to follow instructions. Of equal frustration was the fact that since his return to duty, he and Nesta had been struggling to survive on just one thousand rupees, received as an advance of salary back in mid-October, just before they set sail for India. Not only was his back-pay accumulating, so was the interest on his overdraft.[200] It was hardly the impression of Crown service that he wanted to present to his new wife, but they did their best to make do. Despite several reminders about his pay deficit, matters only got worse when a request for a three thousand rupee advance until his salary was rightly calculated was left un-actioned. By early-February, both Lorimer and Nesta were struggling and feeling the pinch with his pay now almost four months in arrears.[201] There was little sign that the very issues Curzon and the Foreign Department had identified when drawing up his particular special duty, were being considered sympathetically.

Another poor calculation was the fact that Curzon, Dane and even Lorimer himself had grossly underestimated the time it would take to gazette the whole of the Gulf. Not lacking in ambition, Lorimer initially believed that he could perform his special duty in addition to serving in the frontier. He had even expressed an interest in being posted to either Kohat or Hazara as deputy commissioner. Once there, he believed, he would require just one month to be put aside so he could focus solely on the gazetteer.[202] With neither post available, and with some in the North-West Frontier Province's chief commissioner's office reluctant to make an exception in case it hindered their own transfer plans, Lorimer was instead offered the position of district judge in Dera Ismail Khan. He accepted the posting in the hope that this might release his back-pay. He arrived back at the frontier in mid-January but did not assume his judicial responsibilities until early February. Dane had made it clear that he was to focus as much as possible on his special duty while time allowed, rather than receive a protracted handover.[203]

With doubts about his influence and personal agency in the Gulf as an IPS outsider, in Dera Ismail Khan, Lorimer approached Dane, recommending that his statement of information requirements to Cox and the political agents should be sent from the Foreign Department rather than from him. A request from a known and more senior entity was less likely to be ignored or deprioritised.[204] By mid-April, Lorimer had further doubts, this time about his ability to carry out his work on the gazetteer whilst also overseeing court sessions as district judge. It was not just a heavy judicial workload that was hampering his efforts, he had also been struck down several times with fever, an ailment that had stayed with him since the Tochi campaign. During a particularly bad bout of malaise, Lorimer received a visit from district surgeon, Major Macnab, who confirmed his poor state of health. As a remedy, Macnab strongly suggested that the Foreign Department should abandon the idea of the weakened Scot continuing with the gazetteer. This was both an unfortunate and unwelcomed medical prescription, and one that Dane was extremely reluctant to accept. Rather than focus on Lorimer's health, precedence was given to his special duty mission. Dane offered to the viceroy instead, that

> …it will be a bitter disappointment to him not to finish what he has begun, and we shall lose the information that he has acquired during the last five months. I also know of no-one who would be likely to do better, and I venture to suggest that he should be placed on special duty for a year to complete it…[205]

Curzon's reply to Dane's recommendation was to the point, agreeing that Lorimer should continue with the special duty and be immediately relieved of his core duties in Dera Ismail Khan.[206] With the political officer finally being shown some semblance of compassion, both the IMS and Political Department ceded to Curzon's response. Wheels were put in motion to find a successor while Lorimer was despatched to Simla to serve out the last few weeks of his remaining special duty with Nesta, on hand to nurse him should his health fail again.

With a new appreciation of the challenge and all-round acknowledgement that the task required at least another twelve months, it was decided to reset Lorimer's time on the mission. New orders were prepared for a year-long special duty, something that required the secretary of state for India's sanction. Wasting no time or allowing Lorimer a short period of recuperation, on 2 June, a formal request was submitted to Whitehall, seeking the India Office's approval. By mid-August, William St John Brodrick, Hamilton's successor in the India Office, approved the government of India's request. He also affirmed that Lorimer should continue to receive the same deputation allowance as before.[207] It was a gesture that was well-received by the Scot, having only just seen his salary regularised and his arrears finally paid to him.

Despite the lack of spare human and financial resources within the IPS, the importance Curzon had given to the creation of a gazetteer ensured that now back on mission, Lorimer was authorised to appoint a small team of capable officers to help him take forward his task in earnest. Unlike Sir William Wilson Hunter's 1881 first edition of the gazetteer of India, which had been mostly drafted by writers based in Britain, selected for their literacy skills rather than knowledge of the continent, Lorimer looked to recruit locally.[208]

His first request was for Lal Shah, the head clerk in Tochi, to join him. Lorimer considered him to be an excellent administrative assistant and perfect for the role of working through the archives.[209] Unable to secure the head clerk's services however, Judge Jerome Saldanha was, instead, the first to join in June 1904 as Lorimer's assistant.[210] Two years older than Lorimer and with both a Bachelor of Art and law degrees, Saldanha had joined the government of Bombay in October 1892, holding various appointments in the Judicial, Secretariat and Political Departments as a member of the uncovenanted civil service. Based in Simla, he supported Lorimer's grand assignment until the end of March 1906, producing a series of Gulf precis, drawing from treaties, correspondence and official minutes held in the archives in Bombay and Calcutta since the EIC's earliest days in the region. Considering it impractical to record every entry, Saldanha quoted some documents in their entirety, while others were summarised, overlooked or ignored. Where there were ambiguities, he either addressed them by adding his own synopsis and interpretation of events, by making them subject to rhetorical questioning or in extremis, by leaving them unaddressed. As useful as they were as reference books, there were still substantial gaps in knowledge.

While Lal Shah might have been a capable clerk, Saldanha was an obvious person for the role having already précised the affairs in Arabistan in 1903. This established a format and approach that would soon become familiar. In the twenty-one months that Saldanha worked in support of Lorimer's special duty, he was a force of nature, producing sixteen substantial publications, all classified as 'secret'. His perpetual output included a general summary of governmental correspondence (a second volume would follow in 1908) and a volume each on commerce and communications, international rivalries, naval arrangements and the slave trade. He also produced eleven geographic summaries and drafted an appreciation of recent Turkish expansionism. Although both selective and subjective, the various precis, totalling over two thousand five hundred pages of typed foolscap paper, still provided Lorimer with an authoritative foundation on which to build the gazetteer.[211]

Twenty-five-year-old Lieutenant Cecil Hamilton Gabriel was the next to join the mission in September 1904. Gabriel was a relative newcomer to the Gulf, having only been in India since 1902, initially as an officer in the First Battalion Yorks and Lancashire Regiment. A year later, he transferred to the Indian Army's 37th Baluch Lancers, a familiar route taken by young officers considering a career in the IPS. Rather than be actively recruited, Gabriel, at the time on local leave but working as an unpaid attaché in the Foreign Department, volunteered his services when he heard about Lorimer's imminent travel plans. He even offered to travel at his own expense if he could be seconded from his regiment. Despite not having any relevant linguistic qualifications, Gabriel had given a good account of himself, drafting some useful notes when he had accompanied Cox on his recent travels, recording their visit to Sur and Wadi al Tayeen in Oman and Umm Qasr near Babiyan in Mesopotamia.[212] This, and the lieutenant's selflessness, was sufficient for Lorimer to put forward a strong case to support the young officer's request.[213] As a secondment meant the Foreign, rather than the Military Department would have to cover Gabriel's salary and associated costs, it was decided that he should, instead, be deputised to support Lorimer. This ensured that the Indian Army continued to pay his wage and was, Dane considered, an excellent arrangement to keep the Foreign Department's overheads down.[214]

Unlike Saldanha, Gabriel spent most of his time in the field with Lorimer, responsible for providing compass sketches of the routes travelled, writing their descriptions and taking photographs that might help the gazetteering. His first contribution, however, was to draft a precis on arms smuggling in the Gulf, highlighting the prevalent proliferation of weapons through Muscat and Qatar in particular, to India. Smuggled weapons would then find their way to the frontier, to be used by belligerents and tribes against British military patrols and government outposts. It was a thorough report, prefaced by noting that he had written at length to save Lorimer 'the trouble of constantly referring to the recorded collections'.[215] After an eight-month tenure under Lorimer, Gabriel would move on to start his probation in the IPS in Bushire, as a second assistant to Cox.

Gaskin, who had helped set the stage for Curzon's Gulf cruise, joined around the same time. He joined with personal and professional circumstances within the Foreign Department's Gulf network that were arguably unique. Unlike Lorimer or Cox, Gaskin was of mixed heritage or, to be exact, of Anglo-Indian descent. Prior to being posted to Bahrain, he had worked out of the political residency in Bushire as an uncovenanted civil servant. His transfer to the small island kingdom was only meant to be temporary, to provide cover for the local agent, Mohammed Rahim, who had fallen ill.[216] In October 1900, with Rahim still in a poor state of health, Gaskin's posting was regularised and treated to some extent as a covenanted officer, given accommodation, limited notarial powers and representational pay. It was a contentious decision as his superior in Bushire, political resident Lieutenant Colonel Malcolm Meade, considered him unsuitable for the role as 'He [was] not pure European, [was] disposed to intrigue and … mixed up in Bahrain affairs'.[217] The Foreign Department, however, had been unable to find a suitable 'English gentleman' to assume the position, not least because political officers serving in the Gulf generally saw a reduction in their overall pay than if they remained in India.[218] Frustrated with such disinterest among his juniors in taking on the position, Dane complained that though 'many other officers have been sounded [out and] are only too ready to complain of their prospects, they will not go to the Gulf'.[219] There was also the problem that very few officers had the required linguistic skills to be effective diplomatic operators. Meade's reservations were ultimately overruled when no-one from the covenanted civil service stepped forward. With no alternative, Gaskin was allowed to remain there as assistant political agent, overseeing affairs for four years before he was eventually replaced by thirty-three-year-old Captain Francis Prideaux, a veteran British political agent and son of former Bushire political resident, William.[220] Prideaux, like Meade, came with his own prejudiced views which were not restricted to just the uncovenanted service. He was equally critical of some of his covenanted peers, including Shakespear in Bandar Abbas. Saldanha would later include Meade's damning observations uncensored in his precis of Bahrain. Whether it was to record for posterity, the inequality and institutional bigotry of the government of India, or because he too, was prejudiced against Gaskin, is unknown.

It was only after Prideaux was in place that some in the Foreign Department felt Gabriel's posting, in hindsight, had considerable shortcomings. It was deemed that he had lacked the required presence to make an impression on the seasoned Bahraini ruler. There were also concerns that 'his colour prevent[ed] his carrying much weight',[221] leading the Foreign Department to judge that an officer of superior status like Prideaux, was clearly preferable there.[222] Gaskin seemed to have adversaries everywhere as the Ottoman *vali* in Basrah also took exception to his presence in Bahrain and outreach elsewhere, alleging that he was also intriguing with Sheikh Ahmed Al Thani in Qatar against them.[223]

Cox and the Foreign Department struggled to find somewhere to send him after he left Bahrain, as he was now far too senior and experienced to be sent back to Bushire. Cox suggested sending him to either Lingeh or Bandar Abbas as vice-consul, an opinion shaped by his fear that Belgians posted along the Persian coastline were becoming both powerful and influential in that part of the region. He justified his suggestion to Dane by writing that 'we ought to have an Englishman or quasi-Englishman at every place where there is a Belgian customs official'.[224] Alternatively he thought, Gaskin could instead, assume a new position as assistant political agent on the 'Pirate Coast', an alternative name given for the Trucial Coast on account of the Al Qawasim, who threatened commercial shipping passing through the Strait of Hormuz in the late eighteenth and early nineteenth centuries.[225]

Unlike some of his peers, Lorimer saw no deficiency in Gaskin's mixed ethnicity, but rather appreciated the benefits of his experience. With Gaskin's immediate future still uncertain, Lorimer asked if he could join the gazetteer mission for a season on the grounds that he had 'a perfect command of colloquial Gulf Arabic, [was] well acquainted with the chief places and leading men on the west side of the Gulf and [is evidently] able to collect and arrange information'.[226] Gaskin's linguistic qualifications and local knowledge, which were in Lorimer's mind, far superior to the political agents in Muscat, Bahrain and Kuwait was an observation that must have irked Cox as well as Major William Grey, Prideaux and Knox the respective agency incumbents. Rather than defend the reputation of the Gulf political network, Dane agreed with its shortcomings.[227] He supported Gaskin's inclusion, and if he was to end up spending much of his time in Dubai or elsewhere along the Trucial Coast, he considered it an opportunity to test whether it would be possible to permanently post an officer there.[228]

Another member of the uncovenanted civil service working for Lorimer was the experienced surveyor, Khan Bahadur Sher Jung. Unlike the rest of the gazetteering team, his recruitment had not been an easy one. Following an early misunderstanding between Lorimer and the surveyor-general of India, Colonel Francis Longe, they could not come to an agreement on the value of having a surveyor as part of the gazetteering team. Their relationship got so bad, that despite being in the same location, Longe looked through the Scot and wrote a curt note to the Foreign Department demanding 'will you please ask *your* [his emphasis] Lorimer now here, to let me know early tomorrow what he wants done about the surveyor to accompany him'.[229]

Lorimer had assumed that on learning of his forthcoming gazetteering fieldtrip, Longe would agree to sanction a surveyor to accompany him. He had even provided the surveyor-general with an ambitious overview of the ground that he expected to cover over a six-month period, passing through places, to include

> Muskat, Bunder Abbas, Bahrein, Bushire, Koweit, Busrah, Baghdad, Najaf, Kerbala, Mohammerah, Khuzistan possibly Hasa and Katar, the Trucial Chiefs' Coast, the Beni Yas and Manasir country towards Katar, Abu Dhabi, Sharga, Mahdheh, Shinas, some points on the Batinah Coast, Mahot, Wadi Halfein and Sur...[230]

His assumption turned out to be wrong as Longe had not taken the initiative and certainly did not like the idea of taking orders from a subordinate civilian official. With travel due to begin in late November and still lacking a surveyor, Lorimer too looked to the Foreign Department to put pressure on Longe to make the most of the opportunity to finally explore and map the Gulf. Longe was eventually partly persuaded but he was still unwilling to release a British surveyor, which he argued, would be more appropriate to 'ensure [there would be] results of any practical value'.[231] Forced to comply with the Foreign Department's orders given Curzon's close interest, Longe reluctantly deputed Sher Jung.

By the time Sher Jung joined the gazetteers in late 1904, he already had an impressive career as a soldier and a surveyor, having participated in many military campaigns in the frontier region including the 1897 Tochi expedition. From 1899 to 1901, he helped survey over fifty-three thousand miles of Persia, mapping Bushire, Bandar Abbas, Kerman and Shiraz. He was then attached to the Abyssinian Boundary Commission, serving there for a couple of years where he assumed duties typically undertaken by British officers. His next mission was in Tibet where he was mentioned in dispatches. Such was his professionalism that after leaving Abyssinia, he was conferred with the honourable title 'Khan Bahadur', a formal title given as a mark of respect, honour and seniority. In addition to his new title and citation, Sher Jung was also given a substantial financial gratuity and awarded the Black Memorial sword of honour by the RGS for his selfless contribution to geography.[232] Sher Jung's field knowledge and experience was extensive, arguably exceeding the skills of many British survey officers also working under Longe.

In late July 1904, with the full expectation that St. John Brodwick would agree to a new special duty, Lorimer was allocated a contingency grant of nine thousand, two hundred and fifty rupees from the central coffers to fund his gazetteering field work. Another two thousand rupees was allocated from the Secret Service Fund to pay for various gifts that might need to be presented along the way, in return for information or access. An impressive cache was procured with the fund, ranging from silver pencil cases, tobacco boxes and watches, to Norwegian hunting knives, telescopes, Browning pistols and ammunition.[233] For those unlikely to be enticed by material trappings, Lorimer could also use the fund to pay for information in hard cash. Three months later with his travel plans now taking shape, he submitted a request to draw down a thousand rupee advance from the contingency grant to cover unexpected travel costs that he might incur whilst he was in the field. Any expenditure, he asked, should ideally be held in suspense until his eventual return.[234] It was a small request, but one that troubled the Finance and Commerce Department who were unused to government money being unaccounted for, for a prolonged period of time. After some procrastination, the funds were eventually made available to Lorimer, to be collected at the political residency in Bushire with the understanding that whenever he was near a political agency, he was to reconcile his spending immediately with the local accountant.

He would soon find himself at odds again with the accountants when he submitted another request. Not wanting to be struggling again with a lack of salary for the forthcoming months or to face further bank charges for being overdrawn, Lorimer also asked for a five thousand rupee advance of pay so that Nesta would have sufficient funds to live on during the winter months when she was alone in Simla.[235] Again, hands were wrung with apprehension as the pay clerks questioned the need for nearly three months advance of pay when Lorimer could easily draw down his wages whilst on the road, failing to appreciate why and for whom the advance was required. His response, that 'I shall be 6 months in the Gulf and most of that time on the march, out of reach of treasuries, telegraphs and even post-offices. Knowing how easily technical difficulties arise, I am unwilling to embark on such a course of drawing at two treasuries, one some hundred, the other a couple of thousand miles from where I shall be …' gave the accountants something to think about.[236] Either obliged or persuaded, Nesta got her advance.

Although the gazetteering field work was to be just six months in total, productivity was expected to be high. Lorimer and his team would travel in the winter months when the temperatures were a little bit more bearable. While Sandanha worked his way through the archives in Simla, Gaskin, now temporarily back in Bushire but with orders to head north to Kuwait, was set the task of working up a programme for Lorimer.[237] His planning parameters were simple, to make the most of 'gunboats [and] despatch vessels etc, [operating in the Gulf to] avoid the loss of time'.[238] But before there could be any travel, everyone's deputation allowances had to be agreed by their respective departmental paymasters and negotiations concluded about their individual travel rates, calculated on the number of miles covered per day. With Indian daily travelling subsistence rates deemed insufficient given the higher cost to hire mules and camels in the Gulf, local rates were eventually, but again, reluctantly, agreed. The new rates came with conditions: in addition to each man's riding horse, the standard maximum allocation of five camels or ten mules per man if carrying tentage, fewer if not, could be increased to eight camels or sixteen mules with tents or five and ten respectively without, but only if the political agencies were unable to provide their own animals.[239] If the agencies had their own stables or bandobast, a different costing mechanism altogether would need to be adopted. Curzon might have been the authority for the mission, but it was his purse-holders who really had command over the art of the possible and the affordable. Finally on 26 November, accompanied by Gabriel and Sher Jung, Lorimer once again, departed Karachi and headed across the Gulf of Oman to begin the gazetteering in earnest.

The expedition, however, did not start well. Their first port of call was to Abu Dhabi and then on to Sharjah as 'the two most important [principalities] in Trucial Oman'.[240] This was the first time that the term 'Trucial Oman' had been used in official British documents. Originally suggested by Prideaux in the absence of an Arabic equivalent, it was readily adopted by Lorimer as he felt the previous proper noun, the 'Pirate Coast … not sufficiently comprehensive, and [in] the present day … obsolete and even misleading…'.[241] After landing ashore, Lorimer's hoped to parlay with Sheikh Zayed, 'by far the most powerful personality', despite the precarious nature of authority throughout the sheikhdoms at that time.[242] The opportunity was lost when he found the ruler had moved his camp to Buraimi, a renowned 'remarkable oasis' deep within his territory that he had recently become attached to.[243] From the mostly barren and undulating sandy desert of Sharjah, they expected to make a quick transit up the coastline to another oasis, Qatif, described as 'a well-watered maritime tract' in Al Hasa and then travel deeper into the province which was itself, also mostly desert.[244] The lack of physical features aside, Lorimer considered this leg of the mission to be highly desirable as he hoped it would allow him to procure first-hand, the local population's sentiment towards the Turks and the *Wahhabi*s, a contentious term readily used by orientalists to describe inaccurately, the people of the Najd on the presumption of their strict interpretation of Islam.[245] Again, there was disappointment when the party were informed that they had been refused permission to travel inland by the Ottoman government despite the British ambassador in Constantinople, Sir Nicholas O'Conor, receiving initial assurances that Lorimer's mission could pass through their governed territories without being molested.[246] A subsequent Ottoman *demarche* to O'Conor, demanding that the gazetteering team must confine their surveying to the coast meant that a stopover in Qatif would be of little benefit.

The Turks demonstrated again when they heard rumours that Lorimer might instead, plan to head deep into the interior when he was due in Kuwait, possibly as far south as Riyadh 'the principal town of the Aridh district in Southern Najd'.[247] Further untruths, including that British Army officers were disguised as Arabs and fighting alongside Ibn Sa'ud, a rumour allegedly spread by the Russians, only helped to fuel Turkish paranoia that there was more to Lorimer's gazetteering than had been shared with them.[248] Since the summer of 1904, the three provinces of Jabal Shammar, Al Qassim and southern Najd that made up the interior had been absorbed with internecine warfare as Ibn Sa'ud and his rival, Ibn Rashid, battled for supremacy and suzerainty.[249] For over a decade, the Ottoman government had given substantial material support to Ibn Rashid to prop up his claim as ruler of Najd. This support had now been increased with their physical presence, reinforcing his tribal warriors with six infantry battalions, despatched from various garrisons in Mesopotamia to Ha'il, his capital in Jabal Shammar.[250] Through sickness, desertions and defeats, the poorly prepared expeditionary force had been severely weakened by the campaign. When a secondary force was sent to Najd, it too was soon in no fit state to play any part in tipping the balance in the ongoing civil war. The last thing that Turkish political and military leaders needed was for the British to find out, first-hand, how poorly they had performed and to see how little influence they really had, not only in the interior, but also in the Two Holy Cities, which they claimed to be the custodians of.

Reliant on Gaskin and flexibility in his logistical planning, from Trucial Oman, Lorimer and his party sailed past the Al Hasa coastline and headed further north-west instead, arriving at the 'thriving town' of

Kuwait in late December where they finally rendezvoused with Gaskin and the political agent, Knox.[251] It was here where Sher Jung got to work, surveying the entire area from Jahrah 'a considerable village … near the foot of Kuwait Bay' to Safwan, found 'just within the Turkish frontier' and on for thirty miles south to the edge of the sheikhdom.[252] Gaskin, too, got busy with his camera, taking a photograph of the bay for the gazetteer, capturing numerous pearling and fishing vessels grounded along a cluttered beach, overlooked by a scattering of low-level buildings.[253] With time of the essence, the travellers spent just a few days together in Kuwait before they went their separate ways to continue their mission. Whilst in Kuwait, Gaskin's schedule originally included a survey of the northern approaches, in particular Khor Musa, a 'remarkable inlet', Karun River 'the largest river of Persia and the only one navigable by steamers' and Shatt Al Arab, which had been briefly scouted by *Sphinx* and *Lawrence* during Curzon's tour.[254] When Lorimer found that another team of ICS officials and engineers were already in the area carrying out an irrigation survey, it made sense to hand over information-gathering responsibilities to them, freeing up time for their own explorations elsewhere.[255]

While Sher Jung surveyed nearby, Gaskin initially remained with Knox to gather information on Sheikh Mubarak's realm, the tribes who either settled or passed through Kuwait and the various caravan routes that carried trade deep into Arabia.[256] Both Lorimer and Gabriel were in possession of government of India official passports, which were valid for travel through Persia and the Ottoman empire and protected them – on paper at least – from unwarranted molestation, and headed into the Ottoman Caliphate proper. The omission of Gaskin despite his language skills, was likely because he could only travel on a normal passport given his mixed heritage and employment status, which gave little to no political protection.[257]

Accompanying Lorimer in his place was a locally hired interpreter, who in line with Finance and Commerce Department rules, came with his own daily travel rates and subsistence. It was a poor hiring decision as he was soon found to be unsatisfactory and had to be dismissed. As well as terminating his contract, Lorimer also made sure that the interpreter forfeited any potential claim for financial compensation.[258]

Lorimer would instead, need to rely on his own linguistic skills. From Kuwait they travelled north through featureless terrain, broken up only by the occasional melon field to Zubair 'a market town for the surrounding Bedouin tribes' then east to Basrah 'the most populous and important town' in the district.[259] The next waypoint was 'the God given place', Baghdad, achieved courtesy of a passage up the Tigris 'one of the two great rivers of Turkish Iraq' on one of the many boats that worked the river artery.[260] Not long after they arrived, they found they were the source of many rumours and suspicions, 'some of which [were] unfortunately of an anti-English character', rumours fuelled by local Ottoman administrators and remnants of paranoia from Curzon's cruise the previous year.[261] Following a bearing south, their next destination took them through dense palm groves to Musaiyib, 'a town of pleasant aspect … situated upon both banks of the Euphrates River … crossed by the Baghdad-Karbala road'.[262] This was followed by Karbala itself, 'renowned as the scene of the martyrdom, or rather, massacre, of Husain' and finally to Hillah, a fertile town surrounded by fields of wheat and barley which might have explained why it also garrisoned 'a regiment of cavalry, 3 guns and a battalion of infantry'.[263]

Their next destination was through a reddish sandstone plateau to Najaf, 'the most sacred of the places regarded as holy by Muhammadans of the Shi'ah sect,' but with Ottoman assumptions and concerns about Lorimer's potential ulterior motives, sufficient attention was given to his speculative movements to force him to abandon that leg of his gazetteering as well.[264] A cruise on a Lynch mail steamer down the Euphrates River to the Shatt Al Arab 'the only navigable river that enters the Persian Gulf' followed instead, eventually landing them at the 'flat, alluvial and low-lying' town of Muhammerah, having now covered almost a thousand miles, either in the saddle or on a boat.[265] Another ship took them to Bushire, 'the chief seaport of Persia… [sat in] a large bay [with] muddy, ill-defined edges…' which allowed Lorimer the chance to finally reconcile his clutch of receipts.[266] From there, they zigzagged to Bahrain 'which had once embraced the promontory of Qatar and the Oases of Qatif and Hasa', to the 'almost intolerable' town of Bandar Abbas and then to Jashk 'where the air is heavily charged with fine red dust'.[267] After passing through the Strait of Hormuz, they steamed south to Sohar 'an important town on the Batinah coast, and lastly to Muscat, situated 'in the centre of an outcrop of volcanic rock which extends 10 miles along the coast'.[268]

Having seen and recorded as much as they could in Muscat, both Lorimer and Gabriel returned to India on 18 March 1905 just as temperatures started to rise.[269] By the end of the month, Lorimer was back in Simla with Nesta, reconciling outstanding receipts and invoices that needed to be presented to the accountants. Whilst the bookkeepers examined Lorimer's expenses, he carried out an equally forensic task of his own, interrogating his, Gabriel and later Gaskin and Sher Jung's notes, sketches and observations.

For the rest of his special duty, Lorimer would be predominately deskbound in Simla, a move that suited Nesta now the couple had been joined by daughter Jean Mary, born in 1904 and later, Isabella Lockhart (or Bell) in 1906. The same could not be said of Sher Jung who continued to travel throughout the region, sometimes alone, at other times with Cox or his political agents. This would see him pay his own visit to Muscat to survey the mountainous pass that connected the capital to the nearby market town, Muttrah. He would also return to Bushire, as well as to Muhammerah, Basrah and Bahrain to gather new topographical data. It was not without danger given the curious and suspicious nature of the locals when they saw a foreigner surveying their locality.[270] To lessen their curiosity, Sher Jung took notes and spelt names in English rather than in Arabic or Persian, a successful ploy but one that did little to help their eventual transliteration.[271] Gabriel too, returned to the Gulf, visiting Bahrain a second time, this time from Bushire, where he travelled extensively on his own around the island.[272] Gaskin was also kept busy, visiting Muhammerah, Fallahiyeh and Qatar, making best use of his informal contacts and relationships to gather information about the Ottoman-controlled peninsula state.[273]

At the end of 1904, Lorimer and his team of gazetteers faced considerable uncertainty about their mission. News had reached them that Curzon had resigned as viceroy, citing an inability to reconcile with the military autocracy led by commander in chief and military member of his governing council, Lord Kitchener.[274] A successor was immediately found with Gilbert Elliott-Murray-Kynynmound, the 4th

Earl of Minto shipped out immediately to replace Curzon. With his own ideas on governance and reform, the gazetteer's future could have been in doubt had Minto been inclined to make a statement about his own aspirations for governance at the expense of Curzon's. Bringing one of his predecessor's pet projects to a close or calling for its immediate abandonment would have been a sure way to make his mark. Fortunately, he too appreciated the value of having a gazetteer of the Gulf and was content not only to allow Lorimer's field and deskwork to continue, but to agree to extend the term of his special duty until the end of October 1905.

In the one hundred and twelve days that Lorimer had been in the field, even with best intentions and plans, it had been impossible to gather even a fraction of raw data that would be required to meet Curzon's original demands. The areas visited were extremely limited and arguably random, at times, duplicated and influenced by the availability of access and shipping schedules. They were also hampered by the weather and shaped by repeated Ottoman protests. There was also a substantial lack of penetration into Arabia itself even though the interior was to be one of the gazetteer's main areas of focus. Lorimer's frustration, both about the want of time and the various political obstacles put in front of him which had forced him to abandon some of his more ambitious travel plans was made clear in a letter to the Foreign Department.[275] Even though he was not explicit, it was clear that he considered the Foreign Office's longstanding policy of non-interference in the interior, as much as Ottoman obstructiveness, to blame for his lack of progress. With a further expedition unlikely to be supported or financed, Lorimer would instead need to rely heavily on Dane's communication to Cox and his growing network of political agencies to support Lorimer's mission if it was to be a worthy publication and now to the satisfaction of Minto rather than Curzon.

Chapter 6

The Sands of Time

Lorimer was determined that no topographic, demographic, genealogic or petrologic stone should be left unturned. Every political officer directed by Dane, or government official likely to be working in the Gulf, received a list of requirements to help inform the gazetteer. How they sourced their information or assessed the accuracy of their returns was for each to decide but alongside rulers, local agents and translators, agency clerks and spies in government-pay, merchants, caravan-guides, tribal agents and even rumourmongers loitering in the bazaars, all played their part to help populate their inquisitors' returns. Sometimes given freely, at others, persuaded by gifts or money but always unknowingly of the real objective given the gazetteer's confidential status.[276]

Despite the lack of hard borders in Arabia, Lorimer asked for as much information as possible on municipal and tribal boundaries, trade routes and waypoints, the distances between them and the ease of communication between districts, settlements and towns. Details about valleys, mountains and islands as well as their local geology and meteorology were also demanded. Beyond geography, information was sought on the people who inhabited these places, including their tribe or family affiliation, size of population, language, religion, livestock, customs, taxes, occupations and commerce. Historical facts, forms of governance, models of administration and the extent of any foreign interests or representation were also to be pursued. Other key details of interest were the towns and tribes' fighting strength and defences, their number and type of weapons, as well as the extent of any military or police presence; particulars that would equally benefit military planners as they would political ones.[277] Alert to the differences between Gulf Arabic, or *Khaliji*, and the standard Arabic typically used by the government of India, officials were also encouraged to spell names in Arabic where possible. This, Lorimer hoped, would help standardise their eventual transliteration.

Commanded by Dane and armed with Lorimer's guidance as well as an assortment of gifts and money, Cox travelled extensively in late 1905 to gazetteer on his contemporary's behalf. His travelling companion and note taker was once again, Gabriel.[278] In October, they travelled eighty-five miles north-west up the coast from Bushire to the swamp-surrounded port town of Bandar Dailam and then inland to Behbahan, in Fars Province but which was, for the most part, outside of the gazetteer's geographic scope.[279] From there, they passed through the district of Hindayah (Hendijan), before following a canal that led to the Euphrates River, noted in the gazetteer for its 'winding… [and in parts] inaccessible' waterways, until its entry into the Gulf.[280]

Continuing on their way, the ancient port town Bandar Mahshahr, which Cox noted had an artificial appearance given its barren backdrop, was their next destination.[281] After crossing the Jarahi River, which he found was 'fordable in summer in numerous places', he arrived at the busy trading town of Buziyeh 'scattered amidst interminable date groves and intricate water-courses'.[282] Its smaller neighbour, Fallahiyah was next, despite being considered an 'almost intolerable' place during the summer months because of the extreme temperatures and ubiquitous presence of mosquitoes.[283] Despite its considered seasonal failings, Gabriel still photographed one of the waterways that served the town for the gazetteer so any enquiring soul could make up their own mind.

A month later, again with Gabriel but also with Sher Jung, Cox navigated the Bahmanshir estuary, which 'among [the] natives, [had] no general name' to 'a deserted site' known locally as Qubban and then to Muhammerah.[284] In December, he commandeered RIMS *Lawrence* and set out again with Gabriel, bound for Trucial Oman.[285] After landing at Ras Al Khaimah, 'part of the Oman promontory [estimated to be] roughly triangular with its base to the west', he headed down to Sharjah, inland to Dhaid and south to the Buraimi Oasis to record its latitude and longitude. Nearby, Jau, 'a small district of Independent Oman situated between the Oman Sultanate and Trucial Oman' was the next waypoint.[286] Years later, his research there would be extremely important to the British. Their extraction involved taking a challenging route, that took them eastward over the Al Hajar 'mass of mountains' in Oman's interior, through Wadi Al Jizi to Fujairah and finally to Sohar where the steamer waited at anchor to take them back to Bushire.[287]

While Prideaux openly surveyed parts of Bahrain not visited by Gabriel and discreetly, parts of Qatar not covered by Gaskin, Lieutenant Richard Birdwood, Cox's second assistant in Bushire, was sent to Minab.[288] It was, he recorded, 'a comparatively rich and important but not very extensive district' located close to the Strait of Hormuz. He then headed inland in Fars Province, near Biyaban, although why he was despatched there is unclear.[289] From there, he set off east as far as the coastline, following a dogleg route that took him beyond the entrance to the Gulf to Gwadar, which, since the late 1700s, had been 'administered by an Arab deputy of the Sultan of Oman'. Cox's assistant resident, John Bill, who until 1906 had been serving in Bannu in Lorimer's footsteps, also added to the gazetteer, willingly covering familiar ground in Muhammerah, Bahmanshir and the Karun River.[290] The same level of willingness could not be said of Cox's successor in Muscat, Grey. With Sultan Faisal already refusing him permission to trek into Oman's interior, he was more than content to collect and correct information comfortably for Lorimer from behind his agency desk. This changed in 1906, when he was obliged to break out from Muscat and ordered down the Omani coast to survey the volatile Dhofar region, home to 'the two great tribes… the Qaras … and the Al Kathir' where blood-feuds between its inhabitants but also with the sultan, seemed to flourish.[291] As a key feature of the gazetteer was to present the various ruling families' genealogy, with at least five prominent sheikhs governing in or near Trucial Oman, it was also up to Grey to head up the coast to call on the rulers to record their respective family trees and pedigrees. It would prove to be a futile trip. All refused to share personal information with him, considering a family tree to be a dangerous innovation, leaving Grey, Cox and ultimately Lorimer to rely on Abdul Latif, their local agent in Sharjah, and other amenable sources to map the ruling families' heritage.

Like his political agent counterparts, Shakespear, the first British consul in Bandar Abbas, also had to plan his travels around the weather, limiting his gazetteering to the cooler winter months. More eager than Grey in Muscat, by February 1905, having already covered Bandar Abbas, Shakespear managed to visit nearby Hormuz, Larak and Henjam

Islands, which he described as being 'nearly circular in shape', 'oval' and 'nondescript but compact' respectively.[292] In March, he picked up a 'hard and stony going' caravan route, which led him three hundred miles north inland to Kerman, returning through the district of Shamil, situated to the east of Bandar Abbas and Minab.[293] In April, he added Khamir, a sizeable village situated on the coast of Bastak and the practically unoccupied British station in Bassidore on Qeshm, an island he could only describe as being shaped like a fish, to his travels.[294] Ambitious to travel more, in August, Shakespear attempted to survey the 'bold mountain ranges' at Kuh-e-Genu and Kuh-e Fareghan but was defeated by the intense summer heat, confirming, like Lorimer, that gazetteering was a seasonal affair, best done during the winter months.[295]

Gazetteering got even closer to home when Lorimer's brother, Lock, was also sequestered to support his brother's assignment. Lock too, was another newcomer to the region, having only been made vice consul in January 1901, posted to Ahvaz, a 'considerable village on the left bank of the Karun River'.[296] His latest posting followed a brief spell initially as a supplementary assistant commissioner in Ambala, situated between Delhi and Simla, and then Hazara, part of the new North-West Frontier Province.[297] His position was one of the new political billets established as part of Curzon's forward policy, one which was considered ideal for 'the energies of a young and strenuous officer' to hone new skills.[298] Despite a promising beginning, Lock soon understood first hand, the dangers associated with being part of Cox's network. Just a few months after settling in, he had the opportunity to join a section of the Persian Sagvend tribe, who were migrating north from the 'elevated and somewhat uneven' town of Dizful to high ground near Khoremabad.[299] It was a pleasant enough ride. Once there, he was met and escorted by the Delfans tribe who led him safely on to the Saimarra River. On his return to Ahvaz, confidence in the local tribes was high, on account of the hospitality, protection and friendly manner afforded to him throughout the trek.

Several months later, he received a letter from Lieutenant-Colonel James Douglas, the military attaché in Tehran, who was planning to visit Luristan. Lock sought to join him, expecting more of the same tribal hospitality and assistance throughout the expedition despite longstanding concerns about local governance and security in the district. In October, Lock set off with a tribal escort from the Direkvend tribe, who, for a fee of one hundred Persian tomans, provided him with security along the Dizful-Khoremabad road.[300] A few days in, the Direkvend demanded an additional thirty tomans, a demand that threw Lock as their original agreement had been sworn on the Qur'an.[301] Despite the religious guarantee, he had little choice but to pay the revised fee or be left stranded. When Lock and Douglas's caravans rendezvoused several days later to continue their survey together, the Direkvend guides looked again to renegotiate terms by demanding an additional five hundred tomans, on account that their original agreement had only been to escort Lock. Unwilling to agree or to take the risk of continuing their journey alone, the party agreed to set up camp for the night.

On 26 October the next morning, after some renegotiation, the ruthless guides agreed to Douglas's counteroffer of an additional two hundred tomans but then rushed the camp, attacking both men. Lock was shot through his left hand and had a rock smashed into his face, breaking his upper right jaw and damaging his supraorbital nerve. Douglas fared just a little better, shot through his right forearm, breaking bones in the process. With both men incapacitated, the Direkvend stripped the camp clean, leaving the two casualties and their Indian helpers or *sowars* with just three baggage ponies and some blankets. Despite their wounds, Lock, Douglas and their aides found their way to a small village called Chimashk, and then to Khoremabad, where they were helped by a local merchant who accommodated them in his house. There, they stayed in relative safety until 4 November, when they set off again in slightly better health mentally if not physically, arriving two days later in Burujird, an industrial town, for help. By chance, they were found by IMS Surgeon Lieutenant Thomas Williams and Doctor Funk from the American Mission in Hamadan, both of whom were fortunately in the area. As both men's wounds had not been treated since the attack, Douglas had early onset of gangrene requiring him to be knocked unconscious by chloroform before the doctors could treat him. This time, Lock fared a little better as his hand was just oozing pus.

A flurry of telegrams and letters followed as the British and Persian governments bickered amongst themselves who should be held to account, what retribution was warranted and what financial compensation, if any, should be afforded to the victims. As both were aware of the poor security in Luristan, Lansdowne initially questioned whether they were in part, responsible for the unfortunate incident negating any need for financial recompense. After a change of mind influenced by politics rather than sympathy, he later conceded that their survey was in the Crown's interest, which came with inherited risks and dangers.[302] Compensation was therefore, warranted and pursued.

It would take three months before Lock recuperated sufficiently to make his way back to Ahwaz, passing through Baghdad along the way. His return, however, was brief. With his brother's list of requirements still pending, in April and May, Lock travelled north to the ancient fortress city of Shooshter, once a 'flourishing place in the 10th and 14th centuries A.D.' and then north-west to return to Dizful.[303] After another short stay in Ahvaz, he set out again deep into the Persian interior, this time north-east for three hundred and fifty miles to Isfahan, finally returning to the agency in November.[304] Two months later, he was back on his saddle, retracing his route to Shooshter and then to Ramuz which he found amid a 'fertile plain... watered by various streams and springs'.[305] In all, he assessed, over two hundred days had been spent away from his agency building, either in support of Lorimer or trying to fulfil his regular responsibilities. Despite his age and enthusiasm, both tasks were beginning to take their toll on his health. Further opportunities to explore extensively inland were hampered as he was struck down several times with persistent neuralgia, brought on from the lingering effects of the attack although he later managed to take a short trip south to Ma'shur just a mile north of Khor Musa and endured a passage along the Aquleh route of the Jarrahi River.[306]

In Lock's contribution to Cox's 1906 annual report to the viceroy, shared blood only counted for so much as he complained that the gazetteering had taken up so much of his time, it had prevented him from doing some of his routine tasks as a political agent. It was an observation echoed by Cox, who reported with equal frustration, that ten of his twelve political agents were involved in supporting various special duty missions which were impacting on their core work. Four of whom (including Lock), he continued, were already heavily burdened by setting up new consular posts and establishing local networks.[307]

Despite the reservations and complaints about the additional workloads, Lorimer remained efficient if not merciless in his task, continuing to make the best use of any temporary expeditions working in the region if they could usefully supplement reporting. This included pressing doctors von Krafft, Oldham and Pilgrim from the Indian Geological Survey to provide geological data for the gazetteer in addition to their own scientific missions in Oman. Lorimer also leant on the government of India's Archaeological Department when he heard that they were excavating in Bahrain. Ever resourceful, he even called on Lieutenants Ranking and Wilson, British officers in charge of the Isfahan oil guard to take forward some gazetteering duties in addition to their regular security duties, exploring areas that Lock had been unable to visit.

Such resourcefulness was necessary as an implicit condition of Lorimer's various extensions was that he could no longer be solely occupied with the gazetteer. There was an expectation, if not an operational requirement, for him to be on hand to consider wider Gulf matters outside of his terms of reference, given his increasing depth of knowledge on a region that just two years before, had been completely alien to him. This condition was with immediate effect as no sooner had he arrived back in Simla in March 1905, he was asked for his opinion on the extent of the sultan's sovereignty in Musandam promontory. His assessment was needed to support the British position in the ongoing Muscat Arbitration, which saw them at odds with the French at the Permanent Court of Arbitration in The Hague. The British complaint, or rather Sultan Faisal's after he had been persuaded to allow them to submit a complaint on his behalf, centred on the fact that the French were allowing Omani subjects to sail under the Tricolour. As only stateless vessels could be challenged at sea, this prevented them from being boarded by the Gulf Squadron's warships. Had their dhows been inspected, among legitimate cargo, the British were sure that they would have also found illicit arms and slaves on-board some of the vessels. The French in turn, queried the extent of the sultan's authority beyond Muscat and any obligation to respect any treaties that the British had with him beyond his capital.

After reviewing all of the historical documents in his possession, he invalidated Cox's 1902 judgement that the sultan's jurisdiction over

Musandam was so ambiguous that the British government could either recognise or choose to ignore it.[308] Lorimer's research found clear evidence that the small communities in the premonitory did, in fact, recognise the sultan's governance over them. When asked for his view on Lorimer's observation, Cox remained firm in his original observation but decided against defending the accuracy of his judgement. As part of the same request, Lorimer also gave his opinion discounting the very foundation of the French argument that Sur, a large coastal settlement one hundred and twenty miles south-east of Muscat, was independent of the sultan's rule. Although formally acknowledging Musandam as part of the sultan's domain undermined any immediate future British and viceroyal aspirations to establish a naval base there, Lorimer's reasoning was reluctantly endorsed by Curzon who was more inclined to agree with Cox. Unable to argue against the strong evidence at hand, Lorimer's assessment was backed and shared with the India Office, who forwarded it to the delegation at The Hague to complement their legal argument.[309]

If there remained any lingering ill-feelings between Lorimer and Cox, they were put aside four months later when Cox asked Lorimer to take a look at a summary of the history of Qatar recently produced by Prideaux. His precis was going to be an annex to a wider government of India paper on its policy on the Gulf, about to be presented to the Imperial Defence Committee. Although Cox did not doubt Prideaux's work, it had been compiled solely from the Political Department's registry files, which Cox acknowledged, were far from complete. He would be far more comfortable presenting the paper to the committee if Lorimer could check its accuracy first, using the independent sources and material that he had amassed through his gazetteering research.[310] What did concern Cox though, was Prideaux's supporting policy recommendations that the British government should consider recognising Ottoman sovereignty over Qatar, if in return, for the next fifty years, the British were leased the whole of the island's coastline or allowed to administer it.[311] It required little persuasion, and certainly no additional commentary from Lorimer, for Cox to have those suggestions struck from the policy paper.

After Lorimer had peer-reviewed and edited Prideaux's work, with his gazetteering special duty expected to conclude in late October, he requested six weeks leave to start immediately, after which he promised, he would dedicate his time to completing the gazetteer. In the same request, he also gave a firm directive that he would be unable to take on any other work until his return in mid-December, having already been made aware that another request from the Foreign Department was forthcoming, this time asking him to carry out a complete review of Aitchison's Treaties.[312] Although content to do a review given his own concerns about the accuracy of Aitchison's work, Lorimer was clear that it would have to wait until his return from leave. Undeterred or immune to the additional pressure that had been repeatedly put upon him, when pressed how long he would need to carry out the additional task, Lorimer judged that three weeks would be sufficient with a caveat that even if the review was not completed, it would at least be in an advanced stage that could be continued by a less-expensive official.[313] The Foreign Department settled on a month, placing Lorimer once again, on another distracting special duty.

Prideaux's political judgement was in doubt again in early 1906, when men from Abu Dhalouf, a pearling village at the north-western tip of Qatar, attacked a Persian dhow headed for Bahrain and robbed it of its consignment of wheat. Despite there being no British interest, Prideaux threatened the village's headman with retaliatory measures unless reparations were given, a message that was delivered courtesy of HMS *Sphinx*, which loitered offshore. Although the 1820 General Treaty, 1853 Perpetual Treaty of Peace and 1861 Treaty with the Chief of Bahrain obliged the British to supress acts of piracy in the Gulf, it had always been interpreted by the government to be limited to the territorial waters of those who had signed the treaties. As Qatar was a non-signatory to the treaties and the vessel was Persian, the incident was considered to be outside the reach of the Royal Navy's maritime security jurisdiction. There was also an expectation that the Ottoman authorities, as the current administrators of the Qatar peninsula and with over two hundred soldiers garrisoned there, should also share the burden of countering and punishing such criminality. When the matter was raised with the Turks, they were incredulous at the allegation, claiming that rather than it being a criminal act, the Abu Dhalouf boat crews had, instead, been given the wheat in return for their assistance to the vessel that they understood, had been in distress during a storm.[314]

Rather than denounce the Turks' appreciation of events, it was Prideaux who found himself subject to governmental scrutiny. While some in Calcutta agreed that he had acted within the spirit of the treaties, others considered he had been overzealous and unwise in his response, having taken Britain's regional maritime security policy too literally. After reading the exchanges of correspondence, Lorimer was asked for his opinion as the new fount of knowledge on Britain's treaty obligations. Having considered both sides of the argument, he admitted that it was a complicated issue, not helped by the various jurisdictions potentially in play. With over two hundred and fifty permutations of potential acts of maritime criminality to consider, he discouraged the suggestion to introduce a general policy to prevent another incident, as the number of piracies that would demand immediate and direct action was judged to be extremely rare. The only exception he could think of was if a British warship was in the immediate vicinity of an illegal act. His recommendation was one of process rather than policy, suggesting that any disadvantage a local or political agent might feel for not taking immediate action, would be more than counterbalanced by the firmness of the government of India if they were consulted first and agreed with any suggested reprisal.[315] The incident and Lorimer's recommendation were forwarded to Minto and John Morley, First Viscount Morley of Blackburn and the latest incumbent as secretary of state of India, both of whom endorsed his preference to consult first and act later.[316]

Had this advice been considered four years later by Cox and the Royal Navy, the infamous 'Dubai Incident' might have played out differently. The incident began with suspicions that subjects of Sheikh Maktoum of Dubai were involved in trafficking weapons. HMS *Hyacinth* lost five of its crew during a fire fight as they went ashore and searched buildings for weapons. Twelve of the sheikh's men were also killed in the exchange. As the search party withdrew, *Hyacinth* fired into the settlement, killing at least another twenty-five residents. Although a large cache of small arms was seized during the raid, it tainted Britain's relationship with the Trucial Chiefs, who subsequently refused to accept a political agency there. It also fuelled resentment against British Indian traders who plied trade with the various emirates.

In August 1906 whilst in Simla, Lorimer was handed yet another temporary special duty, this time to pull together a report on regional 'pan-Islamism' or politicisation of Islam, which he told Cox was apparently 'in full swing at present'.[317] The request followed a memorandum produced by the War Office a month earlier, on the possibility of war with Turkey and the potential use of religious fanaticism by the Turks as a weapon against British interests.[318] Despite the initial request from high quarters, Lorimer expected little from the network given the very limited physical presence the Ottoman government had there and even less spiritual recognition of the Grand Vizier, Abdul Hamid II as the Caliph. Cox and separately Knox, were both asked for any insight that they might have on the matter. In December, Lorimer received their replies. As the request's findings circulated within the IPS, an annotation appeared, summarising for the casual reader that 'the gist of this report is practically a negation…', confirming Lorimer's initial opinion. In response to further demands, Lorimer would later request reports on Muhammad Ahmad bin Abdullah, the 'Mad Mullah'[319] in British Somaliland, whose influence Lorimer had tried unsuccessfully to check many years back. Enquiries were additionally made about the Senoussi clan who were fighting French colonialist ambitions in Libya and the conservative *Wahhabi* religious movement that dominated Najd politics in the eighteenth and nineteenth centuries. Information was likewise desired on influential spiritual figures or *nagibs* in Basrah and the religious Baghdad *Babist* movement, an offshoot of Shi'a Islam founded in Persia in the mid-1800s, all of which would later inform the gazetteer's appendix on religion (Volume I Appendix H – Religions and Sects of the Persian Gulf Region) as much as government policies.

Despite Lorimer's previous critique of Cox's analysis and the considerable reporting burden that had been put on his network of agents, the political resident was forgiving of his critic, openly praising his peer's sympathetic handling and approach to gazetteering. Cox agreed that the gazetteer would eventually be of great benefit to future generations of political officers. He also acknowledged that the collection of material had itself 'been an education to all officers now serving within the field covered by it'.[320] Several years later however, Cox would himself become the critic when he questioned the gazetteer's definition of Kuwait's southern border, which he considered to have been judged using 'scanty information'.[321] Although a fair observation, his critique overlooked the fact that Knox would have confirmed the boundary and endorsed the gazetteer's judgement as the political agent in Kuwait at the time when the various chapters and annexes were being cleared with the network.

After reading the gazetteer's early drafts, Charles Somers-Cocks, special assistant secretary under Dane, also offered plaudits to the author, calling on Lorimer 'to be congratulated on his succinct and interesting exposition of the facts', while Dane himself echoed the need for congratulations for his protégé for producing a 'clear and most useful account that … has [been] prepared of recent history in the Gulf, which will be a valuable addition to our political records'.[322] As welcomed as these endorsements were, the most meaningful compliment that Lorimer could hope to receive would need to come from the man who commissioned the gazetteer and endorsed his special duty in the first place, Curzon. This duly came when the former viceroy received a draft of the opus from Dane as he was mourning in the United States following the death of his wife, Mary. In an unusually restrained tone, he replied 'It seems to me very well done and to err only in giving to me a credit which I cannot pretend to claim. Apart from that I have no criticisms to make and I shall be glad if you will convey to him my sincere compliments and thanks'.[323] From a man who took great pleasure in correcting the work of fellow explorers and chastising the RGS whenever he saw poor standards of topographical draughtsmanship, this was high praise indeed.[324] In fact, all were honest and genuine appreciations of the thoroughness and quality of Lorimer's work, but also expectations that the gazetteering should now be coming to an end. Even if Lorimer had yet to run the fount of knowledge dry, the government of India's flow of money and wider interest in his research was starting to dry up. From thereon in, the special duty was expected to be about consolidation, consultation and confirmation of the accuracy of the new wealth of knowledge that had been brought together, whilst also indexing, cross-referencing and cataloguing it for ease of the reader, and finally, bringing the grand project to a conclusion.

In late April 1906, as the political agents were reviewing their respective contributions to the gazetteer, the process of wider consultation began. Under cover of letters from Dane, draft chapters on the history of Lower Turkish Arabia (which would eventually become Volume I Chapter 9 – The History of Turkish Iraq) were mailed to the embassy in Constantinople, the consulate general in Baghdad and the political agency in Basrah for a final round of scrutiny. Corrections and remarks were actively encouraged, to be given as soon as convenient as printing was expected to begin soon. As it had been agreed from the very beginning that the gazetteer would be a secret publication, letter addressees were also asked to return their drafts plus any annotations rather than keep them for their own reference, lest they fall into adversaries' hands.[325] O'Conor was quick in his reply, returning his copy a month later, with just a few annotations in red ink confirming that the draft had for the most part, held up to embassy, and ultimately, Foreign Office scrutiny.[326] On the same day that Dane had written out to Constantinople, he also wrote to the legation in Tehran, the political agency in Muhammerah and to Lock in Ahvaz with similar instructions, this time to review the draft history of Arabistan (Volume I Chapter 10).[327] They were also informed that drafts on the history of the coast of Fars, the Gulf Ports, Henjam and various islands, and another on Makran (Volume I Chapters 11 and 12 respectively) would shortly follow by post, all of which would additionally benefit from their timely consideration.

Three weeks later, there was a second salvo of correspondence when the foreign secretary wrote again to O'Conor, this time requesting comments on the history of Qatar, Bahrain and Al Hasa (Volume I Chapters 4, 5 and 6). A combined history of Kuwait and central Arabia (subsequently broken down into two separate chapters, Volume I Chapters 7 and 8 – History of Kuwait and of Najd or Central Arabia) and a draft on epidemics and sanitation (Volume I Appendix M – Epidemics and Sanitary Organization in the Persian Gulf Region) were also despatched with the acknowledgement that the latter paper was far from complete. With presence of mind that the relevant expertise was just as unlikely to be held within the British embassy as it was in Simla or Calcutta, it was suggested to O'Conor that Dr Clemaw, the British delegate at the *Conseil Supérieur de la Santé*, an international body of public health experts based in Belgium, might be able to offer some assistance in addressing the paper's substantial gaps in understanding.[328]

Although under no obligation to do so, O'Conor passed the draft on to Brussels. On the same day, another copy of the epidemics appendix was on its way to Tehran with equal encouragement for contributions to help decrease the knowledge deficit.[329]

In early June, Dane wrote out again to Constantinople and Tehran, asking both to review the draft on Imperial Persian customs (Volume I Appendix O), further highlighting the breadth and diversity of knowledge being gazetteered.[330] Tehran was also asked to consider the draft on arms trafficking (Volume I Appendix N – The Arms and Ammunition Traffic in the Gulfs of Persia and Oman), as were Alexander Tucker, the chief commissioner in Baluchistan[331] and Lieutenant Colonel Harold Deane, chief commissioner of the North-West Frontier Province.[332] Tucker was additionally asked to comment on a segment on Gwadar (Volume I Chapter 2 – History of Oman Sultanate; Annexure No.2 History of Gwadar and Chabbar), with the same handling caveats as his counterparts had been given in Constantinople and Tehran. More correspondence was on its way to Tehran at the end of the month, this time seeking confirmation on the accuracy of the draft on the Indian Post Office (Volume I Appendix J – The Telegraphs of the Persian Gulf in their relation to the Telegraph Systems of Persia and Turkey).[333] Dane's final correspondence was to O'Conor, a trace map of Syria and the Hejaz Railway along with a list of place names. In addition to confirming the railway's route, he was asked if the Syrian place names could be spelt clearly in Arabic, complete with their vowels, to help with their transliteration.[334]

Throughout the summer of 1906, responses trickled in from the various political agencies as well as from Constantinople, Baluchistan and the North-West Frontier Province. At times they confirmed or amended the draft statements, at others, they challenged the accuracy of a piece of text. Some returns included substantially more information than Lorimer could ever consider including in the gazetteer, obliging him to reply that 'even in a secret publication such as the Persian gazetteer, it is not expedient to share everything, and though I have carefully borne this in mind, it is possible that my judgement may have here and there, been at fault'.[335] Nevertheless, all returns, amendments and comments were warmly acknowledged by Dane and Lorimer, regardless of their usefulness or tone.

With the Finance and Commerce Department increasingly doubting the value of continually extending Lorimer's special duty and the rising cost of the gazetteer itself, that September, he was asked to produce a memorandum to summarise his progress on the expected publication.[336] In his response, having recently received comments and supplementary reports from the Gulf network on the drafts, Lorimer was able to report the only outstanding work was to carry out a final review that he planned to take forward in the very near future. He was also happy with his piece on the general history of the Gulf from 1899 to 1905 (Volume I Chapter 1 – General History of the Persian Gulf Region), although he admitted that the intermediate history from 1258 to 1899 was proving to be a struggle, not helped by the lack of material to draw from. It is not clear why Lorimer singled out 1258. That year is referenced twice in the gazetteer, both times in his summary of the 'Khojahs' or Ismailis, a branch of Shia Islam who, until that year, resided in a stronghold in Alamut, a region to the south of the Caspian Sea, far away from the Gulf.[337] The next date in the continuation of the history of the Khojahs is the early sixteenth-century, possibly an indication that Lorimer failed in his efforts to find more material. Transliteration was also proving to be a challenge and he confessed that the editorial process had been slow, with cross-referencing and the bibliography (Volume I Appendix R – Book References) being constantly revised and updated as more material was sourced. That, in turn, had meant that there was still no supporting index. Work had also yet to begin on the appendices on religious organisations (although subsequently helped by his pan-Islamism special duty to become Volume 1 Appendix H – Religions and Sects of the Persian Gulf Region) or trade (there are numerous trade-focused appendices on trade which might partly explain why Lorimer had yet to conclude this work, including Volume I Appendices C – The Pearl and Mother of Pearl Fisheries of the Persian Gulf, D – Date Production and the Date Trade in the Persian Gulf Region, E – Fisheries of the Persian Gulf, G – Transport Animals and Livestock of the Persian Gulf Region and controversially, L – The Slave Trade in the Persian Gulf Region). A chronological list of regional British and foreign representatives was also incomplete (Volume I Appendix Q – British and Foreign Diplomatic Political; and Consular Representation in the Countries Bordering on the Persian

Gulf), but with fourteen articles and seven appendices totalling four hundred and seventy-eight pages, as well as a ninety-seven-page chapter on the contemporary history of the Gulf, Lorimer considered it not an 'unsatisfactory outturn' despite his confessed lack of knowledge of the region.[338] Although initially hesitant to give an exact estimate on the additional time he thought would be needed to fulfil the special duty's requirements, Lorimer unwisely offered to the accountants that the gazetteer would be complete by April 1907.[339] They now had a deadline to hold him to account.

Despite his complete dedication and personal sacrifice to see the gazetteer through to completion, by March 1907 it had advanced little and was still far from being in any state that could be accepted by the government.[340] It was not helped by a constant flow of new information that he felt obliged to include. As it was, Lorimer considered that the index, which remained unwritten, was likely to include nearly thirty thousand unique names and references.[341] Rather than see tangible progress since his September 1906 update, a subsequent write out again to the Gulf political agents in response to their initial returns, had sought clarification on nearly five thousand individual points.[342] Some required responses from several agents, hindering progress further. The topographical portion of the gazetteer had also continued to grow and was now expected to be in the region of two thousand pages, just over three inches in thickness.[343] It was, Lorimer argued when challenged by the financiers, to be expected when gazetteering a continent rather than a country that Curzon had originally presumed.[344]

Struggling to find either the time or a credible way to complete what remained unactioned without compromising the quality of the gazetteer, Lorimer admitted that he was 'sick to death' of the whole project and '"stale", from having been employed so long on the very monotonous and at the same time very exacting work of the geographical volume'.[345] Not wanting to be seen to be either obstructive or overly protective about the gazetteer, Lorimer offered that the publication could be broken down, with topographical and statistical elements finalised immediately as a standalone publication. This could be supported by a shorter contemporary historical part, even if in his eyes, its value after a few years would make it appear 'a curiously isolated and valueless document'.[346] If there really was no room for compromise or negotiation, Lorimer's fallback position was to suggest having no historical element at all. If alternatively, the Finance Department thought cheaper personnel was preferable instead to complete the task, Lorimer peculiarly ventured that Prideaux might be someone to consider despite his evident lack of political nous.[347] As honourable as it was for Lorimer to offer to fall on his sword, it was not a view supported by Dane or the Foreign Department who strongly advised against all of his suggestions, especially reallocating the historical portion given Lorimer's 'very special qualifications'.[348]

The idiom of being sick to death could have been equally used to reflect the feelings of those in the Finance Department who continued to have their doubts about the whole enterprise. Various grants aside, since 1903, the special duty had cost the government of India almost ninety thousand rupees, almost all of which had been allocated to cover Lorimer's salary and allowances.[349] Unsighted and arguably, uninterested in what laid beyond the British empire's borders, they were not persuaded by his argument that Arabia was more equivalent to a continent than to a country. They could also not understand why their political masters had such an interest in something that lay far outside India's confines. As far as the accountants were concerned, the government of India was only showing an interest because the British government was, an observation that was factually incorrect in many ways, not least the Foreign Office's longstanding aversion to the peninsula.[350]

Ill-feelings only got worse when they received another request to extend Lorimer's special duty until October. When further questions were asked about limiting the gazetteer's eventual cost by reducing its scope, omitting the historical context, outsourcing the index to a commercial enterprise and thereby negating the need to extend Lorimer's service, Dane was forced to interject. He argued strongly that the Foreign Department had been misled by the time it would take to prepare the gazetteer, having taken their original parameters from Curzon and the time he claimed it had taken him to write *Persia and The Persian Question*. Although a literary account and general history of the Gulf would have been relatively quick and easy to write, it was Dane's view that the subsequent end-product would have only been suitable for use by the general public or casual tourist. In contrast, he argued, what

Lorimer had compiled was an exhaustive publication of a region roughly fourteen-hundred miles from north-west to south-east and six-hundred miles in width, a huge tract of land that was of increasing political and commercial importance to the British and Indian governments and yet, so little about it was known.[351] Dane did not feel compelled to articulate what these political and commercial benefits might be. Strengthening political relationships meant little to the accountants and despite their wider prosperity remit, it is surprising that they did not question what these increasing gains were. Oil was not yet a major source of income and the coastal pearling industry only existed on coastlines that were already well-known. Nor were the interior's main commodities, camels and dates, likely to make huge profits if exported. Perhaps instead, Dane feared that the Germans might find something commercially profitable as part of their Berlin-Baghdad Railway concessions. Before deciding on a final course of action, the Finance Department was persuaded to invite Lorimer to an interview so he could explain in detail, his work and the issues that prevented the gazetteer's completion. Lorimer was equally persuasive, as the outcome of the informal audit was the agreement to seek the secretary of state for India's sanction for a final extension to the end of April 1908. But the Finance Department's request also came with a condition that any outstanding work on the index by the end of his final extension would have to be compiled without any further public expense.[352] In London, Morley concurred on the understanding that there would be no more extensions.[353]

Although most of Lorimer's peers and contemporaries had been able to meet his and Dane's deadlines responding to any new queries in a timely manner, the same could not be said of the legation in Tehran. In early June 1907, a year after being originally approached, the legation required some polite but stern reminding of their unresponsiveness so far.[354] Despite claiming the legation had faced an unusually busy twelve months analysing internal political changes following the constitutional revolution, their annotated drafts were finally received by diplomatic bag in late July. Their returns were accompanied by an apology from Sir Cecil Spring-Rice, minister of the legation, who hoped that their delayed response had not been an unnecessary inconvenience.[355] There was no denying that their tardiness had stalled progress, not helped by the fact that even when their return was posted, it took over six weeks for it to be couriered to Simla. But in true British manner, the legation was thanked for its comments rather than chastised.

In early April 1908, work on the gazetteer had finally taken its toll. Lorimer, now promoted to political officer 2nd class in recognition of time served, requested leave to take furlough, eighteen months in total, to begin from the first of May. As his application required the foreign secretary's approval, the question was asked if the gazetteer was nearing completion. There was little appetite to keep funding Lorimer's team, and given current work pressures, even less appetite to pass any outstanding work to the Foreign Department. He was also asked if his work on Aitchison's Treaties was in a similar state given the same pressures.[356] Downbeat, Lorimer replied that the gazetteer would not be finalised by the time he planned to take leave but as he had plans to initially remain in Simla, he would continue working on the draft until all that was left was the proof-reading. This, he would do on the voyage back to Scotland, with a view of completing it whilst he was there. He was confident that he could also relieve the Foreign Department from updating Aitchison's Treaties, which additionally remained a work in progress although he made clear that completing the gazetteer was his priority.[357] Even with these assurances, it was with much reluctance that his leave application was approved.

As Lorimer promised, for the next three months he continued working on the gazetteer in Simla despite being on leave. Progress stopped dramatically in late July however, when he was struck down with appendicitis and hospitalised in Walker Hospital, a small military hospital exclusively for western nationals. Bedridden as he waited for his operation, Lorimer wrote to the Foreign Department in good faith, if somewhat naively, with a request. He asked if there was any chance that the time he had spent on leave working on the drafts could be considered as special duty and be extended to October. The reply was sympathetic but given the robust commitment given to the secretary of state that there would be no further extensions, there was a reluctance to forward his request.[358] Although he understood the department's predicament, Lorimer wrote back, saying that this put him in a dilemma. Having given up six weeks of privilege leave in 1905 and now another three months to work on the gazetteer, he was hesitant to sacrifice any more of his time if there was little chance of it being given back. But he also did not want to leave the government with an unfinished and uncorrected draft when they had no other means of completing it in his absence. He accepted that his hospitalisation had only frustrated matters further but closed his reply by saying he would need to reconsider his circumstances and think things over after he had recuperated.[359]

Despite the Foreign Department's initial reluctance, an approach was made to the India Office to test whether they would be sympathetic to Lorimer's unique case.[360] The response was anything but. On the presumption that Lorimer had been consulted and had agreed with the last finish date, it was hard for the India Office to see how he could be exempted from being responsible for the continued delay.[361] With much regret, he was informed that his case would not be reconsidered.[362]

By October, Lorimer, Nesta and the children had arrived back in Scotland to her parents' house in Edinburgh. Having had time to reflect, Lorimer decided to continue to sacrifice both his health and furlough to try to finalise the gazetteer. But to do so, he needed the services of cargo ship SS *Manipur*, which left Calcutta bound for Great Britain on 12 December. On-board were eighteen bundles of papers, securely packaged in a case and insured for one thousand rupees. The consignment addressee was Sir Richmond Ritchie, the political secretary at the India Office, with Lorimer registered as the final recipient. Each bundle correlated to a chapter or appendix, which in addition to a hundred and seventy-seven official and mostly secret reports and papers, consisted of Saldanha's precis, various non-government papers and a smattering of books.[363] A month later, printed draft chapters were also on their way to Lorimer to be proof-read and finalised.[364] These included the latter part of the 'General History of the Persian Gulf region' and the introductory pages to 'Turkish Iraq', 'Arabistan' and 'Persian Makran'.[365]

Although volume one still required some more time, with much relief on Christmas Eve 1908, Lorimer completed his introduction to the *Gazetteer of the Persian Gulf, Oman, and Central Arabia. Volume II. Geographical and Statistical*, partly fulfilling his rather unique special duty, having compromised with the government of India to publish the work in two parts. His introduction was to the point, describing the gazetteer as a

> geographical dictionary, presenting, in a series of alphabetically arranged articles, a detailed account of the physical and political conditions of the Persian Gulf and its surrounding countries', much of which was entirely new, constructed by information that had been collected and compiled for this specific purpose.[366]

For ease, quantitative data was presented in tabular form and where helpful, sources and context were provided through foot and endnotes. In the absence of an index, bold cross references instead dominated the publication, signposting inquisitive minds elsewhere if they required additional information. Fifty-six photographs were also included. For historical background on the region, the reader was also redirected to (the still unfinished) volume one and its supporting appendices. There were caveats, not least on estimations of distance where they were reliant on native or local sources as Lorimer judged that they could not be relied upon. This was especially the case in the remote parts of Arabia where neither the gazetteering team nor political agents had managed to visit.

In early 1909, the Superintendent Printing Office in Calcutta received Lorimer's typed introduction, concluding the work on volume two. The priming of the print machines could now begin, running over nineteen hundred and fifty pages of text, tables and photographs that would allow the enquirer to consult in one place, 791 unique entries recording tribes, family names and places, beginning with Abadilah, 'a tribe of Trucial Oman who have 200 houses at Sharjah Town' to Zubarah, 'a ruined and deserted town on the west side of the Qatar Promontory.'[367]

Chapter 7

Hunter's Map

To illustrate the gazetteer's topographical contributions, Lorimer intended to include a series of complementary maps, hence the request to have a surveyor. In addition to a general small-scale map of central Arabia, his ambition was to include insets or separate maps of Trucial Oman, the area inland from Muscat to Wadi Samail, the Qatar Peninsula, Fars and Baluchistan, all of varying scales and detail.[368] Sher Jung's maps of Bushire, Kuwait, Arabistan, Bahrain and Mesopotamia as far as Baghdad would complete the supplement. The Military Department's Intelligence Branch supported his intent, and despite some initial concerns about classification, gave no objection to the maps ever becoming public documents when they learned that they would not include any meaningful information that could potentially benefit Britain's adversaries.[369] Longe, however, had other ideas, dispensing with the suggestion of a small supplementary atlas, asserting his authority as the Indian government's custodian of topography. He decided instead that there should be a single map tucked into a pocket at the back of the gazetteer and like the publication itself, be classified as secret. Despite its eventual official title, a *Map of Arabia and the Persian Gulf*, the resultant map was commonly known as 'Hunter's map', after its creator and final member of Lorimer's special duty team, Lieutenant Frederick Fraser Hunter.

Like so many who served in India, Hunter's family roots could be traced back to Scotland, although he was himself, a first generation Canadian, born in Durham, Ontario, making the team of gazetteers a commonwealth. Born in August 1876, he seemed destined for a career in the military, having served in the local militia since the age of nine, initially as an honorary boy bugler. When Hunter turned eighteen, he entered the Royal Military College in nearby Kingston, where on graduation, he was offered a commission in either the Imperial or Indian Staff Corps. Deciding on the latter and the greater chance of adventure and travel, in the summer of 1898, he sailed to Bombay to join the Shropshire Light Infantry as a second lieutenant while he waited for a vacancy in the Bengal Presidency Army. A year later, having served his time with a British regiment as part of his probationary obligations, he finally passed through the Bombay Staff Corps and found himself drafted to the Duke of Connaught's Own Bombay Lancers. Hunter enjoyed army life but was yearning for action. In July 1900, he requested a transfer to the 3rd Queen's Own Bombay Light Cavalry which had just received orders to sail to China to quash the Boxer Rebellion. The transfer was a disappointment as his new regiment saw little action in China, although whilst on campaign, his thirst for travel and knowledge increased. On his return to India two years later, he re-joined the Duke of Connaught's, serving with the regiment for another two years, becoming a squadron commander and then adjutant, before his continued frustration with the lack of campaigning forced him to reconsider his future.

Not wanting to leave India or Crown service, Hunter consulted his commanding officer, who tried to dissuade him from leaving the army. Unconvinced with either the argument or options presented to him, he applied to join the Trigonometrical Branch of the ICS's Civil Department of the Survey of India, based in Dehra Dun. It was a decision influenced by having previously participated in survey work when he was in Canada and later in China.[370] In August 1905, Hunter was despatched to Simla on probation as part of Number 18 Party, which was preparing to head into the 'Northern Circle', to continue surveying the numerous districts that made up Punjab and North-West Frontier Province.[371] Fieldwork, accompanied by a comprehensive course of technical training in Dehra Dun, was the route typically followed by new officers as part of their apprenticeship to become qualified topographers and surveyors. Before Hunter had even begun to get familiar with his surveying equipment, the opportunity to serve at the frontier was immediately taken away from him when he received new orders. Issued by Longe on behalf of the viceroy, Hunter's new appointment required him 'to compile a map of Arabia and the Persian Gulf – in conjunction with Captain Tandy and Mr Lorimer of the Foreign Department, [where] Captain Tandy will put you all right professionally and Lorimer will give you all the information. It is strictly confidential…'.[372]

As with the gazetteer, it was greatly underappreciated how much time would be needed to produce the map. Hunter was initially told that three months would be sufficient to complete the task. It was, Longe believed, simply a task of producing a compilation, drawing from existing maps, something that would not require any special qualifications. The nomination of a new joiner, rather than an experienced and more expensive officer, to carry out what appeared to be a routine piece of work, was in Longe's mind a more efficient use of available resource.[373]

Maurice Tandy was just the mentor that Hunter needed. He was a seasoned surveyor and knew parts of the region to be mapped well, having only recently returned from Aden. There, he had helped demarcate a two-hundred-mile border from the narrow strait, Bab Al Mandeb, to a point deep into the desert, at times working alone, at others, as part of a joint commission with Ottoman counterparts. Tandy also understood first-hand the challenges and dangers of surveying missions, having spent over two years in the field in Yemen during which time, he had been stabbed with a spear by an assailant who deeply resented his presence.[374] Even though danger was a constant companion in the field, Tandy also remembered the lighter moments. During a survey of Oman, Tandy claimed to Hunter that he had a daily occurrence with local tribesmen who would gather together like a shooting party and take turns sniping him. It was more a distraction than a realistic threat, even when some of them eventually managed to hit some of his equipment. When one day, their bravery brought them within shouting distance of him, he called out 'Look here, if I was a bad surveyor as you are marksmen, I ought to be killed. Now why don't you go home and learn how to shoot before you attempt to fire at a man you can't hit'.[375] He was not harassed again, although it is open to debate whether it was because they took his advice, they could no longer afford the economic cost of expending valuable ammunition to scare off a crazy Briton or they feared the risk of punitive military repercussions if they ever managed to improve their aim.

With very little experience in the art of map making itself, Hunter also relied heavily on Tandy for technical advice. Their efforts initially focused on producing a general map of the region, with a scale of between fifty to one hundred miles to an inch as Lorimer had instructed. This changed when in receipt of Longe's subsequent orders, they were told to use a thirty-two mile to an inch scale instead. It was a logical change as the new scale was widely used by the Survey Office at the time to map India. The adoption of a singular smaller-scale map frustrated Lorimer further. He had little choice but to transfer most of the new places collected by Sher Jung and the political agents to the gazetteer, converting their locations to text, which just added to his own workload.[376] The alternative, to ignore their contributions, was unthinkable. The revised draft was worked up using Bonne's Projection, an equal-area projection with the central meridian as a straight line and all other meridians curved accordingly. Later drafts would also use the modified Secant Conical, re-projecting the map on four sheets, rather than two. Once completed, the map could theoretically be aligned with those of India, offering officials at a glance if there was a big enough wall or table, an imperial overview from Egypt in the west to Burma in the east, a span of almost five thousand miles.[377] By Hunter's own admission, the pace of progress was initially very slow, partly because of his inexperience, partly because of the change in scale.[378] He was also soon to find that the map was the first of its kind, both in ambition and overall coverage, rather than just a compilation. In the beginning, the sheets were coloured by hand and accompanying text, block printed. A proportional compass, a device designed and used by Galileo in the sixteenth century, was used to enlarge and reduce the map although later re-scalings were done using a pantograph, a parallelogram-shaped mechanical device that could increase or reduce facsimiles with relative ease. All were carried out under Tandy's watchful eye.

Throughout the summer of 1905, Lorimer and Hunter worked out of the Foreign Department's Simla offices, continuing there during the winter months, on reflection a foolish decision despite the avoidance of distractions. As pleasant as Simla's summers were, its winters were known to be 'rough and often unpleasant', where 'dwellings [were] covered with cleaving roofs of snow [and] tall pines fretted … with icicles and frosted with snow drift'.[379] As a result, firewood was always at a premium as the few remaining residents, Lorimer and Nesta among them, were obliged to pay extortionate prices for fuel as they attempted to keep their lodgings and offices warm. The days were dark, long and cold, with both men and their draughtsman, Munshi Karim Bakhsh, working from ten to fourteen hours daily, including on Sundays and public holidays, wearing whatever winter clothing they could muster to keep a semblance of warmth. None of it was conducive to Lorimer's health given his vulnerability to recurring bouts of fever. Easy tasks became cumbersome as did the ability to outline and shade features accurately. Every amendment or addition was a physical challenge, not helped by having to wear mittens and working with inks that regularly froze.[380] As the weather took a turn for the better, so the map started to take shape. In January 1906, Hunter updated his seniors, informing them that 'a great deal of fresh detail of the Arabian Coast in the Persian Gulf from Kuwait to Sazwa Bay … [and] inland … has recently been received which shows great alterations and additions to existing maps…'.[381] By Spring, sufficient progress had been made to print the first fair copies for review, naively in the hope that they would be finalised soon.

Hunter and Tandy might have been happy with their end-product, but the map was far from ready to be sent to the printers. The Tehran legation's late returns bore some responsibility for its delayed production. Lorimer's own forensic approach also did not help, but it was the Transliteration Committee that was mostly at fault for holding the press on the production of both the gazetteer and the map. The committee, an informal body comprised of Lorimer, Doctor Edward Ross, an accomplished linguist from the government of India's Records Department and Captain Charles Gibbon, from the Intelligence Branch, was established when 'Hunter's Guide to the Orthography of Indian Proper Names', a publication used by the Indian government since 1872 to Romanise Indic languages, was found wanting.[382] A new system, one overseen by the Military Department, was to be adopted instead, with both Hunter's map and Lorimer's gazetteer to serve as test-cases for the new approach. As frustrating as it was to redraft every plot, the delay gave Hunter the opportunity to return to Dehra Dun, a one-hundred-and-thirty-mile journey, that he recalled even in May, was rough going over weathered hills following atrocious paths.[383] His successful navigation of the precarious route also allowed him to be nearer to his topographical peers as he revisited his workings. Having suffered financially as well as physically in Simla, Hunter was grateful for the relocation as the cost of living in Dehra Dun was considerably cheaper than in the mountain retreat, although the lack of any allowances whilst his surveying contemporaries in the field were profiting from theirs, was a bone of contention.[384] Lorimer stayed in Simla with Nesta and daughters, managing his time between the family, the gazetteer, the map and any other request that the Foreign Department deemed fit to send his way. Hunter's transfer made exchanges of correspondence with Simla a prolonged affair, an arrangement that Lorimer considered awkward for having to rely on the post office to deliver papers and scribblings.[385] A slow postal service was hardly a concern when Hunter found that there was little urgency to finalise the map while the gazetteer remained subject to its own considerable corrections and amendments.

Hunter had not long settled in Dehra Dun when he received instructions from Longe that deviated from the immediate task in hand. The map was now to include Southern Arabia, with a particular focus on Aden and Hadhramaut. Hunter complied, believing that Lorimer had already been approached and was content with the new parameters. When he found out about the map's likely expansion in areas not covered by the gazetteer, Lorimer wrote in strong terms to Hunter. An explanation was needed for the unexpected deviation as Lorimer had no desire to see either the map or the gazetteer expanded to include the far south.[386] It was not that he intended to thwart Hunter's work he explained, quite the opposite but first and foremost, Lorimer had 'to look after [his] own interests as [he understood] them…'.[387] Hunter was opaque in his response, possibly because he did not know why Longe had demanded the map's expansion, but he assured Lorimer that his 'first and chief duty [was] to produce it as a gazetteer map and in the exact form that [he] would wish it. The additional part [would] not be shown in the gazetteer map … but [was] utilising the opportunity [of] the re-drawing of fair sheets'.[388]

Several weeks later, Hunter received another directive, asking him to share the northern section of his draft map with Longe. That particular sheet was needed to enhance the government's latest edition of their map of Turkestan, Central Asia. The request followed renewed interest from Longe in Hunter's work since it had been rescaled.[389] This time, Longe sought both Lorimer and Tandy's views on the request before it was submitted. While neither objected, Tandy questioned whether classification might be an issue, a view shared by Lorimer who also queried whether new information and detail obtained on Khor Musa and surrounding area would need to be suppressed.[390] Before Hunter could act on the latest directive, in June, the Intelligence Branch stepped in. There was to be no potential enhancement of the Turkestan map covering 30–31 degree Latitude to 48–49 degree Longitude. If any official needed to know more about the geography within that zone, the Intelligence Branch would direct them to Hunter's map once it had been finalised.[391] It was a welcome sign of the military's confidence in Hunter's work.

And yet despite the increasing interest in the map and potential utility far beyond the Gulf itself, both the map and gazetteer seemed to be at a standstill. One of the reasons for the delay was the Transliteration Committee's continuing struggle to agree on a common approach for transliterating places, features, tribal and family names. It was not helped by the fact that they were having to contend with some that were only known in Persian or Baluchi or where native spellings were of such an uncertain derivation that they led themselves open to conjecture and argument. By June 1906, some progress was made when Lorimer and Ross came to an agreement on the way ahead, but Gibbon remained unpersuaded. By July, there was more headway when the intelligence officer finally agreed to Lorimer and Ross's suggestions albeit with some minor, almost petty, compromises. These included the use of Q rather than K, making Katar – Qatar and the use of a final H to denote the *ta marbuta* in Arabic, even if it was silent, as in Basrah. Gibbon also continued to argue for the redundancy of a vowel either before or after an apostrophe, but Lorimer held firm as the more experienced and qualified linguist to prevent any further deviation and delay.[392] At some point in 1907, the new system was finally agreed and adopted, requiring all names to be transliterated appropriately. The only exceptions were transliterations already in use by the Egyptian Survey Department.[393]

Despite the system being agreed by a government of India committee, Lorimer rather than Gibbon or Ross, found himself on the receiving end of critical correspondence from the Gulf political agents. All complained about the revised spelling of places, insisting that their versions were correct. Lorimer may have been sympathetic to the politicals, but this was the government's new doctrine. Two years later, Gibbon, who had been most obstructive within the committee, experienced first-hand the challenges of transliteration when he led a surveying party in Persia. He now understood the difficulty and challenges in trying to correctly spell place names. His recommendation for future topographical missions drew as much from Lorimer's experience in the field with Gabriel and Sher Jung as his own, advising that local government officials should be the first to be approached to confirm a place name which should then be accepted as fact. If that was not possible, given the problems when using a phonetic system, names should, instead, be spelt in Persian or Arabic and then tested against the new transliteration system – although hopefully without the need for them to be agreed by committee.[394]

Outside of committee, Lorimer read extensively, working his way through piles of reports, publications, maps and maritime charts that had been archived in the government's various libraries and registries. His ability to work through Bombay presidency's early hand-written records was particularly challenging. To help him, copyists and section writers were employed to decipher the inked scribbles with papers dating back to the seventeenth century, these proving the most difficult for the clerks to understand.[395] The more that Lorimer read, registered and referenced for the gazetteer, the more that Hunter's map also increased in detail until it eventually became worthy of its official geographical title.[396]

Including the various precis produced by Saldanha and Gabriel, Lorimer referenced six hundred and fifty-five publications and monographs.[397] With some information spread over multiple volumes, the true number of works digested was in excess of seven hundred and seventy although many more must have been read and dismissed. Just eleven publications originally written by non-Europeans were directly quoted as sources. Moroccan travellers, Mohammed Al Idrisi and Ibn Battuta of the twelfth and fourteenth centuries respectively, Turks Mohammed Abu Qasim ibn Haukel, a geographer from the tenth century and countryman, eighteenth-century physician, Cassim Izzedine as well as Persian – or possibly Arab – geographer, Abu Ishaq Ibrahim Al Istakhri, born in the middle of the tenth century, all added to the gazetteer. The Iraqi historian, Al Musadi, born in the late 890s CE and Jivanji Jamshedji Modi, a Zoroastrian priest born in Bombay nearly a thousand years later also contributed. Other Persian geographers, administrators and writers whose work were also reflected in the gazetteer in one form or other included Nasir Khosrau, Abdur Razzak and Mirza Mehdy Khan, offering vignettes in turn from the eleventh, fifteenth and eighteenth centuries. The last of the non-oriental sources quoted was that of Abu Mohammed Al Hasan Al Hamdani, born in Yemen around 893 CE and his monograph, *Sifat Jazirat Al Arab* or 'Geography of the Arabian Peninsula'. Such was the credibility and robustness of Al Hamdani's work that whilst in Baghdad during his special duty, Lorimer saw an Egyptian scholar exploring the city carrying a volume of Al Hamdani's work which, he observed, was consulted as eagerly as a tourist would thumb through a travel guide.[398]

The work of Charles Huber, a French explorer who toured Syria and the Hejaz in 1879 and again in 1893, was of particular interest to Lorimer and Hunter.[399] After recompiling his astronomical observations and correcting his barometric readings by comparing them with the Survey of India's tidal stations in Bombay, Bushire and Aden, Hunter was able to use the revised data and elevations to help make the map's height contours extremely accurate.[400] Such corrections also justified checking the work of other Europeans for their accuracy. The German explorer and cartographer Karsten Niebuhr's sextant readings from his time travelling through south-west Arabia were found to be accurate within a hundred yards despite being taken over two hundred years earlier. Palgrave's credibility, however, continued to be challenged when Hunter considered that his 'records did not appear to … be any more truthful than their reputation'.[401] Another British explorer who failed to impress was Richard Burton, whose illicit pilgrimage to Mecca and Medina in 1853 resulted in him writing a popular personal narrative of his travels and his subsequent rise to fame within orientalist circles. His 'sensational popularity as an Arabian explorer', Hunter mused, '[was] out of all proportion to his actual contribution to geographical knowledge'.[402] There were less doubts about British orientalist Charles Doughty's records though, with the only concerns about his work limited to his height measurements which were judged to be out by approximately five hundred feet.[403] The work of George Bury, a former British soldier cum explorer and naturalist, who worked briefly as a locally employed extra assistant resident in Aden from April 1903 to

August 1904, was also recognised. Bury had a tarnished reputation, having later fallen out of favour with the Foreign Department, but his notes on Hadhramaut were found to be extremely valuable to Hunter.[404] This was despite Tandy's private opinion, doubting the reliability of Bury's information given the various rumours.[405]

The writings of female British travellers, Ladies Isabella Bishop, Anne Blunt, Ella Durand and Mary Sheil Hunter, as well as Ella Sykes (sister of Sir Percy) were also consulted and used. Czechoslovakian, Mathilde Helfer, whose travelogue of her time in Syria and Mesopotamia had been translated into English by Jane Sturge (a prominent translator who wrote under her father's name George Sturge) and Jane Dieulafoy, a renowned adventurer, archaeologist and writer from France, were additional sources of reference. As a religious man, Hunter was confident that Lorimer had also consulted the Bible even if it had not been directly referenced in the gazetteer. The Qur'an was also absent, possibly because such books of faith did not need explicit acknowledgement, as was any of Ptolemy's work, despite being revered by the RGS.

Of more use to Hunter were the maps that sometimes accompanied the publications. He was also reliant on the various maps and sketches that Lorimer managed to extract from official reports produced by the political agent network or military officers travelling 'innocently' incognito on behalf of the Survey Office, War Office or Military Department. Despite their provenance, they too, needed to be treated with caution given doubts about their accuracy, as some of the techniques used by these amateur topographers were dubious. Hunter had considerable doubts about a sketch map produced by Prideaux, which had been compiled solely after interviewing an Arab traveller as he recuperated in hospital having just recently journeyed from Najran through Wadi Dawasir-Aflaj to Bahrain.[406] Arguably, Hunter too was at fault for using questionable sources, at one stage asking if detained Turkish deserters in Yemen could be squeezed for information, but eventually, the Canadian was able to plot and record, nearly two thousand place names, from Abadan to Zughail.[407]

In May 1907, Hunter's time working exclusively on the map came to an end, seventeen months longer than had originally been expected. His next mission was to lead Number 19 Party, working for the Madras presidency surveying the Malabar Hills in Western India, at last experiencing time in the field to fulfil his apprenticeship and to finally start to receive much-needed field allowances. Although now on a different mission, he continued to work on the draft, populating the four sheets with more locations and features as new maps, sketches and geographical information became available. Once he was content with their reliability, new details were forwarded to Munshi Bakhsh Khan to plot the new locations on the map traces. After their names were checked and endorsed using the transliteration system, the particulars were then passed on to the *munshi's* colleague, Tufail Ahmad Khan to update the typesetting. In 1908, the map was as informed as it could be. With the gazetteer expected to be printed in final form soon despite Lorimer's constant struggle to find the time, sanction was given to forward copies of the map sheets to the drawing office in Simla for sign off and publication.

By June 1909, the map was finally ready to be despatched to the political residency in Bushire and its satellite agencies. It would be circulated alone, without its parent publication, as volume II of the gazetteer, despite being in final form, had still not been printed. Shakespear, a good acquaintance of Hunter's, now the political agent in Kuwait, confirmed receipt of a copy of his friend's map just a month after it had been released. In accordance with the King's Regulations, its classification demanded that it should be kept in his personal custody at all times when not secured under lock and key. A few months later, he received a slightly larger scale map, this time of Persia which included a reference to Hunter's work as a major source of information. Despite their immediate incompatibility because of differences in scale, both were of value to him as intellectual tools given Kuwait's location, precariously positioned in the overlapping peripheries of Persia and Arabia as well as those of the Ottoman and British empires. Hunter's work could also help him plan his various expeditions into Najd from Kuwait, which in turn would allow him to provide updates for later versions of the map.

Shakespear dutifully complied with the handling regulations but was surprised when a year later, a letter from Lieutenant-General Douglas Haig, Chief of the General Staff's office made its way to Kuwait demanding the political agent's immediate attention and action.

Within the letter contained a new handling directive, demanding that Shakespear should 'entirely obliterate' the reference to Hunter's map in its Persian counterpart given the former's secret classification.[408] As ordered, the reference to his friend's work was dutifully struck through. Although the map would remain secret, the same could not be said of its general index, a small unclassified reference book that was subsequently produced to be used in conjunction with later versions of the map.[409] Listing every place name identified by the gazetteering, including its location, description and Arabic spelling, but instead started at Aamad Tabar, Jabal (Hill, B3) in Syria and finished at Zureki (Tribal district, H12) in Yemen, further proof of mission-creep, far beyond the map's original scope.[410]

Lorimer considered the map's detail of Najd to be the best of its kind given the sparsity of information on the area.[411] He also sang its creator's praises, claiming never to have met anyone so dedicated to his work, noting in particular, Hunter's energy and industry to make the map 'as nearly perfect as possible'.[412] The government of India too, was initially happy with Hunter's product with Longe acknowledging that the map would be a 'very valuable addition to geographical knowledge … [and was] the best map of Arabia that ha[d] been produced'.[413] Hunter had little time to bask in such approval when Longe's high-praise quickly petered out after the War Office took exception. In a strongly worded letter to the surveyor-general, Longe was told that the map was found wanting and only good 'to turn face to the wall'.[414] No explanation was given for the disapproving observation, although perhaps the use of intuition and heavy reliance on secondary or native sources rather than any doubts about the map's overall accuracy in the absence of any other in circulation at that time, might have been factors. Not wishing to have either his, or his department's reputations smeared, and with Longe's relationship with Lorimer not the strongest, he decided against defending Hunter's work or even to seek a justification for the damning comment. In an act of subservience and self-interest, the surveyor-general decided that his department would not accept responsibility for the map. It was an unusual decision to make given the substantial cost, human resource and expertise that had been invested both by the Foreign Department and the Survey Office. Had Curzon still been in place and explicitly endorsed the map as he had the gazetteer, Hunter's work might not have been criticised by outsiders although the former viceroy would have undoubtedly made his own views known had he considered its quality and accuracy, wanting. But so it was that to anyone who enquired, the map was to be referred to as 'Hunter's map' and no longer a product of the Survey Office despite it authorising its continued production, controlling wider access and maintaining its upkeep for years after Hunter had extracted himself.[415]

Despite its classification and the strict handling instructions imposed on recipients, it came as a surprise when in May 1910, the American Geographical Society announced the imminent publication of a map of Arabia. The bulletin carried a surprising level of detail including acknowledging Hunter as the map's compiler and its development the result of information drawn from all available resources. Although the society could not have seen either the draft traces or the final sheets, it was confident enough to state that the map would finally define the Tuwaiq Escarpment and the Wadi Dawasir system in central Najd, assign a firm fix to the Jabrin Oasis in the Dahna sand belt and reconcile conflicting information currently held on Hadhramaut. Such level of detail could have only come from one source, Hunter, who was a known entity to the society. Hunter visited the society in New York in 1908 whilst on furlough when he was seeking sponsorship for a trans-Arabian expedition that he wanted to lead, travelling across the peninsula from Medina to Abu Dhabi and then on to Mukalla via the Empty Quarter by car.[416] Although the expedition was to be a private rather than an official journey of mental, physical and mechanical endurance, he was eventually refused permission by the Foreign Office who once again put its relationship with the Ottoman government above any topographical benefits that would have undoubtedly been captured during the ordeal. Whatever his motivations had he been the society's source of information, the map stayed classified and remained associated with him in a negative rather than positive sense within the War Office for many years. He was perhaps fortunate that no investigatory measures were ever explored following the society's announcement.

For all of the map's advancements, the main lesson the society observed, was that the work brought home 'what an immense stretch of the unknown still lies in Arabia'.[417] With the Empty Quarter still largely a blank space, the lack of detail beyond any of the immediate coastline and a large void where the eastern edge of Najd met the western periphery of Hejaz, it was a valid observation to make and arguably why Curzon had been persistent about the need to produce a gazetteer. Despite its shortfalls, the map was still a major advance from those that preceded it, most of which had been compiled from simple and sometimes inaccurate compass traverses.

In 1919, a decade after the map had been in circulation and despite the substantial technological advancement of land and air transportation over that time, and improved telecommunications which allowed the faster and greater passing of new information, Hunter observed that 'we still know little more about parts of South Arabia than we do of the moon'.[418] He was certainly right that much of the interior remained unknown or explored by westerners. Three years later, on behalf of the RGS and in partnership with the War Office, renowned British explorer Douglas Carruthers was commissioned to produce another map of Arabia. It was unclear why he rather than Hunter was given the responsibility although Carruthers's war-time employment in the War Office, compiling and producing maps of the Middle East was likely to have been a factor. He might also have been one of Hunter's anonymous critics. The new map included marking the various routes taken by Blunt, Bell, Shakespear, Knox and other prominent explorers as well as new features and places that had been identified and, in some cases, even visited. Its use of a larger scale, despite its incompatibility with many of the Survey Office's catalogue of maps also provided a better topographical appreciation of the region, a task made far easier by drawing from Hunter and Lorimer's original work rather than producing something from scratch.[419] And unlike Hunter's map, Carruthers's work carried no classification once it was released.

Notwithstanding the extensive effort invested to agree on the transliteration, Hunter's map found itself at fault as early editions used 'Katar' in the accompanying key rather than 'Qatar' as it was marked on the map. The variation in spellings would also continue to plague the government of India long after Lorimer and Hunter's work had been finalised and circulated to departments, political agencies and embassies. In an attempt to finally break this habit, in August 1910, Cox wrote to Major Arthur Trevor, political agent in Muscat, setting out his desire to 'remedy the evil' of the continued practice of using alternative name spellings.[420] Although it was Cox's desire to correct such human behaviours, it was a wish that was ultimately formed in response to direct orders from the Foreign Department. For the amount of time, money and human resource invested in producing the gazetteer and new system of transliteration, the government had a firm expectation that the agreed spelling of names should be used rather than ignored. From thereon in, Cox expected all political agents to take their guidance from Hunter's map and volume II of the gazetteer, both of which by then, were in their possession. When in March 1913, Trevor's successor in Muscat, Knox (formerly of Kuwait), continued the practice of irking the political resident and the Foreign Department by using local vernacular rather than official transliterations, a letter was despatched again from Bushire giving the political agent a swift reminder of the orthography expected to be used in all official correspondence and reports. A short, hand-written addition at the end of the letter, 'please speak', so often used by teachers to reprimand an unruly pupil, made clear that Cox planned to emphasise his point orally to ensure that it was understood.[421] It is understandable why Muscat in particular seemed to be the most culpable for its continued deviation in language. Twenty-four years earlier, IMS Surgeon-Major Atmaram Jayakar, Muscat's political agency doctor and at times, a temporary political agent there, had written a respected book on Omani dialect, not too dissimilar to Lorimer's own work on local Pashtu. It had also been one of the many hundreds of books used to inform the gazetteer. Despite its local authority and provenance, there was no real defence for not using the names agreed by the Transliteration Committee even if the explanation of the new system adopted, as set out in the *Gazetteer of the Persian Gulf, Volume I, Historical. Part II Appendix S* had still not been published. Ambassadors, agents and residents alike would all need to wait for another two years before it too, finally made its way to print to understand why a place name was to be spelt as demanded by the Foreign Department rather than what it was known as locally.

Chapter 8

Double-Hatted in Baghdad

In the summer of 1909, it was time again for Lorimer to leave his homeland and return to the Foreign Department. With Cox still firmly embedded in the political residency in Bushire and the viceroy, Minto, yet to signal any intention of moving him on, the only regional posting for someone of comparable grade, seniority and experience as a political agent second class was Baghdad. As His Britannic Majesty's Consul General and Political Resident of Turkish Arabia, it was an equally prestigious role but one that worked to multiple masters: to the Foreign Office through Sir Gerald Lowther, the British ambassador in Constantinople, and, to the India Office and Minto, both directly and via the Foreign Department or Cox. Although reporting to both London and Calcutta (and from December 1911, the new capital in Delhi) would increase his visibility and profile, Lorimer was at times, little more than an extended reference or source in Lowther's formal reporting to Whitehall. He did, however, remain a respected voice with a valued opinion on the Gulf when reporting to India, even though the humdrum of daily life in the residency would become a constant distraction from finishing volume one of the gazetteer.

To Gertrude Bell, Baghdad was the 'biggest and most important Consulate General in Asia', straddling multiple spheres of influence whilst to the Turks, the city was a hive of British intrigue.[422] To downplay its importance and legitimacy, they refused to acknowledge it as a British political residency. It was, instead, recognised as just another consulate, a minor satellite of the British embassy in Constantinople. The British in turn, refused to acknowledge the various Ottoman outposts scattered around the Gulf littoral, including those in and around, Shatt Al Arab, hence why *Lawrence* and *Sphinx* had lowered their standards when transiting the waters several years earlier during Curzon's grand tour. Unfazed by Ottoman remonstrations and churlish attitudes, Lorimer received his movement orders and on 5 November, took over the residency as consul general and political resident, succeeding Lieutenant-Colonel John Ramsay, who had been in post for the last three years. As they made their way up the Karun River, Lorimer and Nesta's transit included staying overnight with Arnold Wilson, the acting consul in Muhammerah and a good friend of Lock. Despite it being the first time that they had met, it was Wilson considered, a most enjoyable visit by 'a very fine man, as much a soldier as a civilian, with a most pleasant wife'.[423] Lorimer's reputation preceded him.

Seated on the banks of the Tigris River, the residency was a grand building, complete with two squat square watch towers and a columned terrace overlooking the river with steps that led down to the water's edge. It was by far, the most comfortable household that Lorimer and Nesta had lived in. Protecting the buildings and garden was a high-walled perimeter, patrolled by a troop of sepoys from India, who ensured that the occupants came to no harm or interference. Moored nearby was the residency launch, the Bombay-built RIMS *Comet*, a one-hundred-and-eighty-two-tonne gleaming-white paddle-steamer that allowed the resident to navigate upriver to Samarrah if *Comet*'s draught allowed and its paddles could outpace the racing tide or with the current, down the winding waterway and marshlands through Kut and Amarah to Muhammerah. With a forty-strong crew and armed with two .45-inch five-barrel quick-firing Nordenfelt guns, Lorimer had a formidable albeit slow gunboat at his disposal, something that riled the local Ottoman authorities.[424] As grand as the residence and its water transport were, only Nesta accompanied Lorimer in Baghdad.[425] As was typical at the time for British families living overseas, both Jean Mary and Isabella stayed in Britain to complete their schooling, staying in Edinburgh with Nesta's parents.

Lorimer was soon to learn how busy the residency was as the gateway to Arabia and Persia. It was both customary and a courtesy for British officials, 'non-official' travellers and explorers alike to pass through Baghdad, either before setting off on their excursions or to seek some immediate comfort, sanity and sanctuary (and hopefully a whisky or two) at the mid or end point of their travels. Such visits allowed Lorimer to help prepare his guests for what might lie ahead, or to tease out of them, information that might then be reported to his various seniors or to others in the wider political network. Lorimer's sister-in-law and wife of Lock, Emily, best summed up the need to entertain at post despite the costs and intrusions. She observed that 'the most important work is done, not in the office but in the drawing-room; you affect universal amiability and waste most of your days and a large part of your nights at social functions of every sort, and in the end if you are lucky, you will trap some worthy minister when he has had too much champagne, or you will worm some state secret out of an indiscreet wife'.[426] With volume one of the gazetteer still a work in progress, held back because of the daily pressures of work, these loose snippets only added to its delay as Lorimer attempted, arguably in vain, to make it as current as possible before it finally went to print. At such a fluid and fast-moving time in Arabia, it was not only proving a challenge to keep up with events, it was also getting harder to keep the demands of the Finance and Foreign Departments at bay, as he struggled to complete the gazetteer.

Lorimer had been in Baghdad for less than a month when his first guest, Lieutenant Gerald Leachman of the Royal Sussex Regiment, arrived unexpectedly, seeking accommodation. Leachman was part of a wider War Office ruse to circumvent the Foreign Office's longstanding ban on official travel into the Arabian interior, by encouraging military officers about to take leave, or in some cases, giving them exceptional leave, to 'innocently' tour areas that they would normally be banned from passing through if they were on a government-sanctioned mission. Their deception, sometimes endorsed or financially supported by private entities such as the RGS or the Palestine Exploration Fund, a private fund under royal patronage set up to promote archaeological, cultural and topographical research in the region, added an additional semblance of innocent cover should the Foreign Office ever make enquiries about what were clearly, military movements.[427]

Once the officer had completed their non-official travel, they were expected to report their observations and findings to the War Office's Directorate of Military Operations' Intelligence Division and to Naval Intelligence. They, in turn, would from time to time, share their fresh information with their equivalents in the government of India's Intelligence Branch, with whom they had sympathy given the Foreign

Office's stubbornness and lack of ambition. Lorimer was generally supportive of the War Office's ploy but the regular flow of unofficial military travellers passing through his patch risked the attention of the Ottoman authorities who watched his own movements closely, potentially compromising the traveller's chance of success, even if they were travelling in disguise.[428] He was also typically given little warning from Constantinople of their imminent arrival on his doorstep from Basrah or elsewhere. This was likely to have been a deliberate move, not that either Lorimer or Lowther ever prevented or discouraged any non-official visitor from their planned wanderings. As a result, both Lorimer and Nesta found themselves constantly hosting, entertaining and even accommodating almost every passing British waif and stray despite not having an allowance to cover the subsequent costs. Nor was the residence an obligatory rendezvous solely for imperial travellers, as Raunkiaer also called on Lorimer before he started his trek to Riyadh.[429]

Leachman stayed with Lorimer for two weeks, lapping up the generous hospitality provided by the political resident and his wife before he headed off to Karbala, where with the help of Muhammed Hassan, the British local agent there, he was introduced to some contacts who might be willing to take him into the interior. After passing through Babylon, Leachman returned to the residence to spend Christmas with the Lorimers, enjoying the festivities with them and the small western expatriate and, diplomatic community. Between the distraction of endless evenings of social events, he only just managed to make plans for his excursion. Once the New Year celebrations were over, Lorimer watched on as Leachman dressed himself as an Arab, complete with scrawny beard and thin cane akin to a more familiar swagger-stick that he would have carried when wearing the King's uniform. Once fully garbed, he slipped away and headed off with a guide to join a caravan destined for Ha'il, along the way, travelling through territory that had previously been visited by Lady Anne Blunt.

Lorimer thought little more of his recent guest until late March, when he received a letter from 'a very fit and very dirty' Leachman dated 22 February 1910, written from ruling emir, Ibn Rashid's camp.[430] Written in haste, it offered Lorimer a short account of his travels into the interior. The note also gave his observations after having been caught up, not in one but two, major skirmishes between Ibn Rashid and Ibn Sa'ud's armies. Such colour of life in the interior supplied valuable context. Lorimer quickly passed on the traveller's account to both Cox and the Foreign Department in Calcutta, side-copying the report to Shakespear in Kuwait given his own recent explorations and travels into the interior. Unbeknown to Lorimer, in late February, Shakespear too, had been in northern Najd and was at one point less than two days ride from Leachman but had avoided at least one of the raids, or *ghazzu*s, that Leachman had been caught up in, and a spectator of. As Lorimer's friendship with Shakespear grew, so did the exchange of informal and demi-official accounts and reports between Baghdad and Kuwait to keep themselves, the draft gazetteer and a few other select political agents, up to date on latest developments, rumours and local conspiracies not worthy of formal reports.

On 18 April, Lorimer too, was on his travels. Accompanied by a familiar if now portly figure, Gaskin, who had found employment at the residency as the commercial attaché, Lorimer headed north to tour the extremities of the Ottoman empire in Kurdistan. A caravan of ponies and mules, the standard military mode of transport rather than camels in that part of the region, were mustered and packed to support their journey. His main aim was to try to find a suitable location for a hill station within easy reach of Baghdad although it also had an ulterior purpose, to provide political, military and topographical information of interest to the Foreign Department.[431] With most of the places he planned to visit beyond the reach of the gazetteer, his subsequent report would add little to the wealth of knowledge already captured and cross-referenced, but with Hunter's map also never far from mind, Lorimer hoped that his subsequent reporting could also be used to confirm locations that thus far, had only been approximately fixed and to correct any other topographical mistakes.[432]

His full report read like a military route card rather than a political despatch, with rendezvous and stations broken down by miles and timed to the minute. Each leg was also supplemented by clear descriptions of the immediate surroundings, obstructions (particularly those that might hinder infantry or artillery movement), population size and religion, watch towers, telegraph lines and food stocks. Lorimer was also able to gauge the reach and political influence of the Young Turks and their Committee of Union and Progress (CUP) who now controlled the politicking in Constantinople. The local governor or *mudir* of Tuz Khumatu was subject to particular attention by the travellers. He was, Lorimer considered, a typical Young Turk, arrogant and threatening, and of the opinion that although the pen was mightier than the sword, the stick was greater still. As if to demonstrate his power and status, when walking with the resident through the local bazaar with stick in hand, everyone was quick to *salaam* him out of fear of potential, and immediate, reprisal or humiliation.[433]

On the afternoon of 23 April, Lorimer and Gaskin entered Kirkuk where they enforced a day's halt to explore the town and its surroundings. On returning to the road, next they passed through Alton Kopru, Erbil and Shaqlawah, and a week later, found themselves in Rowanduz. There, they made camp for three nights to rest, recuperate and research their surroundings, not least as the town was bolstered by a large military base, garrisoning nominally at least, Lorimer found, three battalions that were in a state of readiness to be deployed to Persia. On 6 May, Lorimer reached Aqrah, the furthest point north of his journey and presently home to an Anatolian battalion. Having split from Gaskin the previous day, who had started to head south-east with the caravan, Lorimer arrived on horseback accompanied by Nasir, the local interpreter cum guide or *dragoman* from the British vice consulate in Mosul who met him along the route. As light faded the following evening, Lorimer and Nasir entered Mosul. Not far behind was Gaskin and the caravan. For the next ten days, the party remained in Mosul at the vice consulate although Lorimer wrote little about his surroundings, considering the area already too well known to be worth repeating. Making quick work of the return journey, Lorimer, Gaskin and the depleted caravan took just five days to get back in Baghdad, arriving on 22 May by the easiest means of travel available, on a raft or *kilik*. Their return leg would later be included in the Military Department's publication 'Routes in Arabia', recorded as Route 202.[434]

Having experienced the tribes in the North-West Frontier and heard numerous stories in the streets of Baghdad, Lorimer had expected the Kurds to be equally ferocious. He found them instead, to be more intelligent than 'the brutish Arabs in Mesopotamia' and certainly less effeminate.[435] But he equally found them to be less vivacious than the Pathan tribes and less obsequious than the Punjabis. It was just the type of observation that an orientalist could be expected to make and was a reminder that even Lorimer was not without prejudice. Despite the level of detail in his report, Lorimer failed to note the total number of miles travelled, or time spent on horse-back or raft, but a liberal estimation would suggest one hundred and seventy hours on the move to complete a five-hundred-mile round trip.[436]

Late in the afternoon on 12 March 1911, a notable bedraggled British traveller darkened the steps of Lorimer's river-facing columned terrace. Early that January, Gertrude Bell set off from Victoria Station in central London, bound for her Middle East start point, Damascus. Her final destination was Aleppo, a direct route that would have taken less than a week of hard riding. Bell however, planned to follow an extremely circuitous route via Baghdad. Now a few months in, she was theoretically at her mid-point. Having been in the saddle since before dawn that morning, and with just a snatched lunch-break, she entered the city seeking respite, riding against the flow of men, women, pilgrims and donkeys who jostled along the roads.[437] Unable to cross the Tigris River as the nearby bridge was under repair, Bell hired a boat to take her to the other side, informing the boatman to drop her off at the British residence's waterside steps.

As surprised as Lorimer and Nesta were to see a stranger appear on their terrace, she was at once welcomed inside where she was received by a host of equally surprised stares from other guests who were being entertained at the Lorimers' expense, among them Sir William Willcocks, a British irrigation engineer. After a 'large and very welcome tea',[438] Willcocks offered to take the explorer off Lorimer's hands, and to escort her to a nearby hotel as there was no spare accommodation at the residence. It took little to persuade her to take full advantage of the invitation to stay at the residence two days later when the other guests had gone. For the rest of the week, Bell travelled freely around Baghdad from her temporary base, meeting many officials and representatives who typically kept company with Lorimer, including the *wali* of Baghdad, Nizam Pasha. Lorimer was struck by Bell's energy, sharing with her, his observation that he had 'never met anyone who is in the confidence of the natives in the way [she was]'.[439] This, she immediately and gushingly recorded in a letter to her father, Sir Hugh Bell, adding 'and Mr Lorimer, I should wish you to understand, is an exceptionally able man!' as if to endorse the endorser.[440] Bell was as equally impressed with Lorimer, both in terms of knowledge and the extreme levels of kindness and hospitality that he and Nesta had shown her throughout her stay, a point she made repeatedly in her personal letters and diary.[441] Early on 19 March, after a week of local exploration, pleasure and quasi-diplomacy, Bell, accompanied by Lorimer walked down to the local bazaar where her horse had been stabled, to continue her journey. Although Aleppo remained her final destination, her immediate intent was to head north-east to the Kurdish town of Khanaqin and 'then to slip over into Persia for a day or two [to] see the ruins of Kasr i Shirin [and] then on to Kirkuk and Sharqat'.[442] Together they rode for a couple of hours and then on behalf of Nesta and himself, he bid her safe travels and returned to the luxury of the residence.

Exactly one month later, Lorimer and Nesta also set off for Aleppo, with Constantinople their final destination so the British government's consul-general and Indian government's political resident could finally meet his ambassador in person.[443] Unlike Lorimer's tour of Kurdistan, there was to be no official or day-by-day account of their travels but in a letter to his father, he shared an entertaining tale of endurance and hardship of his and Nesta's journey. Along with two carriages and a baggage cart, their drivers, a camp-hand, two guides and a riding horse for Lorimer, the small caravan immediately settled into a routine when it left Baghdad. This entailed getting up any time between half past two and four o'clock each morning, and after a rushed breakfast and repacking the cart with the camp gear, they were on the move by half past five to make the most of the cool air. After anything from nine to twelve hours on the road, broken up only for an hour's halt to allow the horses to rest, camp would be pitched and dinner prepared, cooked and served before the travellers retired for the night. Another woman destined for Constantinople, Miss Brown, accompanied them, keeping company with Nesta in a carriage which they made more comfortable by padding the interior out with pillows and spreads, allowing them to lie down. The second coach carried Mustaf Ibrahim Bey de Courten and Rushdi Bey, a Moroccan and Egyptian respectively. Both were engineers working for the Berlin to Baghdad railway but had originally been sent to Baghdad to support a river barrage project being overseen by Willcocks. For the most part, Lorimer rode alone with his thoughts on his horse. This continued for eighteen days, filled mostly by the monotony of a dreary and barren landscape or equally dull rocky hills. Only the occasional colourful glimpse of the Euphrates River, which they hand-railed throughout their journey, offered some brief visual stimulation. A different moment of stimulation came when the baggage cart driver overturned his vehicle in deep water whilst drunk. Initial bouts of laughter soon turned to cries of frustration when the Lorimers found that their trunks had also been submerged and for Nesta at least, the need for a whole new wardrobe to replace her spoiled dresses. This mishap aside, the journey was uneventful. In both good health and spirits, the Lorimers arrived in Aleppo on 6 May.

During the next few days of recuperation and exploration in the Syrian city, Lorimer had a chance meeting with the chief German engineer of the Berlin to Baghdad railway who was about to survey potential routes to Baghdad via Mosul, giving him a new appreciation of German ambitions. Adequately refreshed, the travellers continued on their journey, this time by rail to Baalbek, Damascus and ultimately to Beirut. On 13 May, they set sail on the Messageries steamer, *Oceanian*, destined for Constantinople on a course that would pass near the islands of Cyprus and Rhodes as well as an unexpected day's 'leg stretch' on the island of Samos. Four days later, they arrived at the Turkish capital where they were met by an embassy *dragoman* who helped them navigate their way through Ottoman immigration bureaucracy.

Whilst Nesta and Miss Brown toured the city, Lorimer was kept busy by Lowther and his embassy officials, attending meetings, visiting both Parliaments and being introduced to influential Turks, among them the familiar face of Nazim Pasha who had recently become *persona non grata* in Baghdad.[444] On 28 May, Lorimer saw Nesta and her female companion off as she headed back to Edinburgh, arriving there just five days later, while he remained absorbed in the rhythm of daily embassy life. For the next few days, Lorimer was faced with even more meetings, attending garden parties and lunches, but also reuniting with Bell who had just arrived from Aleppo, having finally completed her own epic journey. With little more to be achieved in the capital, it was time to return to Baghdad.

His initial plans were extremely ambitious, taking him by rail to Eregli, over the Taurus mountains by carriage to Adana, by sea to Alexandretta (known to the Turks as Iskenderun) and then on to Aleppo in any way that he could, something that would have taken the best part of a month to achieve. The chance to sail on the Russian steamer *Karniloff* on 4 June straight to Alexandretta, however, was too good to turn down. Good fortune was again with him as he explored the unimpressive 'hot, damp and pestilential'[445] little Turkish port when an engineer from the American Liquorice Company offered to take him by car to Aleppo, reducing a bone-rattling three-day journey by carriage to just a few hours of fast driving. It was a delightful drive, which also passed Lake Antioch, once a site of a major battle between Christian and Muslim warriors during the First Crusade. When he made it to Aleppo, he briefly indulged in the idea of travelling back via the towns of Sanliurfa, Diyarbakir and Mardin, all of which would become consumed in the Armenian genocide in 1915, but persuaded again by both the length of time it would take and the high temperatures, he headed instead for Maskanah, from where he could cruise down the Euphrates to Fallujah and then finally across to Baghdad. It was, he wrote, his loneliest birthday since 1902, not made any easier despite living in an age of posts and telegraphs which had, in fact, only resulted in the constant desire for news.[446]

As Lorimer had expected, the various to-ings and fro-ings at the residence had not gone unnoticed by the local Ottoman authorities, not that the British presence in Baghdad was a recent phenomenon. The first representative was James Morley from the EIC, who established himself in Baghdad in May 1766. It was the briefest of postings and one which soon fell into abeyance before a local agent was chosen to represent the EIC's commercial interests. In 1798, the position was returned to that of an Englishman, but following the amalgamation in 1810 with the British residency in Basrah, Baghdad became a political agency until 1879 when it assumed residency status. Lorimer was the eleventh political resident since its establishment. Although Baghdad had been at the frontier of the Ottoman Caliphate since the early sixteenth century, it had enjoyed relative autonomy under the governance of the Mamluk dynasty.[447] In the 1830s, this changed when Sultan Mahmud II and the Sublime Porte looked to bring Baghdad, Basrah and the wider eastern periphery back into the Ottoman fold. Suspicious of British intentions despite both empires being long-established strategic allies, the local Ottoman authorities frustrated and restricted British interests wherever they could. This policy, however, was at odds with the Turkish desire to modernise and to adopt western engineering advancements, including in areas such as irrigation and dams. Willcocks's presence in Baghdad was solely to help in that journey and was something that only the British were willing to offer in spades to the Ottoman administration in Mesopotamia. It now fell to Lorimer as the latest political resident, to try to deal with these challenges and contradictions.

Since the EIC's earliest days in Baghdad, British commercial interests and opportunities were considerable. One major opportunity presented itself in 1836, when Irish soldier and explorer, Francis Chesney, led an expedition up the Euphrates River, to explore but also to trade, carrying British goods should any commercial prospect arise. Among his party was Henry Lynch, an officer from the Bombay Marine. Although the expedition itself was considered a failure, the entrepreneurial Lynch along with his brothers Stephen and Thomas, looked to exploit the emerging markets.[448] This involved shipping British goods up the river, initially working alongside other British and Indian merchants, and using local vessels to transport their wares.

This continued until 1861, when the Lynch brothers decided to remove the middle man by running their own craft up the Tigris and Euphrates Rivers. The brothers had no permission from the Ottoman authorities to run their own shipping schedule but took full advantage of the licence or *firman* originally issued to Chesney in 1836 and reconfirmed by letter in 1841 and 1846. These gave the British government through the EIC, the right to navigate ships under a British flag up both rivers for commercial purposes. When the Ottoman authorities looked to revoke Chesney's *firman* in 1882, the Lynch brothers relied on British political influence to save its trade routes. To ensure that its operations remained of relevance to the British, the Lynch Company looked to secure both the rights and subsidies from the British government to run mail up to Basrah and Baghdad. It was not long before the Turks too, depended on Lynch's mail service.

The Lynch mail steamers continued to carry both imperial and Turkish mail but were unreliable, sometimes refusing to carry post or postponing scheduled mail runs whilst keeping their more profitable commercial ones. Excuses such as a lack of space, wrong tides, adverse weather or local disturbances were often deployed but in reality, this was solely about the pursuit of profit. When in the early 1900s, their contract came up again for renewal, the Lynch Company argued for greater subsidies to run the mail, citing higher running costs, but was unable to persuade the government of India who saw it as nothing more than an attempt to make more profit. The British government in contrast, saw the establishment and maintenance of a network of imperial post offices to distribute mail as a purpose of empire, as well as a means to combat the trade subsidies being offered by Britain's adversaries. The Ottoman authorities were equally frustrated with the Lynch Company, in particular its claim to have exclusive navigation rights, but they too remained reliant on the mail steamers, seeing fast communications as a corner stone of their own empire and proof of a modern state. Unable to scale back the company's operations or to replace them with their own, the Ottoman authorities, instead, took their frustration out on the British. This included trying unsuccessfully to get RIMS *Comet* decommissioned, by arguing that its presence exceeded the number of British-flagged vessels allowed in the original *firman.*

Despite the overarching ambition to support British commerce and interests in Mesopotamia, Lorimer was not alone in recognising the Lynches' perfidiousness, playing the Ottoman, British and Indian governments against each other. He also questioned their monopoly of navigational rights and their manoeuvring to ensure that all parties remained dependent on the services that their steamers and towed barges provided, whether they were carrying goods, mail or grain. When in the summer of 1910, it looked like the Ottoman authorities were going to reopen negotiations with the Lynch Company, this time not only about navigation rights but also their possible amalgamation with Nahrieh

Steamers, an Ottoman-owned enterprise, the company looked to Lorimer to support their case and to protect their monopoly. With appetite waning in Baghdad and now Whitehall to bolster the Lynch Company's commercial activities, a strong letter was written to the Foreign Office in London, complaining about Lorimer's unhelpful 'open mind' about the future of the service. The company also challenged his inclination not to lobby local influential figures on their behalf unless he was under clear instructions to do so.[449] Lorimer might have been more sympathetic had the Lynches' local agent not complained about him to the government of India whenever he was away from the residence, on official business or not, rather than being there permanently at their beck and call. But it was hard for Lorimer to remain objective despite the personal animosity against him as well as the rancour that he, and Lowther, shared against the Lynch Company.

When finally instructed to lobby, Lorimer followed orders, even though it was against his better judgement. It also bothered him, having to request compensation for the company when their premises were destroyed as part of Nizam Pasha's road-widening project, which had resulted in a wave of destruction in the name of modernisation, throughout the municipality.[450] Had it only been the Lynches' property that had been levelled as part of the *wali*'s scheme, Lorimer might not have been as obliged to press for recompense, but as many British Indian merchants had also seen their properties and investments arbitrarily demolished, he knew it was right to *demarche* the governor in the strongest terms.

Nazim Pasha was extremely fortunate that this remained just an issue of financial compensation rather than a full-blown political incident, or even potentially, a cause for military retribution. Whether by accident or by design, when the *wali*'s work gangs encroached the residency grounds, intent on clearing a route straight through the manicured gardens, Lorimer, Lowther and the government of India protested in the strongest of terms. It was clear to Lorimer that this was politically motivated, a malicious scheme with the intent to not only force a reduction in size and status of the residence, but also a statement of Ottoman power in Mesopotamia, including over foreigners and foreign interests.[451] He also believed that Nazim Pasha's actions specifically targeted British subjects although on this point, Lowther disagreed.[452]

Both, however, acknowledged that left unchallenged, Nazim Pasha's policy could soon extend to the sepoy guards and RIMS *Comet* given that the 'presence of both … [are] highly distasteful to Turkish national sentiment'.[453] At one point, the standoff at the residency even drew crowds who loitered by the walled boundary, watching in suspense to see who would blink first, or to be exact, to see either the local denigration of the British empire through the demolition of the residency wall or their Ottoman masters through the rerouting of the intended road. It was only after Lorimer had successfully *demarched* Nazim Pasha during a leisurely steamer cruise of the Tigris (organised by the *wali*) that he was told in response, that it had all been a terrible misunderstanding, doubtless Lorimer thought, on his part rather than Nazim Pasha's. After assurances were finally given that there would be no breach of the residency walls, Lorimer congratulated himself for having been able to 'avert a very disagreeable incident'.[454]

A very disagreeable incident, however, was just the sort of precursor that some in the Committee of Imperial Defence in London welcomed to revisit discussions of retaliatory military action. When in early 1906, Britain and the Sublime Porte disagreed on the undefined border between Egypt and Syria in the Sinai Peninsula, the arrival of British warships off the coast of Constantinople forced Sultan Abdulhamid II to the negotiating table, ultimately to his, and the Caliphate's, loss. Other actions considered at the time by the committee, included seizing the Nahrieh Steamer Company's vessels, which was in competition with the Lynch Company's Tigris River operations, an action that the Lynches would have strongly endorsed. When it was agreed that the seizures would be 'futile', the potential course of action was overruled.[455]

In May 1911, the suggestion of boat seizures was reconsidered, not because of Nazim Pasha's seemingly anti-British behaviours, but because the anti-Ottoman hawks in London wanted to make the most of the regional turmoil that the Sublime Porte currently found itself in, distracted by fighting an insurgency in Yemen. In an ascending scale of size, other potential military actions included evicting the Turks from Qatar, removing a Turkish lightship and buoys from the Shatt Al Arab waterway and driving the military out of Babiyan and Umm Qasr, all of which stopped short of infringing on any recognised sovereignty rights.

The suggested occupation of Fao and control of the telegraph terminus there, were also considered. The temporary occupation of Basrah, followed by British authority and control of revenues and commercial vessels for the next thirty miles up-river however, was struck through when the committee acknowledged that such actions would be interpreted as a declaration of hostilities.[456] O'Conor's August 1906 letter to the Foreign Office reporting that a British military campaign in Baghdad would be welcomed with open arms, already excited those in London who were looking for conflict.[457] Lorimer's report four years later, confirming that local sentiment towards the British remained unchanged, fuelled the argument further for punitive military action.[458] The hawks were only grounded when the War Office's Director of Military Operations made clear that Britain would not be fighting the Turks along the Euphrates.[459]

The Euphrates River had, in any case, been the focus of other discussions, when the Ottoman authorities made it known that they were looking to modernise their infrastructure in Mesopotamia. This included building a new barrage. The Hindiyah barrage was the latest attempt by the Turks to improve their control over the Euphrates River and the surrounding agricultural landscape. Better control of the river presented both food security and tax revenue opportunities. The project was something that the British too, had an interest in, not just providing the expertise to build the barrage but as a means to feed its subjects in India. As an engineer, Willcocks was a fervent supporter of the dam project. For years, he had promoted it unsuccessfully with the Sublime Porte, but attitudes changed in 1908 following the Young Turk revolution and the injection of ambition. In partnership with British builder and Member of Parliament for Devonport, Sir John Jackson, Willcocks pitched his vision successfully to win the tender rights, beating a French design.[460] Although not prepared to commit sovereign wealth into the dam, the British government nonetheless supported the project, considering Willcocks's success a substantial wedge between the German-Turk relationship.

By the time Lorimer assumed his residency in 1909, construction was already well underway on the dam, sixty miles south in Musayyib. Work stopped just two years later when Jackson's masons and engineers laid down tools. Willcocks had failed to extract the National Bank of Turkey's financial contribution to the project, something that Jackson had always feared would happen.[461] With both the British and the Sublime Porte keen for the project to be completed, the local Ottoman authorities in Baghdad offered their tax revenues collected in Diwaniyah province as payment, rather than see the National Bank default. Lorimer, however, was unsympathetic. He preferred a more aggressive approach, recommending that the Sublime Porte should instead, secure the bank loans, accept responsibility for the project and submit itself to any conditions that the lender might put upon them. Fortunately for the Turks, sufficient funds were found to allow construction to continue. When the Turkish banks continued to struggle with their cashflow a year later, Lorimer again, interjected. But rather than suggest increasing pressure on the Sublime Porte, he wrote to the Foreign Department recommending that the government of India should offer money from their own central coffers. This, he believed, would not only impress public opinion among the Muslims, both in India and Mesopotamia, but 'would also fit in with British policy, as tending to the exclusion of foreign interests from the field of irrigation'.[462] Fearful of British aspirations, both real and perceived, the local authorities always managed to find their financial contribution regardless of the social cost, even if that meant squeezing their provinces for more tax revenue rather than encouraging foreign investment.

In early 1912, Lorimer visited the partly constructed barrage. He was impressed by what Willcocks and Jackson had achieved so far but also noted that building the dam was not in itself, the end to a means. Even when completed and commissioned, substantial work would need to be taken forward to address the distribution of water to irrigate over three million acres of the surrounding land. The authorities would also need to populate the area with a workforce to farm and maintain it before any ambitions to create new revenue could be realised. His honest observation spooked the Ottoman authorities, who feared that would result in the British settling tens of thousands of Indian workers to work the irrigated fields.

These concerns were still unaddressed, however, when in 1913, the two-hundred-and-fifty-metre-long barrage, complete with thirty-six arched openings, each five metres wide, was finally commissioned, opening the floodgates, literally and figuratively, for new commercial opportunities.[463] But not everyone was impressed by this engineering success. The Lynch Company in particular, considered it to be a major detriment to their operations. They argued long and hard with both the Turkish and British governments to cancel the project, claiming that they would no longer be able to steam beyond the barrage, affecting the critical services that they provided to both empires. The Turks saw this as an opportunity to revisit the company's navigational rights and to enforce the breaking up of its monopoly. Turkey's alliance with Germany in the Great War a year later, however, would ensure that the Lynch Company continued to operate the waterways, now supporting the British and Indian armies fighting Ottoman troops during the subsequent Mesopotamia campaign rather than running mail.

Lorimer had his own navigational challenges in Baghdad, albeit political ones, as he learnt how to deal with Nazim Pasha who had set a course for destruction in the name of modernisation. Described by Bell as a civil but 'grizzled old man with rather a striking face, bold and firm…', Nazim Pasha arrived the same year as Lorimer to bring order to Baghdad, Basrah and Mosul.[464] By the Sublime Porte's own admission, there had long been doubts about his wider administrative capacity, but he had a reputation as an effective disciplinarian.[465] Discipline, Bell claimed from her own experience, he had certainly achieved, as the caravan routes and roads she travelled through were now safe from robbers. Even the mention of his name struck fear. But there was also a fear that he was out of control, acting way beyond Ottoman law and the direction set by the Sublime Porte. There was certainly no accountability for the loan that he had secured from the National Bank to fund the roads project. He was soon more than the city could bear, with rumours persisting that he had been encouraged by the Young Turks to be heavy-handed in his plans to modernise Baghdad to advance his downfall.[466] Lorimer too, considered that there seemed to be an invisible hand pushing Nazim Pasha along, most likely by that 'gang of political adventurers' in Constantinople, whose motives were still a mystery.[467]

Nazim Pasha's demolition act was eventually cut short in March 1911, but not before the damage had been done. He received orders to return at once to Constantinople on the very night that he was due to dine with Bell when she was visiting. This meant that the issue of compensation to British subjects as a result of Nizam Pasha's wake also remained unaddressed despite Lorimer's efforts to press the municipality. With responses varying from Nazim Pasha's successor having no instructions or funds to reimburse victims to agreeing to give it consideration in due course but only after a full investigation, there seemed very little chance of reimbursement. Although Lorimer was frustrated by their inaction, the local authorities understood the political consequences if they complied. Had compensation been paid to foreigners, they would then be faced with similar claims from their own citizens who had been even more affected, potentially spilling over into the streets if they felt further disenfranchised.

The reliance on Lynch's mail steamers, British engineering at the Hindiyah Dam and Lorimer's interest in imperial agricultural and commercial opportunities, all helped fuel the Young Turks' paranoia about the empire's true intent in Mesopotamia. A constant stream of articles in Turkish and local papers regularly pictured the scene of Britain's claws cutting into the Caliphate's flesh in Basrah and Baghdad. As a seasoned Ottoman-hand having once served as head of chancery in Constantinople, Lowther much preferred dealing with the old Turks than the new ones,[468] even if Sultan Abdulhamid II supported a pro-German policy. Lowther despaired at the Young Turks' CUP-aligned press which criticised Britain's influence in Mesopotamia, especially when they demanded repeatedly, that Ottoman suzerainty there should be acknowledged. It was hard to see how the Foreign Office's policy of warming up to the new Turkish government towards Britain could be achieved through 'sympathy and encouragement to [strengthen] the reform movement', given such animosity.[469] It was clear to Lowther, that the Young Turks were not the potential political allies that the Foreign Office believed them to be, with a habit of making spurious accusations against the British and Indian governments and then demanding that they deny them.[470]

To discount any impression of a British hand in destabilising the Ottoman regime should anyone be gullible enough to believe the Turkish and local papers, Lorimer took the American consul, Emil

Sauer, on a tour of his consular region to show he was 'a perfectly open and above-board character'[471] and to squash any rumours that his work mainly consisted in orchestrating political intrigue 'heaven knows for what purpose with Arab sheikhs and Persian mujtaheeds'.[472] He might even have convinced the American, but the Sublime Porte and the Young Turks remained unpersuaded. When Lowther retired from the diplomatic service in 1913, Lorimer reflected kindly on his Foreign Office senior despite them not always seeing eye to eye. In a letter to his mother, he wrote that 'Sir Gerald is described as "a regular Lowther", gruff but kind, and a most honourable English gentlemen if not the first of diplomats … [with] honour and honesty and not too much pliability … just the qualities required during these difficult years'.[473] He also applauded Lowther's principle of standing up to the Turks, both Young and Old, and maintaining 'the respect and confidence of all who had to deal with him'.[474] Lorimer could only hope that Lowther's successor, Sir Louis Mallet, would be equally willing to stand toe to toe against the Ottoman regime. As Mallet was a childhood friend of Bell and one who supported her personal travel exploits into Arabia, Lorimer had little to fear.

Chapter 9

Between Bequests, Banquets and Coronations

In August 1825, the King of Oudh (modern day Awadh, Uttar Prudesh), Ghazi ul din Haider, loaned the EIC, ten million or *crore* of rupees. It was the third such loan, extracted by the EIC to help finance its army's campaigning. It was made in perpetuity by the king, along with an agreement that neither he nor his successors could recall, or otherwise interfere with, the terms of repayment. He also set other conditions, demanding that an interest rate be set at five per cent, generating five hundred thousand or five *lakh* of rupees per annum, as well as specific instructions on whom, and how much, this premium should be paid. Initially payable on a monthly basis to just four women named in the agreement, it was a very generous financial return. The agreement also included a particular condition that upon their deaths, one third of their payments could be inherited or willed as they wished. The remaining two thirds were to be paid equally between the 'Nujuf [Najaf] Ushruf, and the other half for Kerbulla [Karbala] to the High Priest and Majawurs, or persons who have its charge …'.[475] Four copies of the agreement were drawn up, two each in Persian and English, so both the king and the EIC had both versions to hand. Once they were signed, dated and sealed, the EIC's copies were archived in its Lucknow registry.

Following the deaths of two of the beneficiaries, both wives of the king, in 1849, one of the agreement's conditions, known as the Oudh Bequest, came into effect, a bequest that required administrating by the EIC. To allay Ottoman fears about the bequest making unbridled payments to multiple Shi'a religious centres of learning in Mesopotamia, it was agreed that Henry Rawlinson, the political agent in Baghdad should distribute the payments as the EIC's local representative.[476] When Rawlinson suggested that he should also have discretionary powers to suspend payments, Lord Dalhousie, the governor general in India, strongly opposed any EIC move to exert additional controls.

For the next fifty years, annual payments of one hundred and twenty-thousand rupees were bequeathed without any British political prejudice. To its recipients, it was an important source of income, but the bequest was not without its challenges as the EIC and later the government of India struggled to administer the payments in line with the bequest.[477] As well as doubts about its translation, it was not clear who the high priest was nor who the *Majawur*s were. Were they separate religious classes or just an adjective covering all religious scholars or *mujtahid*s who lived in, or near, the shrines? Even if the government of India knew who they were, what was to stop recipients from using the bequest for personal profit rather than for charitable purposes?[478] It was only after Lorimer requested that the Persian version of the agreement be retrieved and revisited sixty-one years later in November 1910, that the government's longstanding questions were, at least, partly answered. After comparing the Persian version with the one presented in Aitchison's publication, elements of the agreement were found to have differed considerably to its English counterpart. The English exclusion of the line 'that … mujtahids may distribute it on my behalf to the deserving…', raised a new question: who exactly were the deserving?[479]

Lorimer's reach into the archives for the agreement followed decades of potential misappropriation. He was not the only official, however, to have doubts. In 1902, Newmarch, the political resident in Baghdad, confirmed what many in Calcutta were already thinking; the distribution of the bequest in both Najaf and Karbala was corrupt. With the government of India's backing, an attempt was made to make it fairer, accountable and for the exact purpose the government assumed the King of Oudh had originally wanted. By their own interpretation, this was so that the king would benefit spiritually from the bequests, with prayers for his soul in return. In 1903, a new approach was formulated and introduced by Newmarch's successor, Ramsey. The bequest was to be allocated equally to *mujtahid*s chosen by him, with no fewer than ten and no more than twenty, picked from both religious centres.

By the government of India's own admission, the change was not well-received. Both Mesopotamian religious scholars and Muslims in India alike, remonstrated against the new arrangement. Hardinge in Tehran was also vocal about the bequest's revised method of distribution.

He preferred that it should be used, instead, to further Britain's interests in Persia rather than for spiritual recompense, but like Rawlinson five decades earlier, Lansdowne made clear that it was not to be used for political gain.[480] For the next five years, efforts failed to dampen the increasing discontent as beneficiaries and non-beneficiaries remonstrated against the government's new scheme. Just two months before Lorimer arrived in Baghdad, anxiety about the payments had spilled over into the streets, with religious students demonstrating violently in Karbala, calling on the *mujtahid*s to disgorge their bequeathed money. Having researched and written about the bequest whilst gazetteering, Lorimer was probably the most informed official within the British and Indian governments on its genesis, introduction and distribution. He was also likely among the few within either governments with the mettle to correct the misadministration of the 1825 agreement.

The Foreign Department's opening directive to Lorimer was naïve but signalled their honest intent to resolve the matter once and for all Their recommendation was to show the Persian agreement to Saiyid Muhammed Kazim and Saiyid Muhammed Ismail Sadr, the two leading religious figures in Najaf and Karbala. He was then to ask both men to identify the other leading *mujtahid*s (in addition to themselves) who qualified to be deserving. Although Lorimer agreed with the Foreign Department's inference that the Persian copy of the agreement should take precedence, he questioned the value of sharing the relevant text to any of the Persian-speaking *mujtahid*s. The bequest's literal translation, that *mujtahid*s were 'theological doctors residing at the threshold' made little sense.[481] These were not his only concerns. Was every *mujtahid* in either religious centre or threshold worthy, or just a select few? Did the king of Oudh really care about how his bequest was used as long as the payments ensured his eternal welfare? In short, even if the best *mujtahid*s were chosen, Lorimer believed that, left unsupervised, they simply could not be trusted to distribute the bequest as it was intended.

Having considered the Foreign Department's request fully in light of his own understanding of the bequest, Lorimer replied that it would be 'inexpedient' to consult with either man despite their importance.[482] He also reminded the department that in 1908, Ramsey had written to both *mujtahid*s seeking their advice on the bequest. Kazim had refused to accept the revised conditions or to propose names of other fitting *mujtahid*s while Saiyid Ismali ignored Ramsey's request for over a year. When he did eventually reply, he too refused to engage with the residency on the matter or to appoint another *mujtahid* in his stead.

Lorimer had, in any case, already called on Kazim in Najaf just a month after his arrival in Baghdad, which included a discussion on the bequest. It had been, he considered, both 'vague and unsatisfactory'.[483] Even though he had managed to extract a promise from Kazim to write to him with his reflections once he had thought it over, no subsequent letter arrived. When reminded of his promise in April 1911, the *mujtahid* remained dismissive, saying that he had nothing else to add to what he had already shared with Lorimer.

Apart from stirring the public conscience in both India and Mesopotamia about the Oudh Bequest, Lorimer considered that the Newmarch-Ramsey reforms had been a failure. He looked instead to introduce a new scheme, establishing two committees, one each in Najaf and Karbala, both attended by chosen *mujtahid*s and an equal number of individuals nominated by the political resident. Both committees would be presided over by Muhsin, the longstanding local vice consul in Karbala with a standing agenda to decide who among the deserving should receive payments. To acquire the money needed to distribute onwards, Lorimer suggested that each selected *mujtahid* should allot two fifths of their individual bequest to the committees to be distributed. In time, he could see no reason why their donations to the committees could not be increased to half, with the remainder used as each *mujtahid* saw fit. It was endorsed after he discussed his initiative with the *mujtahid*s in Karbala, most of whom were supportive of the new approach. Although Lorimer had not also consulted their counterparts in Najaf, he was sure that they 'would have probably agreed'.[484] It was perhaps, a rash decision to make given the risk of unrest but was taken to move things along at pace.

Another rash decision was to set up a provisional bequest committee in Karbala even though the government of India had yet to appraise his initiative. He had even managed to get the committee to allot him two hundred rupees a month to cover the costs of hostels and guides for Indians going on pilgrimages to the various Shi'a shrines, a gesture he knew, would be immediately well received. He also hoped that some money could be allocated to fund a hospital and local schools for Indian Shi'as in Karbala.

The deeper Lorimer delved into the bequest, the more he questioned if the current position of making equal payments to the *mujtahid*s was the right one given some were far more powerful than others. Muhsin in Karbala, agreed, offering a simile on the matter, that 'a lion and a fly cannot be placed on the same level together … [it] is still more unjust to give the respective food of the one to the other. The lion requires a greater and better quantity of food than the fly'.[485] To some religious figures in India, Lorimer was seen as an obstructionist, interfering in a flow of revenue that had long been to their financial and social benefit. He persevered nonetheless with his 'revolutionary proposal,' calling on the government to give its full backing to his recommendations, or risk 'a stream which is capable of vivifying thousands [and] left unguided, … will continue to stagnate in a morass of corruption and dishonesty'.[486] Five months later, he received the capital's full support with just one condition, that one Indian *mujtahid* must be amongst the chosen distributors in both religious centres.[487]

With his revolutionary reforms now in place, in March 1912 accompanied by Nesta, Lorimer set off on an official tour of the Two Holy Cities to see the administration of the Oudh Bequest, spending ten days in both locations. Taking in the Hindiyah barrage, Tawairij, Mahannawiyah, Hillah, Babylon, Kifl and Kufah along the way, the journey would see them absent from the residence for just over a month to complete the two hundred and fifty mile round-trip.[488] From Karbala, Lorimer wrote to his mother, reflecting on the handling of the bequest under his new arrangements, which by his own admission, he believed was going very well. With the distribution of three hundred Turkish pounds in relief already given to over eleven hundred people and an additional three hundred more benefiting if their children were included, 'it was a great improvement on the old arrangement under which practically nothing reached the poor'.[489] The visit also allowed him to pay compensation, a total of 5,400 Turkish pounds to be shared with local British subjects in Baghdad and Karbala whose properties had been demolished by Nazim Pasha's modernisation drive. As the local municipality had refused to pay any reparations, the payments were only made possible after Lorimer and Lowther had squeezed the Sublime Porte sufficiently to pay up.[490] It was an extremely satisfying visit, but with so much to oversee and so much still in hand, not least the gazetteer's volume I, Lorimer could only hope of getting some leave in the forthcoming year. As he conceded to his parents, 'a public career is full of private difficulties'.[491]

By the summer of 1913, Lorimer's bequest proposal was in full effect, with both committees fully functional and attended by seven *mujtahid*s and an equal number of resident nominees under Muhsin's chairmanship, each distributing funds in the spirit of the king of Oudh's request. It was a promising start, with nearly four and a half thousand deserving people receiving alms. Bequest-funded guides were additionally taking Muslims on safe pilgrimages to Karbala, Najaf, Basrah, Baghdad, Kadhimain, Musaiyib and Samarrah. Free bread had also been distributed throughout Ramadan in both holy places, money lent to stranded Indian pilgrims and there was the intent to provide warm clothing and fuel to the poor in both Karbala and Najaf during the winter months. Despite the committees' efforts to make the most of their allocations, not everyone was convinced. When approached by Lorimer about the Oudh Bequest, the *wali* in Baghdad refused to allow any Ottoman subjects to sit on the committee despite the political resident's encouragement. As well as potentially benefiting from receiving payments, Ottoman representation Lorimer argued, would also prove that British objectives for the bequest were solely honourable not political. The *wali* remained unpersuaded, declaring that if there were any Ottoman subjects deserving of alms, it was for the Turkish government, not the British, to help them. The *wali*'s vindictive nature seemed to have no bounds when Lorimer found that the local authorities had threatened the Persian consul with expulsion if he agreed to Persian representation on the committees.

Despite these hindrances, Lorimer was proud of the amazing work that the Oudh Bequest was now doing rather than lining a few *mujtahid*s' pockets. He also gave credit where it was due, acknowledging the commitment and selflessness of Muhsin in the face of abhorrence and criticism from the *mujtahid*s who were now without a regular source of easy revenue. Mesrop Thaddeus, the residency treasurer, was also applauded for managing the bequest accounts and the various permutations that calculated individual payments.[492] It was, Lorimer observed, a 'pleasanter and more profitable side [of our work] than our perpetual struggle with the Turks over aggressions on British subjects and interests'.[493]

Lorimer's hope of some respite in early 1912 overlooked his recent visit to India which was as much rest and recuperation as it was representation and work. In October 1911, he was invited to the Imperial Coronation Durbar, to take place in Delhi from 9 to 16 December. The *durbar* was the third of its kind to be held in Delhi. It was also the last to be held in India and the only one to be attended by the British monarch and emperor, in this case, King George V, grandson of Queen Victoria. The first *durbar* was held in January 1877, celebrating the proclamation of (the absent) monarch as empress. It was there, where gun salutes were first introduced to salute principal Indian princes. The second, held twenty-six years later in 1903 to mark the succession of King Edward VII, was delivered under Curzon's watchful eye and was an even grander affair as was to be expected from a flamboyant viceroy. As the king had delegated representation to his younger brother, Prince Arthur the Duke of Connaught, one could have been forgiven for believing that the viceroy rather than the duke was the principal guest of honour. The 1911 *durbar* planned to be the most magnificent yet, where the king would announce the relocation of the capital from Calcutta to Delhi, albeit with Simla remaining the summer alternative.

More a three-line whip than an invitation, it was not one to be turned down without good reason. With Nesta in Scotland since early June, Lorimer agreed to meet her in Karachi so they could travel on to Delhi together.[494] But he would not be travelling from Baghdad alone. Departing the residence on 7 November, he was accompanied by Abdur Rabb Barq, the residency interpreter and two representatives chosen from the local British Indian community, Saijad Ali Khan and Muhammed Taqi Khan, all as guests of the government. After reuniting with Nesta in Karachi, Lorimer made the most of his time in India.[495] Rather than head straight to Delhi, the party took instead, a detour to Lyallpur District in Punjab to see how the Lower Chenab Canal Colony was being managed. Lorimer sought a better understanding about the development of the colony's irrigated land as he hoped that the system could be transferred to Mesopotamia after the barrage had been finished. From there they continued to the outskirts of Delhi, arriving on 4 December at the purpose-built Kingsway railway terminus that served the huge, recently erected tented city.[496]

Allocated to Campsite 8 positioned directly opposite the terminus, the Lorimers quickly settled into their allocated pure-white bell tent. As they mingled outside, they found themselves in the company of other Foreign Department administrators, including Cox, his wife Louisa Belle and Shakespear from Kuwait. Campsite 8 was in a prime location in the central camp, neighbouring the North-West Frontier Province administrators' encampment. It additionally overlooked the two polo fields and football pitch which would soon be focal points for various sports tournaments. Their relative importance and hierarchy within the *durbar* also meant that they were positioned less than a stone's throw from the grand marques which would accommodate the king emperor, his wife, the empress, Queen Mary and the current viceroy, Charles Hardinge, the First Baron Hardinge of Penhurst.[497] With over forty thousand tents scattered over twenty-five square miles served by roads and a light railway, the canvassed-city also boasted freshly laid lawns, flowerbeds blooming with chrysanthemums and lines of picket fences. Communications, so long a symbol of empire were also in abundance with a regular mail service overseen by a purpose-built post office, twenty-four sub-offices and post boxes, and a network of telephones distributed amongst the dedicated camp zones. At night, as fire pickets throughout the campsite stood alert, the temporary city was illuminated by electric lamps with a string of cables running back to an unsightly power station, the only eyesore that spoiled the encampment's little England aesthetics. A night of fireworks added additional colour to the black ink sky as well as fear in those who would have to fight any fires if any of the rockets went awry.

On 7 December, the king emperor and his queen consort finally arrived in Delhi to full fanfare. Following a procession through the new capital city, they arrived at their light and dark blue marques, colours chosen to symbolise the Star of India and the Indian empire. For the next two days, the air was heavy with gunpowder smoke as the constant booming of guns announced the arrival of numerous princes, chiefs and prominent land owners or *zamindars*, to pay their respects of varying degrees of sincerity to their emperor and empress.

To commemorate the grand spectacle, thirty thousand silver Delhi Durbar medals were struck by Calcutta Mint, to be issued to all members of the ICS, the Indian Army, local government officials and to a selection of private individuals.[498] All were accompanied with instructions that it was to be worn the furthest from the left shoulder. Lorimer, like countless thousands of others at the *durbar*, took his time in line to sign for his medal mounted on blue-and-red-striped ribbon at one of the administration tents. It was just as unceremonious for Cox who similarly waited in line, but as he had just been appointed Knight Commander of the Indian Empire, he and his wife at least had the honour of being invited to a dinner reception with their majesties as a more personal token of the empire's gratitude. Knight Commander was a fitting reward for visibly driving through Curzon's ambitions for increasing Britain's presence in the Gulf. Despite Lorimer's own dedication, personal sacrifice and equal commitment, 'the whole [gazetteer] business' the Foreign Department observed, 'had been a disastrous one [for him, having] forfeited leave, lost chances of promotion and distinction in his department, and … tied down for some five years to work of a monotonous and exacting description', not that it could nominate him for a similar award in any case given the secrecy of his work.[499]

Durbar celebrations were not limited to Delhi. In Bahrain, Lock and Emily also toasted the king-emperor's arrival in Delhi with some recently arrived champagne. Emily also welcomed the news of Cox's knighthood although was a little envious of his new title but with 'Sir Gordon and Sir Lockhart' sounding just as impressive, she hoped that one day they too, would receive similar appointments to the order.[500] It is unknown if Lorimer felt any resentment for Cox's knighthood or for him being overlooked for his. His thoughts on the *durbar* he and Nesta had been immersed in are also unknown, although he was happy to reflect that for the rest of his small delegation, they left 'much astonished and impressed by all that they saw in India, and their devotion to the King-Emperor and their enthusiasm for British civilization have received a stimulus which will react on the whole Indian Colony here and will make itself felt in Persian and Turkish circles as well'.[501] Given the money and manpower invested to deliver the *durbar*, it is unlikely that a patriot could have said anything else.[502]

Lorimer's hopes of obtaining some leave in late September 1912, to catch up with his parents and siblings were dashed again when, he was given fresh orders to leave Baghdad temporarily for another special duty. The government of India had decided that it could wait no longer for volume one of the gazetteer to be finalised and put into print. It had been over eighteen months since Lorimer had updated them on his progress.[503] The India Office, too, had become impatient with the lack of progress since the publication of volume two. Sir Arthur Hirtzel, the secretary of its Political Department in Whitehall went so far to acclaim that 'it must have been the best part of ten years on the stocks, and will surely be like one of Winston's Dreadnaughts – old before it is new – if it does not come out soon'.[504]

Lorimer was just as anxious as anyone to see the gazetteer through but with the persistent distractions of work, not least the complete re-administration of the Oudh Bequest, it had been impossible to complete the task in Baghdad. Although the bulk of volume one was already in type, some of the chapters and appendices still needed some work in light of more recent reports. Lorimer was also weighed down by the opening chapter which was key in providing an overview of the region as a whole and ultimately bringing everything together to unite the two volumes. It was, he implored, 'a complicated and continuous piece of work requiring perfect concentration of mind and freedom from disturbance'.[505] Again, Lorimer offered the Foreign and Financial Departments some options to try to resolve the impasse: either use an unpaid attaché to keep it cost neutral in line with the secretary of state's wishes which might result in an unsatisfactory product; or send him to Simla on a short furlough to focus solely on the gazetteer.

The Marquess of Crewe, as current incumbent as secretary of state for India, was the latest to appreciate the value of Lorimer's work and his willingness to consider any reasonable proposal to see it through to completion.[506] Swayed by Lorimer's dedication and suffering, the marquess gave Lorimer five months to complete the task with another ultimatum that any request for it to be extended, would not be approved.[507] Lorimer soon headed back to Simla to extract himself from any distractions. Again, Nesta accompanied him. It did not take long for them to settle into their prettily-furnished little house. Known as the 'Rook's Nest', the house was perched like so many others among the mountainside.[508] While Lorimer retired to the side-office, Nesta kept herself busy, converting what had previously been a bachelor's quarter into something more homely. Despite being new arrivals out of season, their nights were still busy with dinner parties.

By the middle of October, Lorimer was well into his task. While volume two provided the A to Z, volume one gave the context, focusing on the history and geopolitics, the ever-evolving internal relationships within the Gulf but also between the rulers and the Turks, Persians, French, Russians, Germans and of course, the British. A lot had happened since the gazetteering fact-finding missions in 1904–05. Even with a revision, Lorimer could only update some of the draft history chapters with some certainty up to 1907 having had time to appreciate the outcomes. Recent technological advances to telegraphy, the continuing saga of the Lynch mail steamers, sanitation and disease prevention as well as conflicting pearling rights meant that some of the supporting appendices also needed to be reviewed and updated. Working without distraction in the winter retreat, Lorimer was confident that the lion's share would be done by Christmas.

In March 1913, his latest period of special duty came to an end. Lorimer and Nesta left the Rook's Nest and the seasonal capital to return to Baghdad. After making their way to Karachi to pick up a ship, their route back would be familiar to Lorimer at least, firstly to Muscat where his gazetteering had nominally began, before the ship steamed through the Strait of Hormuz to the northern Gulf. Their next stop was Bushire, where he was informed of an unsavoury consular development in Baghdad involving a British citizen who was now being charged in the local courts on counts of bigamy, embezzlement, fraud, false accounting and larceny. It was with some relief to learn the matter had been overseen by Lorimer's deputy, requiring no substantial action on his part on his return as there was still work to do on the draft chapters.[509]

Within days of their return, they had little time to settle back in when Lorimer received orders to set off on RIMS *Comet*, to steam-paddle down to Abadan to visit the Anglo-Persian Oil Company (APOC) refinery, the first and so far, only commercial enterprise to find oil in the region.[510] With *Comet* already burning the company's oil and the refinery shipping crude oil to India, it was already an emerging market. Much had changed in the three years since Lock's early dealings with APOC, its exploration for oil in Arabistan and its negotiations with the Bakhtiari rulers or *khan*s whose territories were found to be hydrocarbon-rich. Lock's concern at the time was that 'the oil people [were] doing the khans in the eye',[511] a view initially shared by the Tehran legation, but later found to be unwarranted when APOC agreed to pay the chiefs three percent of shares in the various companies extracting oil from their land.

On his way down-river, Lorimer had planned to meet Cox in Muhammerah, but it fell through following a nasty turn of events in Bushire. A few days earlier, the Belgian director-general of customs in Bushire had been attacked and his wife murdered as they made their way home one evening from a function. With the Persian authorities unable to provide sufficient security, it was impossible for Cox to leave his residence.[512] Baghdad might have had its issues with the Oudh Bequest, and at one time, been at the mercy of Nizam Pasha, but it was certainly not as volatile as Bushire.

Although the lack of an entertainment allowance prevented Lorimer and Nesta from saving much money each month, it did little to discourage them from enjoying a very social life in the far more agreeable, and safer, Baghdad. If they were not hosting dinners for fellow consuls, travellers or influential expatriate residents, they were regular invitees at reciprocal events. To pass away the time when Nesta was back in Edinburgh in 1911, Lorimer hosted a couple of moonlit picnics on 'a sandy spot on the top of a high bank [on the Tigris], with the river reflecting the moon on one side and a thick grove of young poplars on the other'.[513] The first was a stag affair which included a number of senior Turkish officials. The second was a more sedentary event, enjoyed by resident European families. On both nights, a dining table was set out as it would have been in the residence, illuminated by lanterns hanging from sticks. Both were also rounded off with communal singing.

Lorimer also played his part in organising and part-funding a mounted sports competition on the outskirts of Baghdad, with trials such as tent-pegging, polo and horse jumping among the main events.[514] In February 1912, Lorimer and Nesta pulled out the stops to host a fancy dress dance at the residence which was decorated throughout with flags from *Comet*'s signals store. Many of their guests turned up in elaborate outfits while Nesta played hostess wearing a Norwegian peasant dress. Lorimer, in contrast, took a cerebral approach, dressed as a photograph negative, reversing white for black and vice-versa although he stopped short of darkening his face with soot and powdering his hair. The proceedings ended with both being hoisted aloft above shoulder height to cheers of 'for he's a jolly good fellow'. The standard for entertainment had been set and was in Lorimer's opinion, a great triumph and something that could 'not have been bettered anywhere … nor equalled in Baghdad'.[515]

During 'the halcyon days of summer', tennis was a regular feature on the social calendar, culminating in 1913 with an international competition of singles, doubles and mixed games against other nationalities.[516] Both Lorimer and Nesta played their part to ensure that the British won the tournament, with the Germans as runners up and the French coming in third, ensuring again, Britain's primacy in the Gulf.[517] Even on a quieter evening, bridge or billiards served as an equal distraction from work, and both always found time to read passages from the Bible together for spiritual reflection.

Despite Lorimer's best efforts and hopes to have completed the gazetteer following his return to Baghdad, it still remained in draft. At first, he tried working on the manuscript in the evenings after dinner but was either distracted by necessary social engagements or forced to work on other pressing matters. In early July 1913, he considered slipping away on *Comet* for ten days to finish the outstanding work but felt that 'life on board would rather be a penance in this weather – it is 98° at present in my office room – and I should find an accumulation of work on my return'.[518] By the end of the month, Lorimer had revisited his plan to disappear on the residency launch to finish what remained of the gazetteer even though he was still unsure how his little cabin would fare 'notwithstanding double awnings, wet mats, and all that sailor-like ingenuity can suggest' to keep the temperatures down'.[519]

The constant drumbeat of work was not the only reason why Lorimer sought temporary sanctuary on *Comet*. Throughout June,

Lorimer received a number of letters from colleagues asking if he had put himself forward to be considered as the next chief commissioner of the North-West Frontier Province when the current incumbent went on leave.[520] It was not something that he had even contemplated. On the contrary, he had already made a discreet and informal request to remain in Baghdad until the following year, after which, he planned to take his next furlough. With seniority a major factor in such postings, Lorimer was in any case sensitive to the fact that even applying for the chief commissioner position could be perceived as going over the heads of men far senior to himself. It had also been nearly a decade since he had worked at the frontier but his association with the province continued to be strong. The rumour mill, however, was in full turn with Lorimer caught up in it, requiring him to repeatedly deny any interest in the position. To his eventual relief, John Donald, a year senior to him in service, was soon announced as the successful candidate, putting the gossip and speculation to rest. Donald had, himself, leapfrogged another interested and more senior officer to the position, something Lorimer thought would have repercussions in Peshawar. He was also sure that even if he had been given the position ahead of both of the front-runners, the situation would have been worse. He took comfort, however, in the fact that his name had even been considered and discussed by the appointers.[521]

In October 1913, Lorimer received further news about new appointments. He was ordered to take over from Cox in Bushire as the political resident for a period of nine to ten months so his peer could take over as the foreign secretary in Delhi. This was a disappointing turn of events, and when breaking the news to his father, Lorimer was reluctantly reconciled to his fate and the impact that it would have on his ability to take leave. When he initially challenged the posting, he was told that the residency in Bushire was far more important than the one in Baghdad, at least to the government of India, a point that he was prepared to accept. The addition of an entertainment allowance also helped slightly to sugar the bitter pill. When Lock and Emily heard the news of his imminent move, they questioned why he did not seem to want the role despite 'no-one else know[ing] the Gulf as [he] does and … [is] clearly the man for the job'.[522] But they seemed happy for

Nesta 'who would at least have the pleasure of taking over a clean house well supplied with linen, cupboards and store-rooms and pantries', even though the recent attacks against expatriates played on minds.[523] More enthused about the posting than Lorimer appeared to be, they hoped the move to Bushire might eventually become a permanent one.

At the same time that Lorimer received the news of his imminent move, his successor in Baghdad, Colonel Erskine, was given his own orders. He was to assume charge of the residency in Baghdad in late November. Lorimer may have been frustrated but took comfort in the fact that he was not at least being replaced by a more junior official, given the hierarchal system in force throughout the IPS.[524] He was also content to note that Erskine was several years older than him, again a hierarchical hang-up. Although he had spent some considerable time in the Political Department, Erskine had never served in the Gulf region. This made Lorimer question whether being in Baghdad would suit him, forgetting perhaps that he too, had little frontline experience when he arrived four years ago beyond his brief gazetteering days. Despite their different career paths, Lorimer recalled meeting Erskine briefly at the Delhi *durbar*, and was, he thought, 'a nice fellow'.[525] The same could not be said of Major Percy Sykes, the political agent in Meshad who was disappointed to hear that an outsider had been appointed to Baghdad, having assumed with some arrogance that 'with Curzon and Cromer …busy at home … and Kitchener to Egypt, that only left [him] for Bushire'. Rumours of his current administration being compared to 'a fair Augean stable', riddled with corruption, did little to support his case for such a senior posting.[526]

The almost immediate start in Bushire meant that Lorimer would have very little time to organise a farewell tour of Karbala and Najaf. As Nesta set to in the residence, overseeing the packing of their personal belongings, Lorimer set off on a fine new horse by the name of 'Barbeth'. He was accompanied for most of the seventeen-day return trip by Nawwab Saijid Ali Khan, a senior British Indian figure in Baghdad and his cousin, Agha Taqui. In the first two days they covered an impressive sixty miles, but the rest of the journey was hindered as all three fell ill at different stages along the way. Lorimer was arguably the worst of the three, struck down several times by recurring bouts of fever. At one point, he even had to dismount Barbeth quickly to lie on the ground to rest, much to the bemusement of his fellow travellers. Although not in the best of health and feeling rather 'seedy', they managed to ride to the Hindiyah barrage, which although fully built, was still not in use.[527] Nonetheless, Lorimer remained in no doubt that it was an impressive piece of British engineering.

Once he had completed his farewells in both holy cities and was confident that the Oudh Bequest would remain in good hands, he prepared himself for the return journey, knowing that he was likely to fall ill again at some stage. He was saved from a further test in the saddle by catching a passing steamer which carried him up river to Mussayib and completing the remaining forty-odd miles of the journey back to the residence by carriage. On his return, neither he nor Nesta had time to rest as they immediately began to organise a number of farewell events at the residence although none were as glamourous as their fancy dress affair. After seemingly endless rounds of valedictions and bouquets, their final affair was with the *Comet*'s crew and families, who had always made them welcomed guests.

Looking back, Lorimer had achieved much during his time in Baghdad despite the constant obstruction and friction imposed on him by the Turks and their local agents. The administration of the Oudh Bequest might not have been perfect but was now benefiting the deserving masses rather than the wealthy few. He had also managed to put into perspective, the perceived threat to the British empire from the Berlin to Baghdad Railway. Having travelled extensively throughout the region and spoken regularly to the engineers working on the railway, it was clear to him that London's fears of German and Turkish encroachment on India were hyped up, fuelled by paranoia to the point of being 'fantastic in the extreme'.[528] At best, he observed, the railway would only be of local value, unable to compete with existing mail and communication networks and certainly unable to deliver troops in force and at speed to India.[529] Despite these political successes however, volume one of the gazetteer still remained little more than a bundle of loose-leaved chapters and appendices.

Once their belongings had been boxed and centralised, the residency looked and felt empty. The signal for them to be taken away was only given after Lorimer was sure that nothing classified had been inadvertently packed away. His final duty was to hand over the residency's cyphers and secret documentation, including volume two of his gazetteer, to Erskine. As he thumbed through the few remaining official papers left in his office, one document in particular made him reflect on a final albeit petty political win against the Turks. Rather than destroy what was ultimately an insignificant and unclassified note, Lorimer decided to keep it as a souvenir. It had been addressed to him personally by the *wali* of Baghdad. It was an RSVP to an invitation that Lorimer had recently sent to him, to be his guest at one of his numerous farewell soirees. It had inadvertently been addressed to the 'British Residency'![530]

Chapter 10

Life in the Colony

It had been an exhausting last few days in Baghdad. Since the Erskines' arrival, the Lorimers had been kept busy hosting, with the political resident and designate completing various rounds of introductory calls during working hours, and with Nesta by his side, attending farewell dinners most nights, seldom getting home before two o'clock in the morning.[531] On 25 November, the couple boarded *Comet* for the final time to take them down river, making the most of a short breather that the passage afforded them. Any hopes of a low-key departure were dashed as even their embarkation required them to work their way through a crowd of well-wishers who gathered both shoreside and on-board to bid them farewell. The Erskines accompanied them for the first few hours, meandering down the river until they reached Algaara. There, *Comet* stopped for lunch. Joining them was Mr Tod, Lynch's local shipping agent and his wife, showing that despite their professional difference of opinions, they were on very personable social terms. After both had given their own final goodbyes, the two couples left *Comet* and watched it continue on its way down the Tigris, leaving the emotionally and physically drained Lorimers on-board.

For the next six days, Lorimer and Nesta enjoyed a quiet and restful passage downstream following what would soon be designated by the British and Indian military planners as Route 14.[532] This included passing the ancient settlements at Ctesiphon with its crumbling stone archway of Chosroes, the small but prosperous town of Kut and the much larger fertile town of Amarah. Further downstream at Qalat Salih, the Lorimers saw *Comet*'s successful navigation through the 'Devil's Elbow', a considerable bend in the river, followed by a more sedate cruise to Basrah.[533] There, Lorimer saw the familiar outline of RIMS *Lawrence* at one of the many anchorages that served the town, which was to take him and Nesta on the final leg of their journey to Bushire. As the steamer was not ready to accept them, they remained comfortable in their quarters on-board *Comet* and killed time by walking along Basrah's shore and dining with *Lawrence*'s skipper, Captain Finnis, who they knew as *Comet*'s former captain. They also called on, and dined with, Francis Edward Crow and his wife at the Basrah consulate. Unlike Lorimer, Crow was from the Levant Service but was one of the few who did take a keen interest in their surroundings. He was very familiar with local politicking in Basrah, having served there since August 1903. Once *Lawrence* was ready to accept its latest guests, it slipped its moorings and headed further down the river to Muhammerah.

Unknown to Lorimer, Cox was also in Muhammerah, having travelled up from Bushire as part of his own round of farewells. This included a final call on its ruler, Sheikh Khaz'al ibn Jabir Al Ka'bi before he handed over his position, powers and relationships to his successor.[534] Since the striking of oil in Khaz'al's sheikhdom, he was being actively courted by the British, having recently been made a Knight Commander of the Indian Empire. Although it was understandable why Cox made the call, it was still a slightly discourteous affair as his presence was only made known when he came on-board *Comet* unannounced as the Lorimers were having breakfast. As unexpected as it was, this allowed both men to have some much-needed face-time, having not seen each other since the Delhi *durbar* two years earlier, even though there was only so much that could be discussed away from the Bushire residence itself.

Now joined by Cox, the Lorimers sailed out of the Tigris into the Gulf and immediately ran into some heavy seas, arriving at their final point of disembarkation on 6 December. Although Lorimer was familiar with Bushire and its surroundings from his gazetteering days, he considered it a little disingenuous to call it a port. Described formally in the gazetteer as Persia's chief seaport, he considered it little more than a scattering of anchorages from three to seven nautical miles off-shore. Semantics aside, it was an important location nonetheless.[535] After *Lawrence* dropped its anchor in the inner anchorage, a boat fought the elements to collect the two principals to get them ashore. Nesta stayed on-board overnight so that she could enjoy a more pleasant transit ashore once the weather-front had passed.

As familiar as Lorimer was with his new constituency, he had never considered the disjointedness of his surroundings before. The residence was five miles inland but nowhere near Birdwood, his first assistant's house, the British telegraph station or the military barracks. Mirza Ali Muhammad, the governor of the Gulf Port's local residence and various consulates manned by Britain's allies, contemporaries and rivals were also scattered haphazardly throughout the city. Telephonic connections between the residence, staff dwellings and government offices helped to ensure some level of business but without a carriage, it was impossible to meet in person, at speed or with efficiency. Lorimer was also less than satisfied with the business of the transfer of responsibilities, which were brief and impersonal in contrast to his own lengthy official and social handover with Erskine. Within hours of Nesta's arrival at the residence, the Coxes were gone, leaving the Lorimers to their own devices in their new residence.

Known locally as 'Sabzabad' although with strict instructions that it was never to be used in correspondence, the Bushire residence was a large, sprawling and ugly collection of buildings. In addition to Lorimer and Birdwood, it was typically staffed during working hours by a local vice consul by the name of Chick and a treasury officer who had probably scoured through Lorimer's receipts when he was gazetteering.[536] Another newcomer, second assistant Lieutenant Percy Loch (a role once assumed by Gaskin), military attaché Captain Crosthwaite, residency surgeon Captain Hunt and his assistant, Surgeon Mackenzie, completed the official muster.

Bushire was known by British officials and expatriates alike, as 'the colony'.[537] It was not an affectionate term but an indication of their state of isolation. Nesta soon understood what it meant to live in the colony as even with the addition of domestic staff serving the residence, good housekeeping was a constant challenge. With only brackish water available locally, fresh water had to be run up daily in kegs from a well seven miles away which then had to be locked away and carefully rationed. They had not been there long when Nesta wrote incredulously of having received water that had been originally sourced from the Nile. It had found its way to them courtesy of a steamer that had anchored offshore.[538] Bushire was, she continued, the most unpleasant place to live. Even if their general surroundings appeared dismal, it was not long before she was on top of things, and was Lorimer considered, seemingly more in control of her situation and circumstances than he was of his.[539]

Nesta, however, was not as settled as Lorimer assumed. In a letter to Lorimer's mother Isabella, she feared they would end up being stationed there for much longer than the ten months that had originally been agreed because Cox aside, there was no-one else who had the depth of knowledge, experience or seniority. In the absence of anyone else, Nesta opined, Lorimer might be obliged to assume the role permanently.[540]

In contrast to Nesta's thoughts and concerns, Lock and Emily were only too glad to see their elder sibling in the role. Wilson, Lock's friend and fellow political officer working temporarily in Hamadan in Persia's interior, who first met Lorimer in Muhammerah in 1909, was equally excited about the new political resident's arrival. In his mind, Lorimer really was the epitome of a warrior-scholar and seen as the benchmark for other political officers to aspire to. He was particularly proud that he felt he could hold his own when discussing Classics with either of the Lorimer brothers or with Crow in Basrah.[541] Although Wilson was also respectful of Cox and admitted owing much of his own progression in the Foreign Department to the former political resident, he admitted having doubts about Cox's way of working and leadership. In Cox's final few days in Bushire, Wilson had 'been with him up to the last moment, occupied wholly with [Cox's] work to the virtual exclusion of [his] own'.[542] He was also a little disappointed in Cox as he had been promised a better job, either in India or in the Foreign Department before he left, but neither materialised. Wilson, instead, hoped that he might find employment with Lorimer, possibly as Birdwood's successor who he understood was due to move on the following summer.[543]

Lorimer must have felt equally sold-short by Cox's particular working methods. The fact that Cox had been in Bushire for so long meant that most of his knowledge remained in his head rather than documented in the chancery. Every issue or problem initially presented to Lorimer had a history which required resurrecting by Birdwood or Loch before he could even begin to make a judgement.[544] One of the reasons for producing the gazetteer was to address this very issue. What really frustrated Lorimer, however, was the distance that he now had to travel to meet anyone. Given the poor state of the roads and concerns about security, a three-mile journey could take at least an hour, with just one local meeting potentially taking up half a day. These were now realities that Lorimer had to factor in on a daily basis. But there was also some solace. He found the Persian officials more light-hearted and interesting to talk to than the Turks and Ottoman officials he had previously engaged with in Baghdad. He considered that 'they may say more than they mean but they do not reduce whole assemblies to uncomfortable silence by the lack of ideas or reticence as Turks do'.[545] It was also some consolation that knowledge was no longer a commodity but something that could be shared freely without any expectation of requiring an offering back in return.[546]

Lorimer had been in post for less than a week when he was required to write November's political residency report. The monthly bulletin gave the viceroy and the Foreign Department, a running commentary of developments in the Gulf. Not always relevant or strategic, it gave its readership a colourful picture nonetheless of a political agent's lot. Reminiscent of his early gazetteering, he required contributions from the whole of his network, which now included Knox in Muscat, Shakespear in Kuwait and Trevor in Bahrain. Returns were also needed from Captain A.J.H. Grey in Ahwaz, Captain Lionel Berkeley Haworth in Muhammerah, Thomas George Grahame in Isfahan, Major William Frederick Travers O'Connor in Shiraz, George Mungavin in Lingah, Hugh Vincent Biscoe in Bandar Abbas and consul William McDouall in Kermanshah. Lock in Kerman, too, was obliged to add his own summary alongside Lorimer's commentary of movements in Bushire. As insightful as Lorimer tried to be when drafting his own contribution, it was not an easy task given his very recent arrival. Although the task was undoubtedly delegated to Birdwood, even when considering wider geopolitical issues such as Turkish and Russian activities, Bushire's return seemed trivial in comparison to his wider network's returns. His contribution to the following month's report was also lightweight. It was quickly becoming apparent that although he was in charge of a large network of political officers who provided him with a grand overview of latest developments, intrigue and conspiracies throughout the Gulf, very little was actually happening in Bushire.

Lorimer soon understood the need for strategic patience when trying to get anything done as he better appreciated what his role as political resident meant in Persia as opposed to one in Mesopotamia. In early January, he wrote to his aunt, Caroline Robertson, offering her an informal account of both the workload and frustrations that he was now dealing with in Bushire. The residency was, he offered frankly, little more than a general post and telegram office. With lighting and buoyage of the waterways an example of transactional work dominating his days, he recalled that

> the number of authorities with whom one has to correspond is large and … makes the work complicated. Among these are the Government of India, the British Minister at Tehran, the Naval Commander in Chief (of the Persian Gulf Service) the director of the Royal Indian Marine, our own political officers and consuls in the Gulf and Southern Persia under my orders and the various potentates with whom they are in relations…[547]

This was the bureaucracy and protocol that Lorimer had to comply with to replace just two navigation lights, one each at the telegraph stations at Henjam island near the fish-shaped island of Qishm and Chah Bahar, a small bay on Persia's coastline, approximately one hundred and twenty miles west of Gwadar. Orchestrating, rather than playing, was the price that had to be paid as the political resident and although very capable of being the conductor, Lorimer put *Lawrence*'s crew on notice as he hoped to tour his new parish soon. It would require very little planning as he would look to retrace much of Curzon's 1903 cruise and his own gazetteering tour the following year, to reacquaint himself with the atmospherics and conditions within which, his agents worked.

Back in October 1913, when Lorimer had reconciled with the fact that he would be going to Bushire, he was quick to note to his father that Lock would soon be obliged to engage with him as a senior official as well as an elder brother.[548] It was a comment made in jest, and it was not long before official as well as personal correspondence opened up between the political resident and the political agent. In one exchange,

Lorimer had disapproved of his brother's decision to move from Bahrain to Kerman earlier that year. It is unclear why Lorimer was unsupportive of his brother. One can speculate that it might simply have been because transport links between Baghdad (and later Bushire) and Kerman were limited and dangerous, preventing any family reunion. With Kerman so far inland in Persia, Lorimer might have instead, wanted to deter his brother from having to deal with the frustrations that comes with having to report to both the Foreign Office and the government of India. It might have equally been a personal concern about Lock's repeated poor bouts of health and limited accessibility to medical care or the lack of security more generally given the unfettered activities of the various tribes there. Whatever Lorimer's reservations were, in early January 1914, Lock and Emily were happy to receive a letter from their elder brother who had now forgiven them for their decision. It was, they considered, 'very generous…' of him.[549]

Maritime navigation was not the only thing that fell on Lorimer's desk to administer. As the political resident knew all too well, the empire also needed a global postal service. The government of India's ambition was to increase their network of post offices, including establishing one in Abadan, an island in the Shatt Al Arab waterway. A welcomed distraction from these various strategic if mundane priorities came much further down the Gulf coastline, in Al Hasa, where Lorimer had previously been refused visiting rights by the Ottoman authorities. Since Ibn Sa'ud's recapture of Riyadh in January 1902, he had slowly campaigned against his rival, Ibn Rashid, and his Ottoman sponsors to reclaim territories that had previously belonged to his Al Sa'ud forefathers. In May 1913, Ibn Sa'ud switched interest from capturing more of his former northern domains to the east and the prosperous coastal region of Al Hasa which had been under Ottoman occupation since the 1870s.

As a land-locked ruler deep in the heart of the Arabian interior, Ibn Sa'ud had been of little interest or consequence to the British government. The Foreign Office had even given a clear directive that there was to be no entanglement with the *Wahhabi*s or engagement with their ruler.[550] Shakespear, whilst in Kuwait, had long been Ibn Sa'ud's champion, arguing for the need to engage with the new ruler in Riyadh.[551]

Cox, too, had been sympathetic, endorsing Shakespear's reasoning for engagement but the Foreign Office had always been firm in its position of non-interference in case it upset the Turks. Circumstances changed after Ibn Sa'ud's capture of Al Hasa and its considerable coastline. It now gave him agency with the British as the prominent power and the region's maritime security guarantors. From their different viewpoints, Whitehall and Delhi argued and procrastinated for months over Ibn Sa'ud. As long as negotiations continued between the British and Ottoman governments to agree the Anglo-Ottoman Convention, Ibn Sa'ud would have to remain an anomaly. London's inability to give direction was hampered because the draft convention as it stood, acknowledged Ottoman boundaries in the Arabian Peninsula, including their claim to Al Hasa.

It was only after the agreement had been finalised and signed by both sides, that the Foreign Office finally agreed as the *de facto* ruler of the coastal province, outreach to Ibn Sa'ud was both permissible and defendable. In early December, HMS *Swiftsure* landed Shakespear and Trevor, Lock's successor in Bahrain, to meet the emir in Al Uqayr. During the course of intense discussions on a range of issues of concern to both sides, Ibn Sa'ud repeatedly asked about establishing formal relations with the British. As signs of his good faith, he promised to play his part in preventing acts of piracy along his newly acquired coastline and gave his word not to encroach on, or threaten, Britain's interests elsewhere in the Gulf. Unable to promise anything substantial, the two political agents took away his asks and presented them to Lorimer and to the Foreign Department for consideration.[552]

Lorimer understood both the risk and opportunity of engaging with Ibn Sa'ud. In his own offering to the Foreign Department, he set out that 'every free bargain has two sides and must contain, if it is to be accepted, some element of advantage to both parties'.[553] Although he was sure that an understanding was possible between the British and Ibn Sa'ud, the same could not be said of reaching an accommodation between Ibn Sa'ud and the Turks. After weighing up the options, Lorimer put his weight behind the recommendation to establish a relationship with Ibn Sa'ud. As a gesture to manage any Ottoman grievance, Lorimer also suggested offering to mediate between the new ruler of Al Hasa and the

Turks – that is, if both parties agreed The alternative, Lorimer feared, was to do nothing and allow Ibn Sa'ud to come to some arrangement with the Turks that might ultimately be unfavourable to British interests. If an accord was reached between them, the British might then be forced 'to take such action as is required for vindicating the interests threatened', which might result in alienating both Ibn Sa'ud and the Turks.[554] Recalling Curzon's earlier desire, Lorimer also suggested posting a local agent to Qatif who could initiate and oversee communications between Ibn Sa'ud and Trevor.[555]

This was a considerable change from the directive he had given Cox and Shakespear just a few months earlier when he was in Baghdad. There, he had called for the need for caution before any engagement with Ibn Sa'ud could be considered. Lorimer may have represented both the British and Indian governments equally in Baghdad, but it was clear that the Foreign Office's longstanding position took prominence and was not to be ignored.[556] A month later after the Al Uqayr gathering, both the Foreign Office and the viceroy approved Shakespear's request to meet Ibn Sa'ud again. The political agent's request came as he was nearing the end of his time in Kuwait. Rather than catch a steamer back to England, he planned to trek on camel-back, following a well-trodden caravan trail to Riyadh to meet the ruler. From there, he would continue north-east until he hit the Suez and then on, by ship, to England. To help inform future versions of Hunter's map as well as to shed some light on the still unknown interior, he also planned to send couriered despatches to Lorimer along the way, recording his progress and general observations whenever he had the chance.

A regular distraction for Lorimer from work in Baghdad was the substantial social calendar, either as host or guest. This meant that work on the gazetteer too, was at times, deprioritised for a formal dinner, sports competition or evening ball. Although the posting in Bushire came with an entertainment allowance to offset the personal costs that he had previously had to absorb in Baghdad, Lorimer considered it 'a very retired life' in comparison.[557] Since their arrival, only a few visitors from elsewhere in the region had been hosted at the residence. Among them was a fellow warrior-scholar, Trevor from Bahrain.[558] A morning ride on his horse and short walk in the evening, did little to alleviate the pressure of managing a large network of political agents, each one with their own unique requests and questions requiring his attention. Life in the colony was also more formal. Whereas in Baghdad, a New Year was celebrated well into the early morning with a grand party attended by the great and the good, to mark the first of January in 1914, a clearer head was needed. As the most senior British official, Lorimer was obliged, as King George V's representative, to take the salute from Indian troops based in Bushire's Rishehr garrison, mounted, medalled and in full regalia. The first day of the year was finished off with a small dinner at the officers' mess. Despite the formality, Nesta considered the night a great success. While a regimental band played, uniformed guests, including Lorimer, and their spouses dined and played billiards.[559] As fun as it was, it paled in comparison to their former life.

Lorimer's reputation as a soldier as much as an Indian civil servant had been well earned. Although not expected to carry a rifle when he was in the field, like almost every other political officer, Lorimer carried a fire-arm. It arguably served two purposes, as personal protection but also as a small but subtle statement of status that it – and its ammunition – presented. Having shot grouse many times in Scotland with Lock and partridges and quail in Baghdad with any passing visitor, he was familiar with a range of firearms.[560] In early 1911, he purchased a short magazine Lee Enfield Mark III rifle. His decision to buy a Lee Enfield was because the alternative was to take one from the residency armoury which stored the sepoys' 'ricketty carbines of antiquated design'.[561] Later that year, he also bought a new personal side-arm, a modern magazine-fed, semi-automatic Colt M1911 pistol.

Unlike the standard issue Webley Mark IV and V revolvers carried by most British soldiers and officials at the time, the M1911 was a completely different design. Only in circulation within the American army since its introduction that year, it was as equally a symbol of status as it was a weapon. Lorimer was one of just a few British officials to have got their hands on Colt's latest pistol. Another Briton to own an M1911 was Winston Churchill, who even had his name engraved on the pistol's slide.[562] The M1911 had a particular design feature, making it popular with mounted troops. It was added following a request by the American cavalry who had trialled the pistol on horseback, shooting it at the gallop. As well as the normal safety features, a short grip safety was introduced. This was a large button on the pistol grip that prevented the weapon from being fired accidentally unless it was pressed in by the web of the firer's hand and the trigger pulled. It was a practical modification to save both the rider and his horse from harm.

A few years later, another warrior-scholar, T.E. Lawrence, was to find out about the value of such a safety feature when fighting in the Arabian Peninsula's western deserts during the Arab Revolt. During an attack against Ottoman troops on his camel, he fell hard off his mount after it dropped dead unexpectedly. After initially assuming it had been shot down from under him by the enemy, he soon found that he, had in fact, delivered the *coup de grace*, accidently shooting the camel in the back of the head with his revolver as he lumbered precariously towards incoming rifle-fire. A firearm might have been a status symbol, but it was important to remember that its primary purpose was to take life.[563]

The morning of 8 February 1914 was no different to any other in Bushire. Lorimer and Nesta started their day together, reading from the Bible. After their time of spiritual reflection, Lorimer found that the first item on his itinerary was a meeting with local legislator and *mujtahid*, Mirza Ali Muhammad. Deciding against riding there, Lorimer instead, picked up his telephone handset and called the Persian official. After completing the call, and now with at least two hours of his time that would have otherwise been spent on the road, Lorimer returned to his papers. As he worked through his in-tray, he was informed that the outward mail bag would be closing later that day. As well as serving official correspondence, the mail run was also an opportunity for him to order some ammunition for his Colt pistol, having expended a considerable amount several weeks earlier whilst out practising.[564] As his pistol was upstairs in his personal quarters, he dashed away to his dressing room to confirm the size of the ammunition calibre for his order. His office staff thought little of his initial absence, as did the residence staff who continued with their chores downstairs. His absence only became apparent when papers that had been prepared, required his immediate signature before they could be despatched.

Nesta was the first to discover Lorimer just before midday, collapsed on the floor.[565] At first, she thought that he had simply fainted as his body was warm, his limbs limp and his hands relaxed, and unclenched.[566] When attempts to revive him with water and brandy failed, it was only then she knew that things were serious. Within minutes, Nesta was joined by Loch, Mackenzie and other office staff. Hunt was the last to arrive. As he opened his medical bag, Nesta was ushered away, full of hope that inside might be something that could revive her husband. By the time the residency doctor had arrived however, Lorimer was already dead.

Respectfully, Hunt and Mackenzie removed Lorimer's clothes to examine the wound. A bullet entry was found slightly below and to the left of his sternum with a similarly sized exit wound just to the right of the spine between the eighth and ninth vertebrae. Further examination found that the bullet had also penetrated the diaphragm, ruptured the liver and damaged major blood vessels along its violent route.[567] Its kinetic energy spent, the offending lead slug was eventually found between Lorimer's bloodied shirt and waistcoat.[568] As professional and stoic as both doctors were, it would have been hard for them not to have been affected by their immediate task in hand. It was left to Hunt to record Lorimer's last couple of seconds of life. Possibly in hope, or in sincerity, as much as in medical opinion, he wrote for the record, that from 'the expression of the face [that] was calm and peaceful, [with] death speedily followed by syncope', Lorimer was very likely to have been knocked unconscious immediately through shock, feeling nothing as he fell to the floor.[569]

Nesta must have also felt nothing as she tried to process the last couple of hours. The rest of the office staff, however, would need to mourn later as they turned their attention towards government protocol. Section 174 of the 1907 Criminal Procedure Code required that an immediate enquiry had to be carried out. As the *de facto* senior official in-charge, it was for Birdwood to investigate Lorimer's cause of death with Loch and Crosthwaite helping where they could. The trio also concurred with Hunt's post-mortem and opinion that there was nothing peculiar or inconsistent with the wounds for the death to have been anything other than accidental. Their collective judgement formed and agreed, it was recorded that Lorimer had met his death from wounds caused by the accidental discharge of an automatic weapon.[570]

Chapter 11

Lamenting a Legacy

Lorimer was buried the next afternoon. It did not matter that he had neither served in the armed forces nor carried an honorary martial rank, it was agreed that the warrior-scholar should be given full military honours. It was a remarkable gesture, and an equally impressive feat, given the minimal time available to plan the ceremony. From Sabzabad, his coffin was drawn by carriage to Rishehr garrison, escorted by both British and Indian soldiers from the 102nd King Edward's Own Grenadiers. Many more soldiers of Muslim, Hindu and Christian faith, lined the route. From Rishehr, pallbearers drawn from the sailors and Royal Marines from HMS *Fox*'s crew, carried him the remainder of the way to the Christian cemetery, a small plot of land, put aside and used predominantly by the resident Armenian community. Throughout the procession, bag-pipes skirled laments, with the simple but mournful melody, 'Flowers of the Forest', the most poignant.[571] Birdwood and others from the residency led the way. At the request of Monsieur Loiko, the Russian consul-general, a detachment from the Russian Cossack consular guard with their distinctive fur hats, also contributed to the sombre entourage. Waiting for Lorimer at his final place of rest was a guard of honour, comprised of sailors and Royal Marines, some to serve as the firing party, others with bugles. *Fox*'s final contribution was the addition of its chaplain, Reverend Flower, who led the service.[572]

The French, German, Turkish and Russian consuls representing the whole of the consular corps, offered their condolences to a grieving Nesta on behalf of their governments. European expatriates, Mirza Ali Muhammad, other Persian officials and local residents also gathered at the cemetery to mourn Lorimer's death. Despite the colony's isolation, it was a well-attended affair. It was a testimony, Birdwood remarked, of 'the universal respect felt by all members of the community towards the deceased and the great popularity he had earned during the short period of his incumbency'.[573] Once the coffin had been laid down to the sounds of the pipers playing a final sombre dirge, buglers sounded the Last Post, alerting all who were present, that Lorimer's duty had come to an end.

The next few days were a blur for Nesta. In addition to mourning the death of her husband, the emotional burden and trauma of finding his body followed by the rush in organising his immediate burial, she was also obliged to settle their affairs as best she could before she left the colony less than a week later. Possessions that she did not want to be shipped back to Scotland were put aside for auction while personal papers were hastily bundled together and either packed or destroyed.[574] Only the draft gazetteer chapters were left untouched, although they would soon be sent on to the Foreign Department in their completed state. Crosthwaite helped out as best he could and after securing special leave, agreed to sail with Nesta back to Britain as her consort, leaving Birdwood behind in Bushire to remain in temporary charge of the residence. Obliged to compile January's monthly report, it was hard for the temporary resident to write about Lorimer as if he was still alive, a challenge that was faced across the political network, not least by Lock who failed to submit that month's return from Kerman.

Even before Lock had been informed of his brother's death, he was in a poor state of health, having been struck down by various bouts of fever and bed-ridden several times since assuming the Kerman agency in 1913. He had also recently fallen victim to outbursts of a severe rash, which typically broke out whenever something controversial or stressful was presented to him, which then required him to be nursed back to reasonably good health by Emily.[575] Longstanding ailments and anxiety aside, Lock and Emily's ability to mourn with the rest of the family in Scotland was extremely limited, at first only by telegram, with just a few simple sentences asking if their parents were keeping well given the circumstances. With the mail service understandably slow, it was not until early April, when Emily was finally able to offer her own personal condolences to her parents-in-law. In one of her weekly letters to The Reverend Robert and Isabella, she tried hard 'not to stir up anew the first acuteness avividness of grief that is [now] mercifully subsiding' but felt obliged to acknowledge the impact of Lorimer's death upon them. Even though Lock had tried to carry on with his work with expected British stoicism, Emily noticed that

> a great light of day ha[d] gone from his life and he is recovering more slowly than he'd have done, weighted as it were physically with his grief. But as you say sorrow must only unite us more for love is the only thing that matters or that lasts, over which the grave has no victory and which death loses the bitterness or its sting.[576]

Back in Strathmartine however, it was hard for his parents to draw the pain away from the theoretical sting. Unable to talk about the loss of his eldest son, The Reverend Robert, instead, wrote to his congregation at the United Free Church to share his grief. Then, as now, parents should never have to mourn the loss of their children. This made The Reverend Robert's words hard to put down on paper, but in a short eulogy, he saw in his eldest son 'modesty and self-reliance, the simplicity of the child and vigour of the man, generosity of thought and deed, unselfishness and strong home affections, all unified and graced by an attractive geniality of disposition that gathered to him friends from every class and quarter'.[577]

As a resident second class, Lorimer did not fulfil the government of India's minimum requirements to be entitled to an official announcement condoling his death. That honour was only typically given to first class residents and above. Peers and contemporaries from the Home, and newly named Foreign and Political Departments however, sought an exception to the rule. Correspondence was soon with Hardinge, reminding him of Lorimer's close connections with Persia, the Gulf and India. It was also felt that, regardless of grade, a 'mark of distinction should never be refused to any officer of exceptional merit'.[578] The viceroy concurred, brushing aside the government's usual insistence for protocol officiousness. On 5 March 1914, a suitably worded official release noted 'By Mr Lorimer's untimely death by an accident, the Government of India has lost not only an officer of conspicuous ability, but one who in life maintained the best traditions of his service'.

Such words of respect were of little consolation to Lorimer's family but would, the departments believed, 'be appreciated by his many friends and admirers in India'.[579] Further marks of condolence were inevitable as news spread of his death on the telegraphic wires. His death was particularly mourned in Bahrain where familiarity and a friendship of sorts, had developed over the years with the ruling family, not least with Lock, who had only recently departed the island for Kerman. Whilst Trevor and the political agency staff paid their own respects to their former resident, Sheikh Isa ordered the Bahraini flag to be flown at half-mast at his customs house. The sheikh would also pay his own personal condolences to the political agent. Lorimer's death was also felt among the Manamah community as prominent figures from the resident Hindu, Muslim, Persian and Jewish communities made their way to the agency to offer their commiserations. Further afield, Sultan Taimur, too, paid his respects to the recently arrived Lieutenant-Colonel Robert Benn, Trevor's counterpart in Muscat.

Curzon was one of the last to express his condolences to Nesta, but since the loss of his own wife in 1906, his letter exposed a brief moment of human vulnerability to this self-indulgent egotistic man who had at one time governed India as if it was his personal possession. He felt, in part, responsible for Lorimer's death, confessing to Nesta that by giving her husband the opportunity to distinguish himself within the IPS, it had ultimately led to his posting to Bushire. But it was right for Curzon not to offer an admission of guilt, as Lorimer was always destined to achieve, regardless of Curzon's rather particular special duty. The former viceroy's final words reflected on a man who had a

> strong sense of duty, fine natural abilities, untiring personal severance, and a wonderful aptitude for dealing with the peoples and problems of the East. Such a man was a tower of strength to the cause of British prestige and good government wherever he went; and his loss deprives the government of India of one of its ablest servants.[580]

Not one obituary acknowledged Lorimer's greatest contribution during his time in service, the gazetteer.

In 1978, Harry Victor Frederick Winstone, a biographer of many prominent British figures who were influential in the Gulf at the turn of the twentieth century, saw the release of his latest tome. It was of a companion and former house-guest of the Lorimers, Gertrude Bell.[581] Winstone was at that time, arguably without equal in his field, having already produced a critically acclaimed account on Shakespear two years earlier and in 1982, would see the completion of his biography of Leachman, both of whom were also known to Lorimer. One of his last books considered the actions of various political and military intelligence officers working in the region, both before and during the Great War. Among them, featured Lorimer and Lock.

Shortly after Bell's biography was published, Lorimer's daughter, Isabella (also known as Bell) and son-in-law Francis, a former member of the Sudan political service, contested elements of Winstone's latest work. In a letter to his publisher, they took exception on two points after seeing various references to Lorimer. The first was a minor point, but important nonetheless, observing that the former political resident had incorrectly been given the military rank of colonel. The second, and by far the more offensive, were the inaccuracies written about Lorimer's death and the implication that he had committed suicide. The offending line, that he 'was killed in his office by a self-inflicted shot through the head sustained, remarkably for so experienced a soldier while cleaning his gun' needed correcting immediately.[582]

Winstone could have been forgiven for believing that Lorimer was a military man given his reputation as a warrior-scholar. A casual reader of the India Office's Gulf papers could also have easily confused him with Lock, who retained his military rank after he joined the Foreign Department. But Winstone was an authority on the Gulf political network, its people and its archives. He was at best callous, at worst indolent, insensitive and arguably sensationalist, implying that Lorimer had deliberately taken his own life.

In fairness, the author soon apologised to the Lorimers for any impression he might have given about denigrating their father, but claimed in his defence, any unintentional oversights were because of the lack of archives following their destruction. He ventured that he had also been heavily reliant on circumstantial evidence, with Shakespear's reports in particular, a cause to blame. And yet Winstone was well aware that Shakespear had enjoyed a companionship with both Lorimer and Lock, as fellow political officers, for nearly a decade. It was simply impossible for Shakespear to have reported erroneously, Lorimer's alleged military status. The writer also knew that Shakespear was deep in the Najd desert with Ibn Sa'ud when Lorimer's death occurred and was unaware of his friend's demise until May 1914, when he finally resurfaced in Egypt. By the time that the explorer was back in touch with the world, information about Lorimer's mortal wounds were already known to the IPS. Through numerous local and international media obituaries, the general public, too, knew about the tragic event.

Although Isabella and Francis were not successful in convincing either Winstone or his publisher to pull the books from the shelves given their inaccuracies, the writer did agree to correct any future publications of the biography. In 2004 and true to his word, Winstone re-published the biography, re-phrasing the offending sentence with 'Lorimer was killed by what was officially described as a "self-inflicted gunshot wound"'.[583] Although factually correct, the revised sentence remained open to interpretation and still fell considerably short of the family's expectations. Since every single subject of Winstone's biographies had achieved amazing things, it remains unclear why Winstone felt the need to sensationalise what were already sensational lives.

Winstone's presumptions aside, there was, initially some doubt and uncertainty in Bushire, surrounding Lorimer's exact cause of death. Foul-play was not considered as Lorimer had very few, if any, real enemies and had not long been in Bushire in any case to have made some. The lack of security around Bushire would have also made it far easier for an assailant to attack Lorimer as he was travelling rather than enter a heavily-guarded residence and shoot him with his own pistol. But in the hours immediately following the incident, Birdwood sent two 'immediate' telegrams to Delhi reporting Lorimer's death. The first, that it had been 'caused by a bullet wound which he himself administered',[584] the second that his previous telegram 'should not be read in any way precluding death being due to an accident'.[585] It was only two days later, after Hunt's post-mortem and the obligatory internal enquiry had concluded, that Birdwood revised his initial opinion by reporting 'There [was] every reason to suppose that death was due to the accidental discharge of a Colt'.[586] No proposition was given however, on how the accidental discharge might have occurred.

Given Winstone's confession that he had been unable to find much about Lorimer in the archives, it was unlikely that he would have known that the political resident had suffered from bouts of fever throughout his later years. He was also unlikely to have been aware of Lorimer's heavy workload from the burden of managing a demanding political network, the pressure from Delhi to complete his work on the gazetteer, or of the extent of his fatigue more generally, having not had any substantial leave for several years. But it is doubtful that these factors would have driven Lorimer to resort to reaching for his pistol and deliberately shooting himself in the stomach as a means for a swift death. Simple biology tells us that a bullet to the head or heart would have had a far higher chance of success.

If Lorimer's state of mental health was unlikely to have been at fault, consideration must then be given to the weapon used. The Colt M1911's short-grip safety feature and reliability has made it a particularly safe yet powerful weapon to handle, justifying its continued use in parts of the American military over a hundred years since its introduction. The drill for unloading the pistol is much the same for any weapon, demanding that the handler points it in a safe direction before removing the magazine and bringing the working parts to the rear. These steps ensure that any round chambered, is ejected and allows the handler to see inside the working parts to ensure that it is unloaded. Had Lorimer's magazine been charged, he would not have even needed to follow that drill to check the calibre of the round as a simple removal of the magazine would have sufficed. As it was, when the weapon was examined by Birdwood, the magazine was empty, meaning that the pistol either had a round in the chamber when Lorimer picked it up or he cocked the solitary round as he was checking it. It is not a natural movement for a handler to point the pistol inwards towards themselves. But it is also not uncommon for a weapon to be handled incorrectly resulting in a negligent discharge if the handler is fatigued, distracted or harassed, temporarily disorientated through sickness or a combination of them all.

Had Winstone been familiar with the Persian Gulf political residency monthly and yearly administration reports from 1911 to 1914, he would have seen both Hunt and Birdwood's reports on Lorimer's death. Had he researched the reports further, he would have also found that Bushire was a far from idyllic place to be posted and for some, a posting that ultimately led to suicide. In March 1913, Cox's monthly return reported that Monsieur Dmitrieff, Loika's predecessor as the Russian consulate-general, had deliberately killed himself.[587] Just five months after Lorimer's death in July 1914, the residency diary recorded that Nedjed Rajab, the Turkish consul in Bushire, had also taken his own life.[588] If Lorimer had felt compelled to take his life like several of his foreign contemporaries, he hid his mental state extremely well from Nesta, his co-workers and the wider political network as none of his personal or official correspondence offered any signs of severe depression. Ultimately, however, his cause of death will remain a matter of conjecture, despite Birdwood's enquiry.

A few months after Lorimer's death, Birdwood completed his service in Bushire. This included a brief spell as the temporary political resident until the arrival of Knox, who ultimately got the posting he desired, if not in the manner that he had wanted. On 10 October 1914, Birdwood was in Simla and back as assistant to his former principal, Cox. Cox in turn, had recently been appointed the chief political officer attached to the Indian Expeditionary Force-D (IEF-D) which was about to enter the Great War with a mission to secure the Abadan oil fields. Before both men mobilised to meet the IEF-D in Bahrain as their troop-ships headed further up the Gulf towards Kuwait, there was one outstanding action that needed to be taken.

It was a matter that should have really been taken by Cox, who had been obliged to resume the position as political resident in Bushire following Lorimer's death. Knox was merely officiating in his absence. For whatever reason, it was left to Birdwood to write the introduction to volume one of the gazetteer. It had, he wrote, 'been all but completed for the Press by the late Mr. Lorimer at the time of his death in the beginning of 1914, the only portions in fact of the work then remaining to be written being the "Introduction and the Table of Contents." These have been prepared and the volume completed for the press by the undersigned'.[589]

With a final stroke of a pen, the gazetteer was completed. Despite Birdwood's authorisation to begin printing, it would take another seventeen months before copies of the *Gazetteer of the Persian Gulf, volume I, Historical, Parts I and II* and *Genealogical Tables-Maps, Part III*, were ready to be despatched, in March 1916, almost thirteen years since its initial commissioning. It was a very limited run, with just over a hundred initially printed and distributed.[590] Each had 'secret' stamped in red ink on its first page, which bled through because of the fineness of the paper. Each copy also required appropriate handling instructions as well as a centrally provided serial number with firm instructions that it was not to be amended. Within months of its publication, it was being quoted at length in equally secretive military gazetteers and official handbooks, destined for a far greater distribution.

The despatch of twenty-nine copies of volume one to the government of India's Army Department came far too late to help inform IEF-D's senior commanders as they tried in desperation to extract their troops under siege in Kut. For months, they had been surrounded by opposing Ottoman forces with little chance of being relieved. The siege had been inevitable, following a series of poor command decisions, not helped by overstretched supply lines due to an underappreciation of river steamers capable of navigating the Tigris River. As a result of these bad decisions and poor oversight, thousands of British and Indian soldiers were now dying or starving in the most horrific of circumstances.

From the very beginning, the lack of political will and direction combined with poor military planning had made the Mesopotamian campaign a haphazard affair.[591] Initially bolstered by the IEF-D's early successes in Abadan and Basrah, the political and military planners alike, looked to continue to move north to capture Baghdad. Like the Gallipoli campaign, it was a vain attempt to knock the Turks out of the Great War. The IEF-D's failings and humiliation at Kut soon became a military, political, and ultimately a reputational embarrassment to the British Government. In August 1916, a commission was appointed by Parliament to review the overall conduct of military operations there. Its subsequent report was damning, putting the blame squarely on Sir John Nixon, General Officer commanding British India's Northern Army, Hardinge as viceroy and Austin Chamberlain as the secretary of state for India. The report found that the advance to Baghdad, in particular, had been based on a series of 'political and military miscalculations … and inadequate preparation'.[592] Although not explicitly named for contributing to the disaster, Cox was also named in the report for arguing strongly about the political importance of occupying the city.[593]

He had even supported the recommendation for the continued push with a topographical assessment, that he believed could be achieved through a number of tactical bounds from Basrah, the IEF-D's main staging and logistical base, to the river junction at Al Qurnah and from there to Amarah, Kut and finally to Baghdad.[594] It was an assessment not entirely advocated by Hardinge or Chamberlain but reliant on Cox's supposed depth of local knowledge, and in the absence of anyone else familiar with the region, his recommendation was half-heartedly agreed and the military advance to Baghdad following his suggested route, approved.

Cox's political masters were not the only ones who had doubts about his recommendations. The Right Honourable Aubrey Herbert, the Member of Parliament for South Somerset and lieutenant-colonel in the Irish Guards, recalled meeting Cox in Al Qurnah in April 1916. Although finding the chief political officer to be an amiable man, 'he ha[d] evidently made many mistakes that probably were inevitable since he knew nothing of Turkish politics, or the larger Arab question'.[595] Wilson, who had at one time, hoped to join Lorimer's staff, would later join Cox in Mesopotamia. Although he was far less critical of his superior's style of working than before, he was astounded that the military planners were making more use of Willcocks's irrigation maps and reports than the wealth of local knowledge held in either the consulate in Basrah or Lorimer's gazetteer.[596]

Having spent so long in the region, Cox certainly did have a good grasp of Gulf affairs, but his local knowledge ended at Basrah, the periphery of his political network's catchment. All territory north was squarely in Lorimer's former parish, and the route Cox identified for the big push to Baghdad, was one that his former peer knew well. Had Lorimer been alive at the outbreak of war in the Middle East, it would have been conceivable that he, rather than Cox, would have been the government of India's chosen man and made the IEF-D's chief political officer given his unparalleled knowledge of Mesopotamia. No man is without his faults, but it is the author's hope that Lorimer might not have made the same recommendations or supported such a bold advance. He might have also argued the Turks' invulnerability more generally in Mesopotamia to British military actions, having been privy to the Committee of Imperial Defence's earlier ruminations.[597]

In August 1921, Curzon, now back in government as secretary of state in the Foreign Office, re-ignited his interest in the Gulf when he wrote to Churchill as his ministerial counterpart for the Colonies. It was a plea that the Gazetteer of Arabia should not be allowed to fall out of date.[598] The Gazetteer of Arabia, a military publication produced in 1917 by the government of India's General Staff (rather than Povah's 1887 publication), was one of the first to be produced drawing heavily from Lorimer's gazetteer and then complemented with information that made it more suitable for planning military operations rather than diplomacy. Similarly published in small numbers, but unlike Lorimer's gazetteer, there was always the intent for it to be updated and then distributed more widely. A lack of suitable personnel during the closing stages of the Great War however, had made it impossible.[599]

Curzon had approached the Colonial Office, as with the exception of the Hejaz, the rest of Arabia now sat within its geographical area of responsibility. Despite the government of India's continued presence through its political network, much had changed since Curzon's time as viceroy. He was only made aware of the new relationship custodians with Arabia after he had initially approached the India Office with the same request.[600] But as a military intelligence publication, it was now the responsibility of the War Office rather than the Colonial Office, to update the Gazetteer of Arabia. Before any update could happen, it first required the Army Council's approval. Curzon however, declined to approach the secretary of state at the War Office or the chief of the Imperial General Staff. Although supportive, Churchill, too, understood that such an exercise would come at a financial cost, something that could not be justified by either the Colonial or War Office in a post-war era.[601]

The government of India and the India Office might have been dismissive of offering to update Lorimer's gazetteer or any of its progenies for their former political master having committed considerable funds over the years to cover the cost of its production. The same however, could not be said of their political agents in the Gulf who had been carrying out their own revisions and annotating their issued copies in the expectation that the gazetteer would be a living document. Some had even forwarded alterations and additions to Bushire for onward transmission and consideration by the Foreign and Political Department.[602] Each update was broken down by page, letter and line just as Lorimer would have liked it, should either volume ever be scheduled for a further run. With little appetite in Delhi to revisit the gazetteer, their letters were left unactioned, put away and archived.[603] Soon, interest in its upkeep, waned.

Attitudes looked to have changed in September 1928, when Haworth, formerly part of Lorimer's network of political agents and now a colonel and knight of the Indian empire, arrived in Shiraz to take on the political residency. Having just left as resident in Bushire and previously of Muscat and Arabistan in addition to Muhammerah, he was a very experienced officer of the region.[604] He, too, suggested that Lorimer's gazetteer should be updated, and in his opinion, pressed for an officer to be sent immediately to the Gulf to carry out that very task.[605] It was a strong statement to make to the Foreign and Political Department, particularly given that he was unwilling to release any of his own staff to carry out the work, offering instead, a short-list of suitable officials who might be up for the job.[606] As many times before, it fell to the Finance Department to decide. True to form, the bookkeepers were initially reluctant to commission a special duty as it would require finding additional funds.[607] But surprisingly sympathetic to Haworth's observation about its necessity and immediacy, they agreed that a review could take place as long as the financial burden was absorbed by the Gulf residency from any savings it could make from its 1929 budget.[608]

On 9 January 1929, Major Edward Noel, one of the officials on Haworth's short-list, was given orders to be attached temporarily to Bushire on a four-month special duty to revise the gazetteer.[609] Noel immediately took to the task, requesting to see the agents' archived correspondence as well as any other documents that the Foreign and Political Department felt it would be worth considering.[610] The department duly complied and along with the small bundle of letters and exchanges, it forwarded a catalogue comprised of the Persian Gulf's Administration Reports from 1908 to 1928. A background note on the history of the Dhofar region currently in circulation within the network was also shared with Noel for him to work through.[611]

Although Noel was familiar with the gazetteer, having served briefly in Bushire as the second assistant a few months after Lorimer's death and later as vice consul in Ahwaz, he had not served in the Gulf for a decade and soon seemed detached from his special duty. Either overwhelmed or underappreciative of the true scale of the task even if it was only to update and refresh the history sections, he turned down the offer of a full-time typist to work with him, deciding instead, that he would use the Bushire clerks outside of their normal office hours should any typed work be necessary.[612] Although dated, Noel's familiarity with the region was a useful qualification. A far greater requirement, however, was the ability to source, research, collate and process new information, and as Lorimer had proved, the need for patience and endurance.

Like Lorimer before him, Noel found himself predominantly desk-bound, slowly working through various piles of papers and reports that had been forwarded to him. But unlike the gazetteer's author, he was not accountable to his own high expectations or subject to constant pressure from the Indian capital to complete his task. Beyond Haworth's initial interest, Noel was mostly left to his own devices. He was even able to extend his special duty until 9 June 1929 with little challenge from Delhi. Just before his special duty concluded, he spent a few days at the Muscat political agency, following the Gulf coast down from Bushire by ship just as Lorimer had done before, both with Curzon and on his own over a quarter of a century before. It was Noel's only time out in the field. Shortly after his return, he moved on to Kerman to assume the role of consul, having never used Bushire's administrative staff.

Noel's brief foray was the last chance that the gazetteer had of being updated. Unaware of the special duty's lack of delivery, a year later, enquiries were made by both the Gulf political network and the Army Department about obtaining updated versions of the gazetteer.[613] The Foreign and Political Department's reply was to the point, 'there is no question at present of revising Mr Lorimer's Gazetteer or the Persian Gulf, but that [your] request [has] been noted…'.[614] There would be no second edition.

Chapter 12

Finis Coronet Opus

From its inception, the British and Indian governments were aware of the potential power and influence of the information contained within the gazetteer, both positive and negative. They were equally alert to the possibility that some of their embassies, consulates and legations likely to receive the gazetteer, might be 'un-accustomed to the ways of the Government of India, from duly appreciating the value of the "Secret" denomination given to [it]'.[615] Even with the highest possible classification and handling requirements, Dane and Minto felt the necessity to omit certain passages from Lorimer's early drafts that were still considered too sensitive to be included in the finished product.[616] Despite these sensitivities, in June 1922, the gazetteer's classification was downgraded from secret to 'F.O.U.O.' (For Official Use Only), which in theory, allowed greater access to the wealth of information held within.

In November 1933, twenty-five years after volume two's publication, the Tehran legation tested the revised classification requirements by asking the Foreign and Political Department if Abdulaziz Bey Al Modhaffer, the legation's first secretary, could borrow the gazetteer.[617] Al Modhaffer had first become aware of the publication in 1920 when he was working for the British administration in Mesopotamia. He had even managed to take some notes on various unclassified and classified reports referenced in the gazetteer despite the strictest of instructions at the time on privileged access.[618] Although the revised classification gave local custodians the discretion to share or to show the gazetteer to 'approved persons', there was no guidance or definition on who these persons might be. The only regulation heavily emphasised was that it was not to be communicated, either directly or indirectly, to the media or to anyone not holding an official position within government.[619]

While not explicit, it had never been considered that foreign nationals working for the British or Indian governments would fall within the approved readership catchment even though Lorimer had been assisted by numerous colleagues from the Un-covenanted Civil Service when working on the gazetteer and Hunter's map. The legation's request caught the department off-guard. The only exception that it knew of anyone outside of government seeing the gazetteer had been Lorimer and Lock's friend, Wilson, who had been allowed access in 1922 shortly after he had retired from Crown service, but that hardly set a precedent. Consultations followed at the highest level, including between the viceroy, Rufus Isaac the Earl of Reading and Curzon in the Foreign Office who in light of the nature of the information it contained, agreed that non-British subjects should not fall within the 'approved persons' catchment.[620] The legation's request was refused. Had they been more flexible in their interpretation, the gazetteer might have continued to have been updated informally.

In June 1944, the gazetteer's classification was again subjected to scrutiny. Rather than a further relaxation of the rules, there was a reversion back to secret when the government of India considered that much of its contents were still too sensitive. It was not to be made 'available outside limited official circles [and yet] sufficient precautions are not being observed by holders to prevent it from falling in the hands of unauthorised persons'.[621] It was also a sign of the government's increasing frustration with the way that the gazetteer was being accounted for. A signal was sent around the Gulf network, seeking confirmation of the current locations that should have been in receipt of the gazetteer. Particular attention was given to those previously issued to agencies and consulates that were no longer in existence.[622] It was a pitiful return with only the political agent in Bahrain and the residency agent in Sharjah able to confirm safe custodianship of their gazetteers to the Residency in Bushire.[623] The government was no longer in control of the gazetteer or its potential power.

Two years later, despite being able to account for just a few of both volumes still in the government of India's possession, the gazetteer's secret classification was reaffirmed. But times were changing. The reaffirmation was accompanied by new handling instructions that allowed institutions such as the RGS to obtain copies provided the books remained in secure storage and would only be made available to authorised persons, not that there was any indication who these might be.[624]

Former political resident, and now retired, Haworth was amongst the first to make use of this partial relaxation, when in July 1949, he requested access to the gazetteer whilst researching his own history of the Gulf.[625] There was, he considered, nothing in the publication that could still be considered to be confidential now that it was over thirty years old.[626] As the India Office ceased to exist in 1947 and with it, its papers and library, the Foreign Office was left as the sole custodian in Whitehall but with just a single complete set of the gazetteer. It was, arguably, one of the most prestigious ever in circulation as it had originally been issued to the Arab Bureau in Cairo. Even with Haworth's career in service and close links to the gazetteer, it still took time before he was finally permitted to visit the library to record what he needed. But he was also reminded that it remained a secret publication, and if any of its contents were going to be quoted in his research or memoires, he was to submit his manuscript to the Foreign Office for approval first, before it was published.[627] Had he known that fellow political officer, Wilson, who he had replaced as consul in Luristan in 1911, had donated his copies of the gazetteer to the London Library in St James's Square in 1938, he might have saved himself the trouble of having to abide by the Foreign Office's controls and censorship. Wilson's donation was in itself, odd as it begs the question why he requested access to the gazetteer back in 1922. Whether Haworth ever submitted any of his work for approval is unknown, but four years later, and five years before the Public Act of 1958 had been introduced which governed access to historic public records, the gazetteer was completely declassified.

When the United States entered the Second World War, the gazetteer was classified F.O.U.O. Although never shared with the Americans, it was just the publication that their Office of War Information (OWI) would have exploited to its own advantage in the Gulf. Since the OWI's creation, its immediate remit overseas was tactical, propagating support for the Allied war effort, using whatever information, intelligence and means at hand to spread its propaganda. In some ways, it replicated the activities of the Arab Bureau in the Great War. It also had a longer-term strategic objective, to promote a strong image of America and its role as the new world leader at the expense of the old colonialist powers, including its ally, Great Britain.[628] Like the Arab Bureau, the OWI's Middle East outpost was in Cairo. Within its ranks was the American Arabist, George Rentz, who set up and managed its Department of Research and Translation.

In January 1946, Rentz left Cairo and the OWI to join the Arabia American Oil Company (ARAMCO). ARAMCO was a fairly new entity, founded after Ibn Sa'ud and the Standard Oil Company of California signed a concession agreement in 1933 to survey his territory for oil. After five years of fruitless exploration, oil was finally struck in Dammam. This led the way for further surveys in Arabia, including in territories whose sovereignty had yet to be defined or agreed. In addition to overseeing relations between ARAMCO and the Saudi government, Rentz was also the head of the company's Arabian Research and Translation Division, which provided more direct support to the Saudi government, a feat he managed whilst completing his doctorate on the history of Saudi Arabia in the eighteenth century.[629]

In 1949, he wrote 'The Eastern Reaches of al-Hasa Province'. It was written as much for the Saudi government as it was for academia which was, in the opinion of Arnold Robert Walmsley, a Foreign Office Arabist, 'wildly inaccurate'.[630] Two years later, Walmsley stayed with Rentz in Dhahran when he was part of a British delegation visiting Saudi Arabia to negotiate borders. Whether deliberate or by accident, during the course of his stay, he came across piles of statements produced by his American associate which included transcripts of hundreds of Bedouin who had been interviewed in Buraimi and surrounding areas, territory that the British considered to be under the emir of Abu Dhabi's governance. He also saw for the first time, a copy of Lorimer's gazetteer. When Walmsley refamiliarised himself with a revised copy of Rentz's book on Al Hasa years later, he found that it been corrected substantially by drawing from the gazetteer. It was a fearful realisation that it made ARAMCO and the Saudis nearly 'as knowledgeable about the area as our protégés…'.[631]

As being able to present detailed knowledge, both on the people and the topography would be critical in any future boundary negotiations, ARAMCO's assiduousness in gathering information both for itself and for the Saudis, was a cause for concern.[632] Walmsley was strongly of the view that future reports were not to be shared with the American government in case they were forwarded to ARAMCO and by extension, the Saudi government. Although the American government maintained an anti-colonialist stance that undermined British regional interests, it was not in their interest to see the British completely driven out of the Gulf. Its security was a burden that had to be shared. Saudi Arabia was the centre of Washington's focus to ensure continued access to oil reserves if there was ever a war with the Russians. Its eastern coast was also an area being considered to base the American Pacific naval fleet. To try to balance America's commercial and political investments with both the British and the Saudis, the State Department tried, but was unsuccessful in encouraging Ibn Sa'ud to be reasonable with the British. In an effort to distance itself from any Foreign Office resentment, the department claimed convincingly, that they thought it unlikely that ARAMCO really was the driving force behind Saudi Arabia's sovereignty claims.

As condemnatory as Walmsley was about ARAMCO's actions, he had nothing but praise and respect for Rentz's 'wonderful nose for new material… [and considered it] a fine achievement on his part that he had a microfilm copy of Lorimer long before … [British] oil company officials got access to it…'.[633] Walmsley's only regret was that the Foreign Office had allowed the company to photograph the whole of the publication without questioning why, when it had just been declassified.[634] He must have also been impressed by the fact that either Rentz or a colleague, would have spent months producing a facsimile of the gazetteer's 6,317 pages, twenty-one genealogical trees, a map of pearling banks between Ras Tanurah and Diba and the four large sheets that made up Hunter's map.

Walmsley was not alone in having concerns about Rentz and ARAMCO's research to strengthen Saudi Arabia's otherwise ambiguous territorial claims.[635] For some time, there was already apprehension within other parts of the Foreign Office as well as within the Iraq Petroleum Company as a competitor of ARAMCO, about the activities of both. These earlier concerns were only realised when it came to light that Rentz and his team's research on Oman and the Trucial Coast was the foundation of Saudi Arabia's decision to send ARAMCO prospectors to territory in Abu Dhabi that the Saudis notionally claimed to be theirs. This led to the 1949 'Stobart Incident', named after Sharjah's political agent, Patrick Stobart, who along with a couple of armed levies visited ARAMCO's site when they became aware of their presence and demanded that they stop their operations.

Lorimer's gazetteer was ideal for answering the various questions about sovereignty in parts of Arabia when the Ottoman empire and its Caliphate collapsed in 1922. With some expectation, the British naturally assumed that Ibn Sa'ud would automatically become the successor of Ottoman territories in the peninsula and therefore, be equally bound to the boundaries identified in the 1913 Anglo-Turk agreement. Ibn Sa'ud, however, had refused to accept this understanding as he had always been clear of his intent to reclaim as much of his family's ancestral territories as possible, whilst respecting its own treaty obligations. When the British government's own lawyers advised that much of the territories were in fact, not yet owned or claimed or in legal parlance, '*res nullius*', they continued that it was for the various contesting states to prove that they had sovereign rights.[636]

The matter was partly resolved in 1927, when the British and the Saudis signed the Treaty of Jeddah, recognising Ibn Sa'ud's sovereignty in Najd and Hejaz.[637] With the gazetteer recording a *Wahhabi* presence in western Arabia and Hejaz since 1765, it was able to reconcile Ibn Sa'ud's interpretation of history with their own. Eight years later, both sides attempted to agree Saudi Arabia's south and eastern borders with the British proposing a straight-lined boundary that started at the coast east of Abu Dhabi and down to the Empty Quarter. They called the demarcation, the Riyadh Line. The Saudi counter-proposal was more curvaceous, but for the most part, paralleled the Riyadh Line except in the north-east where it diverted to include Khor Al Udaid, a stretch of coastline belonging to Qatar. In 1938, with neither side willing to reconcile or compromise, dialogue finally broke down. They did not return to the negotiating table until 1949, after Stobart's intervention checked Saudi advances.

When talks reopened, the Saudis presented a new boundary that differed considerably to their 1935 proposal, one that swept up a vast amount of Abu Dhabi, absorbing the Liwa oasis to the south and east as far as Buraimi. To encourage negotiation rather than conflict, the British reverted back to the Anglo-Turk 1913 boundaries. They also put the onus on the Saudis to produce evidence to support their new territorial claims beyond the treaty's boundaries, knowing that the gazetteer would be able to counter any spurious Saudi claim. With neither side willing to submit detailed evidence of their respective positions, in February 1951 it was decided that a joint-fact-finding commission should visit all the areas in dispute to appreciate the position on the ground and following consultations with the peoples who lived there, it would present its findings and objective recommendations to both governments. Until that time, it was agreed that no military or commercial activities under either government's control should take place in the disputed areas.

Before the commission was organised, it was agreed that there should be a second conference. Hosted by the Saudis in Dammam from late January to mid-February 1952, it was here that both sides finally presented detailed statements of their respective claims. The Saudis argued that the major tribes in the disputed areas owed allegiance to Ibn Sa'ud and paid tax or *zakat* to him on their camels. The British delegation, led by political resident Sir Rupert Hay and accompanied by Sheikh Zayed bin Sultan Al Nahyan of Abu Dhabi, and Sheikh Ali bin Abdullah Al Thani of Qatar, countered that the tribes claimed by the Saudis had, instead, always pledged allegiance to the sheikh of Abu Dhabi. Such allegiance and loyalty were evidenced by the *zakat* that was paid on their date groves, pearling and fishing rights, in return for protection. To reinforce the sheikh's argument, historical official reports from earlier political residents and the gazetteer were quoted at length.[638]

Keen to come to an agreement, the British delegation offered what they considered to be a generous concession, by returning to the Riyadh Line. The Saudis, however, 'refused to moderate in any way the extreme limits of their wildest claim which they had put forward in 1949'.[639] To add insult to the gesture, the Saudis also denied that they had previously proposed a boundary which for the most part, corresponded closely to the Riyadh Line. This was despite records of the discussion as well as an unofficial Saudi government note later shared with the British being in the possession of the Foreign Office. In the absence again of any compromise or rationality, it was agreed to resume discussions at a later date.

Although the Dammam conference failed to deliver a mutually agreed boundary, it exposed that much of the Saudi claim weighed on the supposed allegiance of the tribes found inland in Liwa, Jiban, Jafurah, Mijan and Agal near Khor Al Udaid.[640] And yet despite both sides' claims, beyond the gazetteer and the odd report to the Foreign Department, little was known about the various expanses and peoples. When British diplomat, Martin Buckmaster subsequently visited to familiarise himself with the disputed area, both he and the Trucial Sheikhs relied heavily on Lorimer's work, which was itself, mostly formed from Cox and Gabriel's visit there in 1905. The more recent findings of the British explorer, Wilfred Thesiger who had travelled extensively throughout the disputed areas, also helped them appreciate their surroundings.[641]

Once confident of the sheikh of Abu Dhabi's sovereignty claims, the British considered how best to approach future negotiations.[642] This included presenting the original documents recording their 1935 boundary discussions which the Saudis had previously denied had happened. They also pulled out the various treaties and agreements that had been agreed over the years with the Al Sa'ud. Among them were an exchange of letters between Pelly and emirs Faisal and Abdullah Al Sa'ud in 1866, the 1915 Treaty of Darin and 1927 Treaty of Jeddah, none of which confirmed the Saudi claim of sovereignty in the disputed areas. Lorimer's gazetteer was also presented as evidence that the tribes in Abu Dhabi and Qatar were independent of Saudi domination.

If the boundaries could still not be agreed, the British believed that consideration should then be given to the current allegiance of the permanent tribes in the disputed areas and settlements, whilst ignoring any loyalties that the nomadic tribes might pledge.[643] The change in tactic was a sensible one given the lack of other options, but as both they, and Rentz knew from the gazetteer, the great Arab sheikhs ruled by influence rather than as absolute monarchs. Their subjects, even those who were settled, only voluntarily accepted their rulers' dominion if it was beneficial to do so.[644] Allegiance and loyalty were fickle, precarious and at times, little more than transactional affairs.[645]

In late August 1952, when the heat of the desert was at its most intense, a Saudi convoy carrying armed soldiers and administrators drove to Buraimi, exercising in their minds at least, legitimate governance

John Gordon Lorimer in Foreign Office diplomatic uniform with his Companion of the Indian Empire medal and India medal with Punjab Frontier and Waziristan clasps.

Left David Lockhart Robertson (Lock) Lorimer in his Queen's Own Corps of Guides uniform.

Below left Some of the Lorimer family
Top row, left to right: Hilda, John Gordon, Emilia
Middle row, left to right: The Reverend Robert, Isabella, Major General David Robertson (Isabella's brother)
Bottom row, left to right: Charles, Florence

Below Right John Gordon Lorimer's medals.

Above RIMS *Hardinge* and accompanying East India Squadron during Curzon's grand tour.
Below Durbar on-board HMS *Argonaut* at Sharjah.

Above A less than grand landing at Kuwait.
Below Sheikh Mubarak Al Sabah's carriage, the only wheeled vehicle in Kuwait waiting for Curzon's arrival.

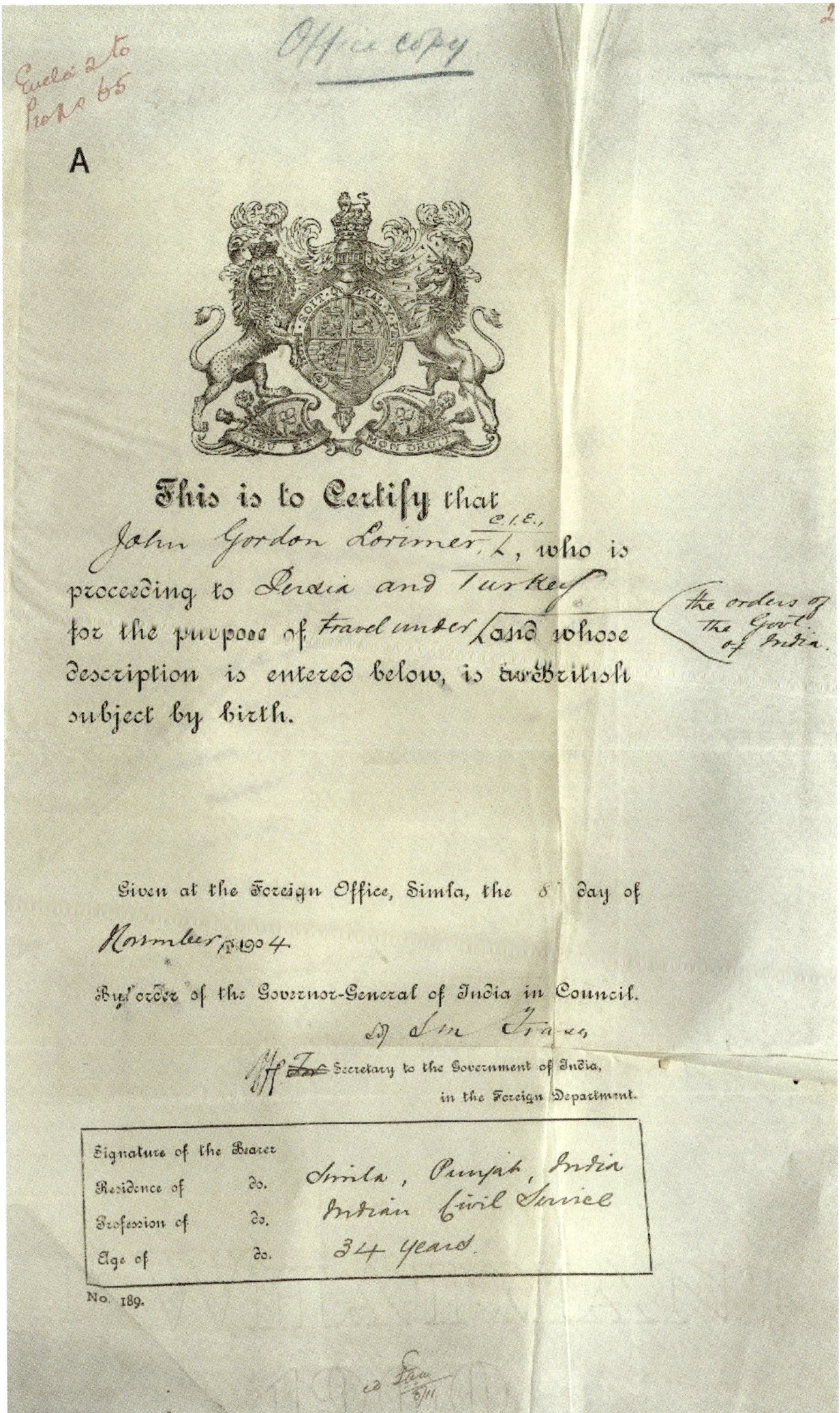
Office copy

Encl. 2 to Pro. No 65

A

This is to Certify that John Gordon Lorimer, C.I.E., who is proceeding to Persia and Turkey for the purpose of travel under the orders of the Govt. of India and whose description is entered below, is a British subject by birth.

Given at the Foreign Office, Simla, the 8th day of November 1904.

By order of the Governor-General of India in Council.

Sd. S. M. Fraser

Offg. Secretary to the Government of India, in the Foreign Department.

Signature of the Bearer		
Residence of	do.	Simla, Punjab, India
Profession of	do.	Indian Civil Service
Age of	do.	34 years

No. 189.

Lorimer's passport for travel in Persia and Ottoman-controlled territories.

Above The newly-built political agency in Manamah, considered to be one of the best buildings in the Bahraini capital at the time.

Below The political agency and residence in Muscat alongside the Sultan's palace.

Above & *Right* Bushire coastline, known locally by British officials and expatriates as 'the colony'.

Below Political residency and RIMS *Comet*. The presence of both was a constant irritant with the Ottoman authorities.

Above Bushire residency in Kuti, one of the town's four principal wards.

Below Troops on parade at Rishehr garrison, Bushire. Many would later form part of Lorimer's funeral precession.

over three settlements in the oasis on the basis that each had previously paid *zakat* to Al Sa'ud tax collectors in the nineteenth century. Lorimer's gazetteer offered a different understanding of Buraimi's history, observing that in 1905, although at that time independent, the influence of the sheikh of Abu Dhabi was strong and increasing. At a turn of a page, the gazetteer could also list the number of settlements, population size and tribal affiliation, size of livestock, extent of agriculture and trade. It even knew what the inhabitants' regular diet consisted of. Most importantly, it recorded that a regular tribute was also paid to the sheikh.

The villages targetted by the Saudis, however, were no longer under Abu Dhabi's protection, but belonged to a section of the Na'im tribe, who gave their loyalty to Sultan Sa'id ibn Taimur in Muscat. A tense standoff ensued as the sultan and Mohammed Al Khalili, the Imam of Oman, mustered their troops in Sohar and in the interior to lay siege upon the Saudi invaders. Trucial Oman Levies (TOL) were also mobilised in Abu Dhabi, ready to defend the oasis and soon, RAF Vampire jets patrolled the skies overhead.[646] Through tact and diplomacy, sufficient mutual face-saving was eventually found to avoid any further escalation. A standstill agreement was drawn up and signed by the British and the Saudis on 26 October. Both sides would test the spirit of the agreement. Whilst the British and their local allies blockaded the Saudi presence, several TOL soldiers including its British commander were murdered by assailants under Saudi influence.

In September 1955, the Buraimi Arbitration Tribunal met in Geneva. Its mandate was to resolve the sovereignty issue but it ultimately failed to achieve its objective. There is one argument that the British abrogated the tribunal when it became increasingly clear that their case was not as strong as they had hoped.[647] Another holds that Saudi bribery of the local tribes, attempted subversion and intimidation, including of some of the tribunal panel members was sufficient for proceedings to be suspended.[648] When the arbitration was discussed in Parliament, it was believed that one local sheikh had been offered thirty million dollars to pledge loyalty to the Saudis.[649]

Regardless, when the British concluded that the arbitration was dead, it was agreed that the memorials presented by both the Saudi and British delegations, should be secured in a jointly funded safety deposit box held by the Union Bank of Switzerland in Geneva. It came with clear instructions that neither side could access the box's contents without prior agreement from the other.[650] The sovereignty of the oasis has long since been resolved. While Buraimi itself sits within Oman's territory, Al Ain, one of the oasis's settlements, sits just across the border in the United Arab Emirates. Despite the oasis's resolution, the box remains under lock and key in Geneva. In addition to both memorials, its contents include tribunal meeting minutes, audio tapes and transcripts, press cuttings, a large, framed object wrapped in brown paper, three green leather-bound volumes of the Gazetteer of Arabia and both volumes of Lorimer's gazetteer.[651]

The year 1949 would see the Foreign Office involved in another negotiation over territory involving a Gulf state. Newly founded and independent Pakistan also asked for British assistance, having expressed an interest in reacquiring Gwadar, which the gazetteer observed, had at one time been administered by a *wali* appointed by Muscat, supported by twenty local soldiers or *askaris*. Supportive in principle to Pakistan's request, not least to demonstrate Britain's leadership within the new commonwealth, the Foreign Office, as the new custodian of Gulf affairs, found itself in a difficult position. It felt uncomfortable putting pressure on the sultan to relinquish the enclave given recent Saudi encroachment on its subjects in Buraimi. When the sultan was eventually made aware of Pakistan's interest, although not dismissive, he was unprepared to negotiate, or at least, to enter into dialogue directly.[652]

With little progress made, in January 1953, Gwadar was raised again with the British. This time, there was a sense of urgency as the Pakistanis had heard rumours that the sultan intended to sell or lease the enclave to the government of India, a move that Karachi considered, would be a most 'unfriendly act'.[653] Again, they expressed their desire to purchase the enclave, and upped their stake by refusing to recognise the sultan's sovereignty, contradicting their previous position which acknowledged the inhabitants as his subjects.[654] As with the Buraimi talks, the historic payment of tribute or *pishkash*, made by Muscat to the *khans* of Kalet whose jurisdiction previously included the enclave, was central to their claim.[655] With so few documents in the India Office's archives to confirm the suzerainty of the enclave, it was left to the gazetteer to inform officials on the British position. Lorimer's segment on both the district and the town, was considerable. Drawn from Captain Edward Ross's reporting from his brief tenure there as assistant political agent in 1869 and Ralph Hughes-Buller's 1907 gazetteer of Baluchistan, there was little to support Pakistan's claim, which was subsequently judged to be 'little deserving of countenance'.[656] That was not what the Commonwealth Relations Office, a new ministry formed from the disbanded India and Colonial Offices, wanted to hear, but was one that its own legal advisors agreed with when presented with Lorimer's gazetteer, even if there were some who harboured doubts about the exact circumstances of the sultan's possession.[657]

Indirect negotiations about Gwadar's future were taken forward nonetheless with the disinterested sultan, whose attitude changed when the possible presence of oil became a consideration. By late 1955, it had also become a political priority for British prime minister, Anthony Eden, who had been openly criticised for not being as supportive to Pakistan regarding border discussions over Kashmir and Afghanistan as the Russians had been of the Indians.[658] With the sultan, himself, unsure of the extent of his enclave and the Pakistanis of the understanding that it was limited to the port and immediate surrounding area, the gazetteer was again consulted to pinpoint Gwadar's boundaries. When Lorimer's findings were relayed to the Pakistanis, they remained unpersuaded but had limited room to challenge given the lack of supplementary evidence of their own.[659] Peeved by the sultan's continued obstructiveness, and now agitated by rumours that he had awarded oil concessions in Gwadar,[660] the Pakistani Prime Minister, Chaudhry Mohammed Ali, attempted to threaten Morrice James, the British Acting High Commissioner that 'it was within his power by a single whisper to the Press to create so much doubt about the international position of Gwadur that no oil company would proceed'.[661] Ali's officials also let it be known that they had other levers of persuasion, not least a customs cordon that would soon stop any revenues from the enclave reaching Muscat. There was nothing to stop them from simply taking it over as it had no defences, something that they had resisted so far because they had no wish to embarrass the British, not that Britain's regional military superiority had any influence in their reasoning.[662]

Sensitive to further negative press, the British continued to support Pakistan's case. In late February 1956, this included James discussing Lorimer's extract on Gwadar with the Pakistani prime minister, the outcome of which was a tacit acknowledgement of its boundaries. As part of their due diligence, a copy of the gazetteer and supporting documents were requested by the Pakistani ministry of foreign affairs. It is unclear if they received them given the British government's ambiguous handling requirements. Negotiations continued slowly until the summer of 1958 when the Pakistani government applied direct pressure on the sultan, refusing to allow any of its nationals in his armed forces to serve in combatant roles.[663] This was a substantial blow as it affected the sultan's ability to fight the Jebal Akhdar rebellion being led by Imam Ghalib Al Hinai (Imam Al Khalili's successor), reducing his ability to put men on the ground to clear areas strafed and bombed by RAF Venoms.[664] On 1 August, with Britain positioned as mediator, both sides finally agreed to the terms of the sale. One month later, a payment of three million pounds (three hundred thousand of which would be paid in US dollars) was made by the Pakistanis.[665] The complete transfer, or return, of ownership followed six days later.

In 1969, now over six decades old, the gazetteer was still far from being a peripheral publication in contemporary global affairs when it was lent to Signor Winspear Giuccardi, a United Nations Representative. Despite being in the public domain for sixteen years, when the United Kingdom's United Nations mission in New York handed the publications over, they erroneously stated that it was 'strictly speaking, still classified'.[666] It is an understanding that continues to exist today in some parts of the Foreign, Commonwealth and Development Office, the latest successor to the Foreign, India and Colonial Offices. Rather than be used to support a territorial claim, the decision to share the gazetteer with Giuccardi was to help him understand the history of Bahrain ahead of a UN-sponsored survey the following year, the outcome of which would declare that rather than remain under British governance or to be placed under Iranian control, the people of Bahrain wanted independence to determine their own future.[667]

It should have been of no surprise to the British mission in New York as it was preparing Giuccardi's briefing, that Arabic translations of the gazetteer were also in existence and starting to be used in global politics.[668] If Lorimer's work was mostly ignored by British policy planners in the late 1910s and early 1920s, it had substantial influence and weight in the 1950s and 1960s, informing decisions about border disputes and shaping the region. By association, it was also allocating potential hydrocarbon reserves and wider economic benefits. Through Rentz, the Saudis had their version of the gazetteer and were trying to use it to their advantage. Translating its contents into Arabic, however, was a mammoth task that came with risks, not least syntax, context and the need to reverse Lorimer's transliterations. This was something that the Qataris potentially found to their cost, when they used a translated version of the gazetteer to support their case at the International Court of Justice (ICJ), claiming sovereignty and territorial waters already claimed by the Bahrainis. These claims included the Hawar Islands, Janan Island, the shoals of Al Dibal and Al Jaradah and the district of Zubarah. With blatant errors such as the gazetteer's 'fort of Arad on Muharraq island' translated into 'the fort of Arathy on Mohammerah island', the quality of proof-reading and fact-checking of the gazetteer held by the Qataris, left much to be desired.[669]

As well as relying on a gazetteer that was pocked with inaccuracies as the foundation of their claim, the Qataris were also alleged by the Bahrainis to have submitted eighty-one false or forged documents.[670] Some contained factual inaccuracies but if accepted at face value, confirmed Qatari sovereignty over the disputed areas. Although the Qatari authorities took exception to Bahrain's allegations and detailed forensic reports in response, they 'decided … [to inform the IJC] to disregard all the challenged documents for the purposes of the present case, so as to enable the Court to address the merits of the case without further procedural complications'.[671]

Throughout the 1990s, both countries continued to quote the gazetteer extensively in their memorials, counter-memorials, rights to reply and rejoinders to assert their respective claims.[672] When the ICJ gave its final judgement on 16 March 2001, it found that while Bahrain had sovereignty over the Hawar Islands, Al Jaradah and Zubarah, it was persuaded by the evidence presented that Janan Island and Al Dibal belonged to Qatar, just as Lorimer had recorded in the gazetteer.[673] A single maritime boundary that divided the various maritime zones was also established and in doing so, resolved Qatar and Bahrain's territorial dispute. Not only did the ICJ's final judgement also quote Lorimer, so did five of the fifteen judges on the panel in their individual declarations and opinions.

Ownership of the Hawar Islands had first been subject to the government of India's scrutiny in 1936. Its decision in late 1940 to recognise Bahraini sovereignty of the islands, was not without its critics. Charles Prior, political agent in Bahrain from 1929 to 1932 and political resident since 1939, considered the decision unfair and unlikely to carry any weight with an Arab, Bahraini or Qatari.[674] It was both his and Lorimer's opinion that the islands belonged to Qatar.[675] Compelled to consult the gazetteer themselves, the India Office replied that it was hard to deduce any sovereignty or propriety rights from the gazetteer, as the only reference made to them was limited to one of the islands adjoining Qatar's western coast. But if consideration was given to current occupancy and use of the islands, the weight of evidence appeared strongly in Bahrain's favour.[676] Sixty years later, the ICJ concurred.

By the time that the gazetteer was declassified, it was already nearly half a century old. Although Lorimer had exercised great due diligence throughout his years of torturous authorship, some of the sources that survived his scrutiny were dubious, as were some of its assumptions. And while some were accompanied by honest caveats about their spurious provenance, others were written, and accepted, at face value. When the gazetteer was first reprinted in 1970, it was finally subjected to a book review. The author of the review was Robin Bidwell, who from 1968 until 1990, was secretary and librarian of the Middle East Centre at Cambridge university, as well as the editor of the journal, *Arabian Studies*. With his own substantial grasp of the region and its history, he observed that it lacked scholarly impartiality and assumed the 'wisdom and benevolence of Imperial policy'.[677] The gazetteer had also glossed over or omitted altogether, events that denigrated the empire or its behaviour.[678] But he also noted that despite being an official document, it contained pen portraits daubed with 'splendid frankness' and displayed other human touches, was 'a masterpiece of thoroughness, … a mass of invaluable information [and] indispensable for anyone seriously interested in the Gulf [even if] not all … can be accepted without checking'.[679]

Many recent academics and historians have similarly questioned the impartiality and accuracy of some of the gazetteer's contents. Lorimer has been blamed for introducing or reinforcing nomenclature, myths and falsehoods in the Gulf, not least by Mohammed Al Qasimi, the emir of Sharjah, who criticised him for using the term the Pirate Coast despite Lorimer clearly questioning its use back in 1905.[680] It has also been claimed that it was produced to consolidate Britain's informal rule in the Gulf, deliberately misrepresenting the history of the Gulf and fixing territorial boundaries 'in the region's turbulent tribal hinterlands' to the empire's advantage.[681] Lorimer's characterisation and perceived strengths and weaknesses in key individuals relative to their relationship to the empire, was also seen as a form of selective recognition. Not specific to Lorimer's work, questions have been asked more generally about the historical accuracy of gazetteers as references as some locations were only defined as such for the purpose of the publication or because of an occurrence of some kind formalising its identity.[682] Here at least Lorimer accepted that in some cases, some locations did not have a local name. And yet despite the objective challenge in some quarters of academia and the sneering in others, almost all have quoted it extensively in their work to add valuable context and background in the absence of any other material. Whatever the gazetteer's faults, Rentz was not alone in believing it to be the 'most important single reference on the area for the nineteenth century'.[683]

It is understandable why the question of updating its contents was never meaningfully answered. Even today with greater access to archives, modern communications and digitalisation, it would be a mammoth task to bring the gazetteer up to date.[684] Despite Noel's brief dalliance with the gazetteer, it was hard to identify anyone within the IPS's Gulf network in the years after Lorimer's tenure and death who could have meaningfully and respectfully continued his opus maximus. Thirty-seven days after volume one's introduction had been typed and despatched to the government printers in Calcutta, Birdwood was killed in Mesopotamia after being struck by shrapnel from Ottoman artillery somewhere in Abadan who were firing on Indian and British IEF-D troops as they fought through the island and marshlands to secure the oil-fields. Two months after the loss of Birdwood, Shakespear was gunned down in a major tribal clash in Jirab deep in the heart of the Najdi interior, on his own special duty as a political envoy to Ibn Sa'ud, tasked to persuade the emir and the tribes to support Britain's military objectives in Abadan and beyond. Leachman was fortunate to survive the Great War. After successfully leading some of the IEF-D's cavalry from Kut in December 1915 before they were surrounded by Ottoman forces, he continued to operate in his unique style, mostly in the Syrian interior and around the fringes of Mesopotamia rather than in Arabia but in August 1920, he too was killed, murdered by Sheikh Dhari ibn Mahmud of the Zoba tribe in Fallujah as he tried to resolve local tensions.[685] Another former house-guest, Gertrude Bell, also played an active role in Mesopotamia during the Great War, working with Cox and others as an oriental secretary in the Arab Bureau, initially in Cairo but subsequently in Basrah after the IEF-D had recovered from its failings in Kut and was again on the advance to capture Baghdad. On 12 July 1926, she was found dead in Baghdad, believed to have overdosed on sleeping tablets. Prideaux, previously acknowledged by Lorimer as a potential replacement to complete the gazetteer when the Finance Department winced about the rising costs although not one who could count on Cox's confidence, disappeared from the Gulf political network in 1909. He would not return until 1924, following his father's footsteps as the political resident in Bushire, retiring from the service three years later. Gabriel, despite a brief return to Bushire in 1919, spent the rest of his time in India. Lock, the brother who nearly died in the pursuit of knowledge for his older sibling, continued his service in the region, joining Bushire in 1916 until 1920. His final post as political agent was in Gilgit, in the princely state of Jammu and Kashmir, eventually retiring in 1927.

In April that same year, distinguished British orientalist, archaeologist, wanderer-scholar and president of the RGS, David George Hogarth, delivered a speech to the society, appreciating the life of Gertrude Bell. Among those in the audience, sat Bell's father, Cox and Brigadier-General Gilbert Clayton, former chief of the Arab Bureau. The primary topic of the presentation was Bell's journey to

Ha'il in March 1914. After talking through her detailed notes, those present were asked to appreciate the importance more generally about collating detailed information about Arabia. Cox, too, stood to speak about the great British Arabian explorers, attributing much of the hard work and success from the Blunts and Doughty to Lawrence, Leachman, Shakespear, and of course, Bell.[686]

Had classification allowed, or indeed, had he even been inclined, Cox might have been equally generous in offering praise to Lorimer, not just because of his gazetteer, but also as a result of his own travels and exploits in the pursuit of knowledge. One can only hope that Cox consciously and benevolently, included his former contemporary when commenting more generally about other Arabian travellers that evening. Given Lorimer's modesty, it is, perhaps, more fitting that it was left to the American academic, Rentz to consider the gazetteer the most important single reference for the history of the Gulf. That Bidwell, whose own scholarly work on the Middle East is required reading in academia, considered Lorimer's work to have been a masterpiece and invaluable despite its flaws and biases, is also testament to the man and his work.

Bell was buried at the British cemetery in Baghdad's Bab Al Sharji district. Leachman, too, was laid to rest in Baghdad, at the British War Cemetery. Shakespear's body was never recovered, but he shares the Heliopolis (Aden) memorial in Cairo, wrongly commemorated along with over six hundred other soldiers who died in the defence of Aden. Birdwood was buried in what is now, the Commonwealth War Grave in Basrah. Birdwood, like Bell, Leachman and Shakespear, never married. It was, therefore, the final duty of his parents to choose the epitaph on his headstone. They decided on 'Finis Coronat Opus' – the end crowns the work. It is an apt final mark of remembrance to their son. It is, arguably, an equally-fitting idiom to commemorate Lorimer and his gazetteer.

Summary of the Gazetteer

Gazetteer of the Persian Gulf. Vol I. Historical Part IA & IB
J.G. Lorimer 1915

Vol.1 pt.1a Historical pp.1-778

Vol.1 pt.1b Historical continued pp.779-1624

Gazetteer of the Persian Gulf. Vol I. Historical Part II
J.G. Lorimer 1915

Vol.1 pt.2 (c) Historical continued and appendices pp.1625-2741

Appendix

A Meteorology and Health in the Persian Gulf (pp.2205–2211)

B Geology of the Persian Gulf (pp.2212–2219)

C The Pearl and Mother of Pearl Fisheries of the Persian Gulf (pp.2220–2293)

D Date Production and the Date Trade in the Persian Gulf Region (pp.2294–2307)

E Fisheries of the Persian Gulf (pp.2308–2318)

F Sailing Craft of the Persian Gulf (pp.2319–2332)

G Transport Animals and Livestock of the Persian Gulf Region (pp.2333–2348)

H Religions and Sects of the Persian Gulf Region (pp.2349–2385)

I Western Christianity and Missions in the Persian Gulf Region (pp.2386–2399)

J The Telegraphs of the Persian Gulf in their relation to the Telegraph Systems of Persia and Turkey (pp.2400–2438)

K Mail Communications and the Indian Post Office in the Persian Gulf (pp.2439–2474)

L The Slave Trade in the Persian Gulf Region (pp.2475–2516)

M Epidemics and Sanitary Organization in the Persian Gulf Region (pp.2517–2555)

N The Arms and Ammunition Traffic in the Gulfs of Persia and Oman (pp.2556–2593)

O The Imperial Persian Customs (pp.2594–2625)

P Cruise of His Excellency Lord Curzon, Viceroy of India, in the Persian Gulf [1903] (pp. 2626–2662)

Q British and Foreign Diplomatic Political; and Consular Representation in the Countries Bordering on the Persian Gulf (pp.2663–2699)

R Book References (pp.2700–2736)

S Explanation of the System of Transliteration (pp.2737–2741)

Gazetteer of the Persian Gulf. Vol. I. Geneaological Tables-Maps Part III J.G. Lorimer 1915

Vol. 1 pp.1–21

Al Busaidi of Oman and Zanzibar
Qasimi of Sharjah
Al Bu Falah (Bani Yas) of Abu Dhabi
Al Bu Falasah (Bani Yas) of Dubai
Al Ali of Umm-Al-Quwain
Al Bu Kharaiban (Na'im) of Ajman
Qasimi formerly of Lingeh
Al Thani (Ma'adhid) of Doha
Al Khalifah (Atbi) of Bahrain
Salman senior branch
Salman junior branch
Abdullah branch
Al Sabah (Atbi) of Kuwait
Al Sa'ud (Anizah) of Southern Najd
Anizah branch
Farhan branch
Thanaiyan branch
Muhammed branch (ruling)
Mashari branch
Al Rashid (Shammar) of Jabal Shammar
Abul Khail (Anizah) of Buraidah, Qasim
Salaimi (Sabai) of Anaizah, Qasim
Qadiriyah (Saiyid) of the Naqibis, Baghdad
Pearl Banks chart between Ras Tanurah and Diba

Gazetteer of the Persian Gulf. Vol. II. Geographical and Statistical J.G. Lorimer 1908. pp.1-1952

LORIMER INTRODUCTION. PP. I–IV

A

Abadilah; Abbadan; Abbas (Bandar); Abdullah (Khor); Abriyin; Adai (Wadi); Adam; Adan; Adan (Barr al); Adi (Bani); Aflaj; Ahin (Wadi); Ahram; Ahwaz District; Ahwaz Village; Aid; Ain (Wadi al); Ainain; Aja or Ija (Jabal); Ajaira Wiyah; Ajaj (Qal at al); Ajirub; Ajman Town & Principality; Ajman Tribe; Akhdhar (Jabal); Ali; Ali (Abu); Ali (al or ahl); Ali (al Bin); Ali (Balad Bani Bu); Ali (al Gharbi); Amamarah; Amarah Qadha; Amarah Town; Anafijeh; Anaizah; Andam (Wadi); Angali; Anizah; Aqal; Aqdah; Aqili; Aqq (Wadi al); Arab (Shatt al); Arabah (Bani); Arabi; Arabistan; Arabistan (Northern); Arabistan (Southern); Arad; Araqi; Aridh District; Aridh Village; Arzanah; Asalu; Ashraf; Asis (Badd al); Asuh (Darveh); Ataibah; Atub; Audhan (Zor al); Auf (Wadi Bani); Awabi; Awal; Awamir; Awazim; Ayun; Azair; Aziziyah Qadha; Aziziyah Village. pp.1–193. 70 entries

B

Badi; Badiyah; Baghdad City; Baghdad Qadha; Baharinah; Bahlah; Bahmanshir; Bahrain Island; Bahrain Principality; Bahriyah; Bai'ah or Bi'ah; Baidhah (Khor al); Bait al Falaj (Wadi); Bakhtiyari (Tribe); Balarud or Bilarud; Baluchi Tribes; Band i qir, Bandakil or Banaudeh, Baqa'a; Baqa qalah; Buraimi Oasis; Buraimi Village; Barkah; Ba'rur (Um al); Basidu; Basrah Qadha; Basrah Town; Bastak; Batih; Batin or Batain; Batinah; Battash (Bani); Battash (Wadi Bani); Bawiyeh; Bayasirah; Behbehan; Bgahilah; Bidyah; Bilad al Qadim; Biyaban; Biyadh; Boshar (Wadi); Bubiyan; Budaiya; Buqum; Buraidah; Burazjan; Busaitin; Bushehr Peninsula; Bushehr Town; Buziyeh or Biziyeh or Buzi. pp.194–351. 51 entries

C

Chah Kutah; Chahbar Bay; Chahbar Town; Charak; Chiru; Clarence Strait. pp.351–357. 6 entries

D

Dabaisi; Dagharah; Daghmar; Dahanah; Dair; Daiyinah; Daiyir; Daliki; Dalmah; Dam or Ildam; Daraiyah; Daru; Das; Dashti; Dashtistan; Dawairij; Dawasir Islands and District; Dawasir Tribe; Dawasir (Widyan); Dha'ain; Dhabi (Abu) Principality; Dhabi (Abu) Town; Dhafir; Dhafrah; Dhahiyah; Dhahran (Barr adh); Dhahuriyin; Dhaid; Dhakhirah; Dhaluf (Abu); Dhank Town; Dhank (Wadi); Dhawahir; Dhrumah; Dhufar or District; Dhufar or Proper; Dibah; Dibai Principality; Dibai Town; Dibdibah; Dih Kuhneh; Dilaim; Dilam or Dailam; Dilam; Dima (Wadi); Dimnah; Diwaniyah Qadha; Diz River or Ab i Diz; Dizful District; Dizful Town; Dohah; Doraq or Doraq; Doraqistan; Dukhan, Jabal ad; Durugah or Durudgah; Duvvan. pp.357–493. 56 entries

E

Euphrates or Furat; pp.493–510. 1 entry

F

Fadhul; Fahaihil or Fahahil; Fahal; Faid; Failakah Island; Failiyeh; Fakkan (Khor); Falaij (Wadi); Fallahiyeh District; Fallahiyeh Town; Fallujah; Fantas; Fao; Fara (Wadi); Farangi (Kut al); Fars; Farsi; Faruq (Wadi); Farur; Farur (Nabiiyu); Fasht (Fasht Khor); Fawars; Fujairah; Fuwairat. pp.510–556. 24 entries

G

Gabandi; Ganaveh; Gargar or Ab i Gargar; Gat'ah; Ghafalah; Ghafir (Wadi Bani); Ghallah; Ghanam (Jazirat al); Gharaf (Shatta l); Gharif; Ghubbat Gazirah; Ghuraib (Abu); Ghuwar; Gulf Ports; Gulshan; Gupal; Gwadar District; Gwadar Town; Gwatar. pp.556–591.19 entries

H

Habib (Bani); Habl; Habus; Hadd (I); Hadd (II); Hadiyah; Hafar; Haffar; Hai Qadha; Hai Town or Kut al Hai; Hail; Hail (Abu); Hail al Ghaf; Haiyad; Hajar; Hajar and Khatt Hajar; Hajar (Eastern); Hajar (Khor al); Hajar (Western); Hajir (Bani) or Huwajir; Hajriyin; Halaifah (Abu); Halfain (Wadi); Halul; Ham (Wadi); Hamad; Hamaid; Hamaidat;

I

J

K

al); Khojah Sect; Khurmaj; Kibisah; Kifl; Kubbar; Kufah; Kumait; Kumzar; Kung; Kunud; Kurd Tribe; Kurd (Al Bu); Kuria Muria Islands; Kut al Amarah Qadha; Kut al Amarah Town; Kuwait Bay and Town; Kuwait Principality; Kuwarah (Al Bu). pp.947–1077. 70 entries

L

Labibah; Laft; Lailah; Lajal (Wadi); Lam (Bani); Larak; Lingeh or Lingah District; Lingeh or Lingah Town; Liravi; Liwa Sub Wilayat; Liwa Town; Lur Tribe; Lusail. pp.1077–1112. 13 entries

M

Ma'adhid; Ma'awal; Ma'awal (Wadi); Mabrah (Wadi); Madain; Madhahakah; Madinah; Mahadrah; Mahair (Al Bu); Mahandah; Mahmadi or Muliammadi; Mahmadshahi or Muhamadshahi; Mahmudiyah; Mahot; Mahra Tribe; Mahram (Wadi); Mahur (Halat Abu); Maih (Wadi); Majar al Kabir; Majma; Makran (Coast of Persian); Malik (Bani) (I); Malik (Bani) (II); Manah; Manamah; Manana'ah; Manasir; Mansah (Wadi); Maqdam (Khan); Maqla (al Bin); Maqlab; Maqniyat; Maqta; Maradim (Umm al); Marar; Marru (Qira al); Masakirah; Ma'shur; Masirah; Masna'ah; Masqat Bay and Town; Masqat District; Mas'ud; Matrah; Matti (Saba Khat); Mazara'; Mazara'i District; Mazarai Village; Mi'aidin (Wadi); Mi'aijil (Dhula al); Mijlas (Wadi); Minab or Minau District; Minab (Khur); Minab or Minau Town; Mirbacheh or Madapchiyeh; Miskin; Mistal (Wadi); Miyali (Wadi al); Miyanab or Miyandab; Miyayahah; Morrah (al); Moz (Birkat a); Mu'adhdham; Mu'awdah; Mubaraz; Mudhaibi; Mugam or Muqam; Mughu; Muhaisin; Muhamad (Al Bu); Muhammareh District; Muhammareh or Muhamrah Town; Muharraq Island; Muhharaq Town; Mulla (Dih); Mund; Muntafik; Muraikhat; Murbat; Musa (Bu); Musa (Khor); Musaiyib; Musallam (al); Musallamiyah; Musandam; Mutair or Umtair; Mutaya (Sabakh at al). pp.1112–1291. 87 entries

N

Na'ab (Bani) or Nu'abah; Na'air (Sir Bu); Na'alah; Na'asan (Umm); Nabahinah or Nahban (Bani); Naband; Nafud; Na'im; Najaf Qadha; Najaf Town; Najd; Najd (Southern); Nakhl; Naqbiyin; Nasiri or Nasiri

O

P

Q

R

S

or Sulaib; Salwa (Dohat as); Samad Town; Samad (Wadi); Samail (Hisn); Samail (Wadi); Samait (Al Bu); Samawah Qadha; Samawah Town; Samhan (Jabal); Sanaisal (Wadi); Sanam (Jabal); Sanau; Sanfan al Hanna; Sarrami (Wadi); Sha'am; Shabadi; Shabankareh; Shafan (Wadi); Shah Abul Shah; Shakail (Bani); Sham (Khor ash); Shamailyah; Shamil or Shamilat District; Shamil Village; Shamin (Jau); Shamiyah Desert; Shamiyah Qadha; Shammar (Jabal) or Northern Najd; Shammar (Northern); Shammar (Southern); Shammar Toqah; Shamshamiyah; Shaqiq (Khor); Shaqq; Shaqrah; Sharaijah; Shararat; Sharifat; Sharjah Principality; Sharjah Town; Sharqiyah; Sharqiyan; Sharsah (Wadi); Shatait River or Ab i Shatait; Shatrat al Amarah; Shatrat al Muntafik; Shatrat al Muntafik Town; Shatut; Shatvar; Shaur River; Shi'aibah; Shibkuh; Shifathah; Shihuh or Shihhiyin; Shinafiyah; Shinas Sub Wilayat; Shinas Town; Shiqqaq; Shivuh; Shu'aib (Shaikh) or Jazirat ash Shaikh; Shura'awah; Shush; Shushtar District; Shushtar Town; Sib; Sikandariyah; Sikar (Qal'at); Sir; Sirhan (Wadi); Sirr (Wadi as); Sirrah (Qasr as); Sirri; Sitrah; Siyabiyin; Sohar Wilayet and Sub Wilayet; Sohar Town; Suraih (Qasral); Sudah; Sudan; Sultan (Al Bu); Sulutah; Sumaismah; Summan; Suq Ash Shuyukh Qadha; Suq Ash Shuyukh Town; Sur; Suwadi (Jazair); Suwaiq; Suwairah. pp.1618–1852. 122 entries

T

Taff; Tahiri; Taimah; Tamim (Bani) (I); Tamim (Bani) (II); Tanaij; Tangistan; Tanurah (Ras); Tarut; Tathlith or Tathlithah (Wadi); Tau (Wadi); Tawailah; Tawairij; Tayin (Wadi); Tigris or Dijlah; Tiwi or Taiwi Village; Tiwi or Taiwi (Wadi); Tunb; Tunb (Nabiyu or Nabi); Turuf (Bani); Tuwaiq (Jabal). pp.1852–1914. 21 entries

U

Umr (Bani); Umr (Wadi Bani); Umr al Gharbi (Wadi Bani); Utub or Itbah (Bani). pp.1914–1919. 4 entries

W

Wabrah; Wadyan; Wafi; Wahaib (Bani); Wahibah (al); Wais; Wakrah; Warai'ah: Warbah; Washam. pp.1919–1931. 10 entries

Y

Z

Images

Earl Canning in Elphinstone inlet, Ruus al Jibal – Gabler (pp.1604-1605)
Wadi Samail, Hisn Samail – Cox (pp.1668–1669)
Jabal ash Sham (pp.1694–1695)
Sur port – Cox (pp.1848–1849)
Bilad as Sur – Cox (pp.1850–1851)
Wakrah fort, Qatar – Cox (pp.1926–1927)

Endnotes

Prologue

[1] Telegram R., No.651–S, 23 June 1923, CO 727/6

[2] Lorimer, J.G. *Gazetteer of the Persian Gulf. Vol. II. Geographical and Statistical*, pp.324–5

[3] Telegram R., No. 651–S, 23 June 1923, CO 727/6

[4] Daly, C.K. to Knox, S.G. letter of 19 June 1923, Ibid.

[5] Telegram P., No. 649, 23 June 1923, Ibid.

[6] Shuckburgh, J.E. letter of 11 July 1923, Ibid.

[7] Lorimer, J.G. *Gazetteer of the Persian Gulf. Vol. II. Geographical and Statistical*, p.1283

[8] Anglo-Al Sa'ud Treaty of Darin signed on 26 December 1915

[9] India Office to Colonial Office. letter of 28 July 1923, CO727/6

[10] Ibid.

[11] Young, H. to India Office. letter of 23 August 1923, Ibid.

Introduction

[12] Alston, R. and Laing, S. *Unshook Till The End Of Time*, p.9

Chapter 1 - Terra Incognita

[13] Curzon, G.N. *Persia And The Persian Question*; *Volume I*, pp.viii–ix

[14] Curzon departed Paris in September 1899.

[15] Ansari, A. *A Mirror For Princes? British Orientalists and the Persian Question*, in Kidd, C. and Rose, J. *Political Advice, Past, Present and Future*, p.123

[16] Curzon, G.N. *Persia And The Persian Question; Volume II*, p.398

[17] Ibid., p.467

[18] Ibid., p.397

[19] Ibid.

[20] Burn, R. The Imperial Gazetteer of India, *Journal of the Royal Society of Arts*, Vol. 56 (1908), pp.364–373

[21] Penck, A. Der Krieg und das Studium der Geographie, *Zeitschrift der Gesullschaft fur Erdkunde zu Berlin* (1916) pp.158–176; 222–248

[22] Wang, H. Stein's Recording Angel: Miss F.M.G. Lorimer, *Journal of the Royal Asiatic Society*, Vol.8 (1998), pp.207–228

[23] Reilly, B. Arabian Travellers, 1800–1950: An analytical bibliography, *British Journal of Middle Eastern Studies*, 43:1 (2016), p.81. Other nationalities included: 4 Americans, 3 Italians and 1 each from 7 other European countries

[24] Ibid., p.77

[25] *Proceedings of the Royal Geographical Society of London*, Vol. 9 (1864–1865), pp.195–274

[26] Frere, in Rich, P. *Creating The Arabian Gulf; The British Raj and the Invasions of the Gulf*, p.227

[27] Pelly, L. 'A visit to the Wahabee Capital, Central Arabia', *Proceedings of the Royal Geographical Society in London*, Vol.9 (1864–1865), p.295

[28] Philby, H, *The Heart of Arabia: A Record of Travel and Exploration*, pp.117–158

[29] IOR/R/15/6/29 File XXIII/5 'Travels in Oman. Intending Travellers', p.8; IOR/L/PS/10/259 File 1202/1912 'Arabia:- Travellers. Capt. F.F. Hunter. Herr Runkiar (Danish Expedition). Capt Shakespear.'

[30] Shakespear, W. to Cox, P. telegram C-23 of 9 March 1912; IOR/L/PS/10/827, File 2297/1919 'Persian Gulf Residency Monthly Reports. 1912–20.' 487v

[31] IOR/L/PS/10/259 File 1202/1912 '*Arabia:- Travellers. Capt. F. F Hunter. Herr Runkiar (Danish Expedition). Capt Shakespear.*' Foreign Department letter to the Marquis of Crewe, 10 October 1912, p.41 & p.75

[32] *The Geographical Journal*, Vol.46 (1915), p.479

[33] When Lord Salisbury became Foreign Secretary in 1878, negotiations with the shah never materialised into any meaningful

commitment to serve as a buffer despite British efforts to influence and to support internal development. See Greaves, R.L. British Policy in Persia, 1892–1903, *Bulletin of the School of Oriental and African Studies,* Vol. 28 (1965), pp.4–60. Ingram, E. Family and Faction in the Great Game in Asia: The struggle over the Persian Mission, 1828–1835, *Middle Eastern Studies*, Vol.17 (1981), p.305

[34] IOR/R/15/1/722 '*Persian Gulf Gazetteer, Part 1, Historical and Political Materials, Precis of Bahrain Affairs 1854–1904*', pp.1–2

[35] Ironically, Turkey and its own empire had at one time also been part of the British empire's wider security equation against the Russians.

[36] Curzon, G.N. *British Government in India*, Vol. 2, p.69

[37] Firdous, N. Curzon and British Strategy for the Persian Gulf, *Proceedings of the Indian History Congress*, Vol.67 (2006–07), p.880

[38] Curzon papers, III/159/59/204, F1/12, cited in Roberts, *Salisbury*, p.768

[39] Ronaldshay, Earl of. *The Life of Lord Curzon*, p.318

[40] Howard, C. Splendid Isolation, *History* Vol. 47, (1962), p.32

[41] *Hansard*, HL Deb 05 May 1903, Vol. 121 cc1329–54

[42] Ibid.

[43] Meade, M.J. to Al Sabah, letter of 23 January 1899, Confidential Print, Vol.17, Document 64 – enclosure in Document 62

[44] Harcourt, R.V. *Memorandum Respecting Kuwait*, Confidential Print, Vol. 17, Document 62

[45] Whigham, H.J. to Cox, P. Sir Percy Cox papers: Box 1: File 1: Item 3, MECA

[46] Hill, to Foreign Office, letter of 14 March 1904, FO 78/5354

Chapter 2 - Competition Wallah

[47] Dickson, H.P. *The Arab of theDesert:AGlimpseintoBadawinLife in Kuwait and Sau'di Arabia*, p.172

[48] The name Lockhart was carried down the family through five generations.

[49] Founded there shortly after the 1843 'Great Disruption' which saw a split within the Church of Scotland and the foundation of the Free Church of Scotland, an evangelical group which advocated more missionary work in Scotland and overseas as well as the weakening of links with the state.

[50] Gordon, J. *The New Statistical Account of Scotland / by the ministers of the respective parishes, under the superintendence of a committee of the Society for the Benefit of the Sons and Daughters of the Clergy. Mains and Strathmartine, Forfar*, Vol. 11, p.58

[51] In February 1984's *London Review of Books*, it was said that William's translation was not one of piety as he had lost his faith as an undergraduate but an attempt to rehabilitate the Scots language.

[52] Where practical mathematics, Latin and sometimes French and Greek were taught. Gordon, J. *The New Statistical Account of Scotland / by the ministers of the respective parishes, under the superintendence of a committee of the Society for the Benefit of the Sons and Daughters of the Clergy. Mains and Strathmartine, Forfar*, Vol. 11, p.64

[53] Lorimer, R. letter of 22 February 1914, Mss Eur D922/1

[54] Institutional opinion at the time was that most Irishmen could not be trusted to govern the British empire because of their potential political and/or religious beliefs. Less than 5% of Haileybury alumni were Irish. This increased to 24% in the first ten years of open competition which alarmed the public service commissioners. The same logic however did not apply to them defending the empire with between 40–50% of British regiments stationed in India and beyond being mostly made up of Irishmen.

[55] Lorimer, J.G. *Gazetteer of the Persian Gulf. Vol I. Historical. Part IA & IB*; IOR/L/PS/20/C91/1, p.123

[56] The Macaulay reforms.

[57] Campbell in Vasunia, P. Greek, Latin and the Indian Civil Service, *The Cambridge Classical Journal*, Vol.51 (2005), pp.35–71

[58] *The Times*, 7 November 1864

[59] Article II, Edinburgh Review, CXXXIX, April 1874 in Spandenburg, B. The Problem with Recruitment for the Indian Civil Service

During the Late Nineteenth Century, *The Journal of Asian Studies*, Vol.30 (1971), pp.341–360

60 *Irish Times*, 22 August 1870

61 No subjects were obligatory. Candidates could choose 7 subjects from a range of branches of knowledge but had to be appreciate that some subjects carried more weight than others. A 'smatterer' was a candidate who, in the absence of any meaningful knowledge in the subjects on offer, would attempt to sit a highly-weighted subject in the hoping of getting some correct answers. Civil Service of India Open Competition, Regulations, Examination Paper, Table of Marks, And Statistics

62 Godley, A. Under-Secretary of State for India to Courthope, Civil Service Commissioner, India Office, 23 August 1889, *Godley Papers*

63 Spandenburg, B. The Problem with Recruitment for the Indian Civil Service During the Late Nineteenth Century, *The Journal of Asian Studies*, Vol.30 (1971), pp.341–360

64 1 of 11 'scholars' to be accepted alongside a further 8 'exhibitioners' and 57 'commoners'. Foster, J. *Oxford men & their colleges. Illustrated with portraits & views. Together with the matriculation register, 1880–1892*, p.431

65 From 1887 to 1891, Oxford and Cambridge provided 5% and 15% respectively of new ICS probationers. When further changes were made to the examination process in 1892 increasing the weight of Classics, for the next 4 years, Oxford accounted for 32% of new probationers while Cambridge's increased to 25%. Vasunia, P. Greek, Latin and the Indian Civil Service, *The Cambridge Classical Journal*, Vol.51 (2005) pp.35–71

66 While Wren and Gurney offered services to support entry into Crown service more generally, William Baptiste Scoones' crammer school based in Garrick Street, London focused almost exclusively on preparing young gentlemen seeking employment in the Foreign Office.

67 *The Times*, 25 August 1888

68 Letter, 1886, quoted in A. Cock and D. Forsdyke, *Treasure Your Exceptions: The Science and Life of William Bateson*, p.25

[69] Kirk-Greene, A. (2002). 'Not Quite a Gentleman': The Desk Diaries of the Assistant Private Secretary (Appointments) to the Secretary of State for the Colonies, 1899–1915. *The English Historical Review*, 117(472), pp.622–633

[70] Other subjects that he could have been examined in included Geology, Bengali, Burmese, Tamil, Mara'hi (spoken in the Western state of Maharashtra, India), Telugu (a dialect spoken in South-East India) and Sanskrit.

[71] In 1893, 124 candidates applied for 63 vacancies, Spandenburg, B. The Problem with Recruitment for the Indian Civil Service During the Late Nineteenth Century, *The Journal of Asian Studies*, Vol.30 (1971), pp.341–360

[72] In 1852, statistics showed that the sons of clergymen from the Church of England accounted for 145 of the 600 EIC employees while the sons of 'other ministers' accounted for another 39. In all, 27.5% came from religious backgrounds. The Aristocracy in contrast accounted for just 67 or 10% of the EIC civil service. Ibid.

[73] Lorimer's other exam results were: 74% in Law, 76% in the History and Geography of India and 66% in Agricultural Chemistry.

[74] Lorimer's Arabic exam result is not recorded in his personal file.

[75] IOR/L/PJ/6/308 File 1874; IOR/L/PJ/6/309, File 1885

[76] Lorimer's official joining date.

[77] IOR/L/PJ/6/304, Lorimer, J.G. letter of 30 August 1891 to the India Office

[78] Ibid., Lorimer, J.G. letter of 7 September 1891 to the India Office. In this exchange, he also asked for an update on the Arabic exam marking error.

[79] Ibid., Lorimer, J.G. to Undersecretary of State for India, letter of 21 September 1891

[80] From the remainder of Lorimer's cohort, 9 would join Bengal Province, 6 to Bombay, 8 to Madras and 9 to Burma.

[81] *Civil Service of India Open Competition, Regulations, Examination Paper, Table of Marks, And Statistics*

[82] Local government administrative units included tahsils, districts, divisions and provinces or states.

[83] Baha,L.'*The Administration of the North West Frontier Province 1901–1919*', p.33

[84] IOR/R/1/4/1052 File Con Est A 1919

[85] Ibid.

[86] Ibid.

[87] '*Gazetteer of the Peshawar District, Punjab Government'*, p.253

[88] His time in Lahore also included a brief special duty in the Punjab Civil Secretariat.

[89] IOR/R/1/4/1052FileConEstA1919

[90] Ibid.

[91] Lorimer had originally asked if he could sit his Arabic exam in the UK before he sailed out to India but his request was turned down.

Chapter 3 - The Very Model of a Modern Waziri Political

[92] IOR/R/1/4/1052 File Con Est A 1919

[93] Ibid.

[94] Ibid.

[95] The others being the Tirah campaign from September 1897 to April 1898, the relief of Malakand garrison in July and August 1897 and the Mohmand campaign from August to October 1897.

[96] '*Frontier and Overseas Expeditions From India, Vol. 2*', p.434; Kemball, G.V. '*Operation of the Tochi Field Force in 1897–98*', p.7

[97] 12 mounted soldiers from the 1st Punjab cavalry, 200 from the 1st Sikh Infantry, 100 from the 1st Punjab Infantry and 2 guns from the No.6 Bombay Mountain Battery.

[98] Kemball, G. V. '*Operation of the Tochi Field Force in 1897–98*', p.8

[99] Ibid., p.18

[100] Miranshah would later become an RAF base. T.E. Lawrence was briefly posted there from May 1928 to January 1929

[101] Kemball, G.V. '*Operation of the Tochi Field Force in 1897–98*', p.49

[102] '*Punjab Frontier Administration Report for 1898–99*'; '*TochiV alley Administration Report for 1898–99*'. From 4–20 December, Lorimer was able to take some leave, returning to as Political Officer, Tochi Field Force until June 1899. IOR/R/1/4/1052 File Con Est A 1919

[103] Ibid., Dane, L. to Secretary to the Government of India in the Foreign Department, Letter No.1090 of 22 July 1899

[104] Ibid.

[105] IOR/R/1/4/1052 File Con Est A 1919, Barnes, H. to Curzon, note of 5 August 1899, Frontier A August 1899, No.7–10

[106] Ibid.

[107] *Proposed Establishment of New Posts on the Afridi Border near Peshawar to be garrisoned by the Khyber Rifles. Instructions asto the conduct of Political Business in the Khyber, Government of India, Military Department, Disturbances–B*, Proceedings March 1900, Nos. 1208–1211; *Arrangements under which the Khyber Pass is being held and enquiry as to the responsibility of the Lieutenant General Commanding the Forces, Punjab in the event of an uprising, Government of India, Military Department, Disturbances – B*, Proceedings April 1900, Nos. 1294–1295

[108] Another demonstration of the strong Indo-Scot links. Fort William was first built in the late seventeenth century by the East India Company and rebuilt eighty years later to garrison troops and home to Bengal Government House.

[109] Information was presented in two sections: the first recording Muslim customs and the second, Hindu ones. Headings included: Tribal and Family Connections, Betrothal, Marriage, Guardianship and Minority, Succession, Bastardy, Wills and Legacies, Special Property of Females, Gifts and Partition. The Hindu section also included Adoptions, a custom not practised by Peshawari Muslims.

[110] When an attempt was made in 1929 to repeat the exercise, none of the Muslim communities agreed to be questioned, arguing that they followed Sharia rather than tribal custom. A subsequent survey of the Hindu communities resulted in just three amendments to Lorimer's aide memoire.

[111] Bhattacharya, S. The Men Who Ruled India, 1899–1901 (A sketch by Lord Curzon). *Proceedings of the Indian History Congress,* 18, pp.209–216

[112] Hamilton to Curzon, Deal Castle, 31 August 1899, *Hamilton Papers*, Vol. 1 No.35

[113] Lytton to HM The Queen, 25 March 1875, Suez, *Lytton Papers*, Vol.1

[114] Curzon, G.N. to Hamilton, 5 April 1899, C.C. vol.158

[115] Goudie, A.S. George Nathaniel Curzon – Superior Geographer, *The Geographical Journal*, Vol. 146 (1980), p.203

[116] Curzon deliberately avoided engaging with Mackworth-Young as he believed that the diminution of prestige would result in Mackworth-Young being obstructive and rallying political support in London.

[117] Ali, G., Ali, H., Hussain, I. and Zhiban, H. A Comprehensive Analysis of R.I. Bruce Maliki System: A Case Study of Mahsud Tribe 1888–1896, *PSAKU International Journal of Interdisciplinary Research*, Vol. 9, No. 1, p.2; Ahmad, D and Mohyuddin, A. Role of Malik in Pukhtoon Tribal Areas, *Journal of Studies in Social Sciences*, Vol. 5 (2013) p.240

[118] Quoted in Howell, E. *Mizh: A Monograph on Government's Relations with the Mahsud Tribe*, p.29

[119] *Hansard*, The North-West Frontier Of India debate, House of Lords, Volume 54, 7 March 1898

[120] Curzon, G.N. minute in Howell, E. *Mizh: A Monograph on Government's Relations with the Mahsud Tribe*

[121] IOR:R/15/2/51File II/I *Appointment of Political Agents*

[122] IOR/R/1/4/1052 File Con Est A 1919, Cunningham, W. to Lorimer, J.G. letter of 15 May 1900

[123] Ibid.

[124] *The Gazette of India*, January to June 1902, p.39

[125] Lorimer, J.G. note of 11 November 1899 *Military Department Notes No.180, Future garrison and management of the section of the frontier between Kohat and the Gomal Valley – Report of the*

Committee assembled to report on the organisation of the tribal militia in Waziristan

[126] Ibid., p.7

[127] Ibid., p.6

[128] Ibid., p.7

[129] Comprising of the Commanding Officer, Second in Command and a joint Quartermaster/ Adjutant.

[130] Lorimer, J.G. note of 11 November 1899, *Military Department Notes No.180, Future garrison and management of the section of the frontier between Kohat and the GomalValley – Report of the Committee assembled to report on the organisation of the tribal militia in Waziristan*, p.10

[131] Referenced by Captain Hugh Daly, Deputy Foreign Secretary on 28 November 1900, *Frontier B, Foreign Department Notes, Matters Relating To The Officering of The Khyber Rifle Corps*

[132] In November 1897, the 8th Rajputs changed from being Bengal Native Infantry to Bengal Infantry as the term was phased out.

[133] Curzon, G.N. note of 6 December 1900, *Frontier B, Foreign Department Notes, Matters Relating To The Officering of The Khyber Rifle Corps*

[134] There were meant to be six British officers commanding the Khyber rifles: a Commandant, two second-in-commands, a Quartermaster and an Adjutant. The amalgamation of the latter two positions reduced this to five while the Political and Military Departments negotiated delegating the responsibilities of the commandant position to the relevant political officer.

[135] IOR/R/1/4/1337, Lorimer, J.G. to Barnes, letter of 31 December 1901

[136] Roos-Keppel, G.O. to Leigh, H.P.P. letter of 10 October 1901, Ibid.

[137] Dane, L.W. note of 19 January 1903, Ibid.

[138] Daly, H. note of 19 January 1903; Curzon, G.N. note of 21 January 1903, Ibid.

[139] *Frontier and Overseas Expeditions From India, Vol.2*, p.441

[140] *Despatches Regarding the Mahsud Blockade operations, Military Department, No.972*, August 1902, Lorimer, J.G. *Political Officer's report on the work of the Sarwakei Military Column*, 30 November 1901

[141] Ibid.

[142] 644 Martini rifles and 569 Snyders. Military Department, *Arms* A, Proceedings March 1901, Nos. 1835–1843

[143] IOR/R/1/4/1052 File Con Est A 1919, Merk, W. to Deane, H. letter No.817B of 20 March 1902

[144] Lorimer, J.G. *Grammar and Vocabulary of Waziri Pashtu*

[145] IOR/R/1/4/1052 File Con Est A 1919, Curzon, G.N. to Hamilton, G.N. letter of 20 March 1902

[146] *The Gazette of India*, 1904, p.464

[147] *Civil Service Regulations* Article 291; *The Gazette of India*, January to June 1902, p.84

[148] Lorimer, J.G. to Lorimer, I.L. letter of 14 June 1911

[149] IOR/R/1/4/1052 File Con Est A 1919, Somaliland Campaign, or Anglo-Somali War

[150] Ibid.

[151] Ibid.

Chapter 4 - Curzon's Grand Tour

[152] Curzon, G.N. *Persia and the Persian Question Vol.2*, p.465

[153] *Hansard*, HL Deb 05 May 1903, vol 121 cc1329–54

[154] Lorimer, J.G. *Gazetteer of the Persian Gulf and Oman, Vol.1, Part 2*, p.2626

[155] Sharma, Lord Curzon's visit to the Persian Gulf 'politics of pageantry', *Proceedings of the Indian History Congress* Vol. 29, Part II (1967), pp.230–233

[156] Curzon, G.N. *Persia and the Persian Question Vol.1*, p.464

[157] Formally known as the 1820 General Treaty with the Arab Tribes of the Persian Gulf but more commonly referred to as the General Maritime Treaty.

[158] Dane, L.W. letter to Curzon, 14 September 1903. The squadron was also visited on an almost daily basis by HMS *Lapwing* which carried out mail runs.

[159] Simla telegram to Viceroy's camp, 12 November 1903

[160] Simla telegram to Viceroy's camp, 13 November 1903

[161] Such were the gun-crews'enthusiasm to pack their cannons with powder and wadding that the fort's masonry and fortifications were once recorded to have become loose and tumbled into the sea after a particularly violent volley.

[162] Cox, P. letter to Dane, L.W. 3 November 1903; Dane, L.W. telegram of 9 November 1903

[163] Known as the 'Unshook treaty' of 18 January 1800

[164] Douglas, Commander-in-Chief Royal Navy East Indies Station to Meade, Political Residency, 17 February 1899

[165] Curzon, G.N. telegram 20 October 1903

[166] IOR/R/15/1/553 File 59/15C (A15) *Muscat Miscellaneous*

[167] Lorimer, J.G. *Gazetteer of the Persian Gulf and Oman, Vol.1, Part 2*, p.2636

[168] Ibid., p.2637

[169] Dane, L. 9 October 1903, Government of India, Foreign Department, Proceedings, February 1904, Nos. 33–127

[170] Haller, A.N. Selective Recognition as an Imperial Instrument: Britain and the Trucial States, 1820–1952, *Journal of Arabian Studies*, 8:2, p.282

[171] Lorimer, J.G. *Gazetteer of the Persian Gulf and Oman, Vol.2*, p.9

[172] Lorimer, J.G. *Gazetteer of the Persian Gulf and Oman, Vol.1, Part2,* p.2644

[173] Curzon, G.N. letter to Broderick, Secretary of State for India, 17 December 1903

[174] Lorimer, J.G. *Gazetteer of the Persian Gulf and Oman, Vol.1, Part 2*, p.2646

[175] Curzon, G.N. letter to Broderick, Secretary of State for India, 17 December 1903

[176] Although the governor of Fars would have undoubtedly spirited some of the money away had it been paid, such was the level of corruption within the Persian Army at that time that soldiers and to a lesser extent, officers, went months or even years without being paid their salaries. To survive, many took up paid jobs outside of the military and would only return to put on their shabby uniform and rifle if they received at least some of their back-pay which the government just could not afford as it suffered from substantial economic decline. Tousi, R.R. The Persian Army, 1880–1907, *Middle Eastern Studies*, Vol. 24 (1988), pp.206–229

[177] Lorimer, J.G. *Gazetteer of the Persian Gulf and Oman, Vol.1, Part 2*, p.2652

[178] Ibid., p.2654

[179] IOR/R/15/1/709 *Persian Gulf Administration Reports 1883/84 – 1904/05*. Lorimer, J.G. *Gazetteer of the Persian Gulf and Oman, Vol.1, Part 2*, p.2649

[180] Dane, L.W. letter to Kemball, 13 August 1903

[181] Curzon, G.N. letter to Broderick, Secretary of State for India, 17 December 1903

[182] Lorimer, J.G. *Gazetteer of the Persian Gulf and Oman, Vol.1, Part 2*, p.2662

[183] Mohsin, M.H. to Newmarch, L. letter of 12 December 1903

[184] Goldberg, J. *The Foreign Policy of Saudi Arabia: The Formative Years, 1902–1918*, p.52

[185] Mss Eur F111/358 *Notes Prepared for Reference during Curzon's Tour of the Persian Gulf, and Other Papers on Persia and the Persian Gulf*, p.103

[186] Goudie, A.S. George Nathaniel Curzon – Superior Geographer, *The Geographical Journal*, Vol. 146 (1980), p.203

[187] Dane, L.W. telegram to Kemball, 15 October 1903

[188] Dane, L.W. demi-official letter to Commissioner of Sind, 10 November 1903

Chapter 5 - A Rather Particular Special Duty

[189] Colvin, E.G. to Dane, L. 16 August 1903, Government of India, Foreign Department, Proceedings, January 1904, Nos. 30–31

[190] Goudie, A.S. George Nathaniel Curzon – Superior Geographer, *The Geographical Journal*, Vol. 146 (1980), p.205

[191] IOR/R/1/4/1052 File Con Est A 1919, Dane, L. note of 22 October 1903

[192] Ibid., Curzon, G.N. note of 23 October 1903. Colvin had also identified Talbot, another experienced officer who could potentially complete the settlement work on the same terms and conditions Dane endorsed his other choice.

[193] *Summary of Principal Events and Measures Of The Viceroyalty Of His Excellency Lord Curzon Of Kendleston, Viceroy and Governor-General Of India* The Foreign Department. I. January 1899–April 1904. II. Mss Eur F111/531 Volume IV. *Persia And The Persian Gulf*, p.73

[194] Curzon, G.N. *Persia and The Persian Question Vol. 2*, p.398

[195] Dobbs, H. to Wheeler, H. memorandum No.2626-E.B of 17 July 1907

[196] Fraser, S.M. Letter of 5 November 1903, Foreign Department, General A, Proceedings, July 1904, Nos. 1–14

[197] By the name of Fink.

[198] Dane, L.W. letter of 14 May 1904, Foreign Department, General A, Proceedings, July 1904, Nos. 1–14

[199] Lorimer, J.G. telegram of 14 December 1903, Ibid.

[200] Ibid.

[201] Lorimer, J.G. to Russell, L. telegram of 3 February 1904, Ibid.

[202] Lorimer, J.G. to Dane, L.W. telegram of 16 December 1903, Ibid.

[203] Foreign Department, General –B, Progs October 1905, Nos. 200/202

[204] Lorimer, J.G. to Dane, L.W. telegram of 16 January 1904, Foreign Department, General A, Proceedings, July 1904, Nos. 1–14

[205] Dane, L.W. note of 17 April 1904, Ibid.

[206] Curzon, G.N. note of 22 April 1904, Ibid. By late 1906, the chief commissioner's office of the North-West Frontier Province had given up any hope of Lorimer returning there as an administrator. Foreign Department, Secret-E, Proceedings, March 1907, Nos. 729–738

[207] St J. Brodwick, W. to Curzon, letter of 19 August 1904, Foreign Department, General-A, Proceedings, October 1904, Nos. 14

[208] Burn, R. The Imperial Gazetteer of India, *Journal of the Royal Society of Arts* (1908), p.366

[209] Lorimer, J.G. to Dane, L.W. telegram of 30 December 1903, Foreign Department, General A, Proceedings, July 1904, Nos. 1–14

[210] Lorimer, J.G. to Foreign Department, letter of 9 September 1905, Foreign Department, External-B, Proceedings, December 1905, Nos. 143–146

[211] Saldanha would later request that he be given a certificate of appreciation of his work on the gazetteer. The government refused, suggesting instead that he go through official channels. It is not known if he continued to pursue his request. Foreign Department, Deposits – G, Programmes 1910, January 1910, No. 11

[212] Lorimer, J.G. '*Gazetteer of the Persian Gulf. Vol. II. Geographical and Statistical*', p.1503

[213] Lorimer, J.G. letter of 3 September 1904, Foreign Department, General-B, Progs. October 1904, Nos. 66–68

[214] Dane, L.W. note of 3 September 1904, Ibid.

[215] IOR/L/PS/20/C237, Gabriel, C.H. *Persian Gulf gazetteer. Part 1. Historical and political materials. Précis on arms trade in the Persian Gulf*, p.6

[216] Onley, J. *The Arabian Frontier of the British Raj; Merchants, Rulers, and the British in the Nineteenth-Century Gulf*, p.170

[217] Meade, M. telegram to Dane, L. 18 October 1899, *Persian Gulf Gazetteer, Part I Historical and Political Materials, Précis of Bahrein Affairs*, p.138

[218] Ibid.

[219] Foreign Department Notes External-B, November 1904, Nos. 19–21

[220] From 1876 to 1877

[221] Fraser, S.M. note of 17 September 1904, Foreign Department, External B, November 1904, Nos. 19–21

[222] IOR/R/15/1/330 File 19/118 (C7) *Bahrain*, Foreign Department to St. John Brodrick, letter of 21 April 1904, p.2

[223] Government of India, Foreign Department Proceedings, May1903 Nos. 64–87

[224] Cox, P.Z. to Dane, L.W. letter of 17 September 1904, Foreign Department Notes External-B, November 1904, Nos. 19–21

[225] Parts of the gazetteer reinforced the name even it is debatable whether the Al Qawasim were involved incriminality or exercising an acceptable charge for safe passage.

[226] Lorimer, J.G. telegram of 10 October 1904, Ibid.

[227] Ibid.

[228] Dane, L.W. 10 October 1904, Foreign Department Notes External-B, November 1904, Nos.19–21

[229] Longe, F.B. to Russell, L. telegram of 16 October 1904, Foreign Department Notes, External-B, January 1905, Nos. 84–88

[230] Deputy Foreign Secretary to Surveyor-General, letter of 19 October 1904, Ibid.

[231] Longe, F.B. to Dane, L.W. telegram of 31 October 1904, Ibid.

[232] He received a gratuity of thirty-eight pounds, six shillings and six pence. In 1907–08, he returned to South Persia surveying an area of 25,000 square miles as far north as Herat in the North-West Frontier Province.

[233] Gifts and money were also allocated to Prideaux, Lock, Knox and Cox to be used in much the same way. Enclosure 3, Pro. No.118, Foreign Department, External-B, Proceedings, January 1906, Nos. 114–121

[234] Lorimer, J.G. note of 20 October 1904, Foreign Department, General-B, Progs November 1904, Nos. 259–261

[235] Lorimer, J.G. note of 15 October 1904, Foreign Department, General-B, Progs December 1904, Nos. 155–157

[236] Lorimer, J.G. note of 1 November 1904, Foreign Department, General-B, Progs December 1904, Nos. 155–157

[237] Trevor, A.P. to Dane, L.W. letter of 5 November 1904, Foreign Department, General-B, Progs. November 1904, Nos. 291–292

[238] Lorimer, J.G. telegram of 10 October 1904, Foreign Department Notes External-B, November 1904, Nos. 19–21

[239] Foreign Department External-B, Progs April 1905, Nos. 63–65

[240] IOR/R/15/1/709 '*Persian Gulf Administration Reports 1904/05*', 5r; Lorimer, J.G. '*Gazetteer of the Persian Gulf. Vol. II. Geographical and Statistical*', p.1425; Ibid., p.405 & p.1757

[241] Ibid., p.1427. This refutes the claim in Sugata Bose's *A hundred horizons: the Indian Ocean in the age of global empire* that Lorimer had reinforced the use of 'the Pirate Coast'.

[242] Lorimer, J.G. '*Gazetteer of the Persian Gulf. Vol.II. Geographical and Statistical*', p.409; Onley, J and Khalaf, M, Shaikhly Authority in the Pre-Oil Gulf: An Historical-Anthropological Study, *History and Anthropology* 17:3 (2006), p.191

[243] Lorimer, J.G. '*Gazetteer of the Persian Gulf. Vol.II. Geographical and Statistical*', p.260

[244] Ibid., p.1535; p.643

[245] Lorimer, J.G. letter of 7 November 1904, Foreign Department, General-B, December 1904, Nos. 64–73

[246] Mss Eur F112/450 '*Memoranda Regarding Other External Affairs Volume II*', p.3; see also Cetinsaya, G.'*Ottoman Administration of Iraq: 1890–1908*', p.144

[247] Lorimer, J.G. '*Gazetteer of the Persian Gulf. Vol.II. Geographical and Statistical*', p.1592

[248] IOR/R/15/1/476 File 53/7C (D6) '*Koweit Affairs, 1903–1904*', p.48

[249] Lorimer, J.G. *Gazetteer of the Persian Gulf. Vol.II. Geographical and Statistical*, pp.1313–1314

[250] Ibid., p.600

[251] Ibid., p.1048

[252] Ibid., p.1060; p.896; p.1642; p.1059

[253] Ibid., p.1048a

[254] Ibid., p.1276; p.982

[255] IOR/L/PS/20/C247 *Précisof correspondence on International rivalry and British policy in the Persian Gulf, 1872–1905*, p.95

[256] Ibid., p.23, p.1591

[257] Both Lorimer and Gabriel collected their passports in Karachi. After some consideration, the Government of India decided to waive the one rupee fee per passport given that their movements were official.

[258] Lorimer, J.G. to Assistant Secretary, Foreign Department, letter of 31 March 1905

[259] Lorimer, J.G. '*Gazetteer of the Persian Gulf. Vol. II. Geographical and Statistical'*, p.1951; p.269; File 1855/1904 *Koweit:- H.M. Govt and Political Agent at Koweit. (Representations from Turkish Govt & temporary withdrawal of Agent* Pt 1, p.53

[260] Lorimer, J.G. *Gazetteer of the Persian Gulf. Vol.II. Geographical and Statistical*, p.196; p.1880

[261] IOR/L/PS/10/87 File 3131/1905 '*Mesopotamia:- Irrigation*', Newmarch, L.S. Diary for week ending 6 March 1905, p.2

[262] Lorimer, J.G. *Gazetteer of the Persian Gulf. Vol.II. Geographical and Statistical*, p.1281

[263] Ibid., p.975; p.713

[264] Ibid., p.1309

[265] Ibid., p.759; p.94; p.1256; p.116

[266] Ibid., p.1455; p.339

[267] Ibid., p.233; p.9; p.1455; p.1130; p.915

[268] Ibid., p.1838; p.1383; p.1179

[269] Ibid., p.5

[270] It was impossible to work discreetly in populated areas given the extensive paraphernalia typically carried by a surveying party, which included: theodolites housed in large wooden boxes, plane tables, beam compasses and diagonal scales, numerous watches, lamps and lanterns, pocket compasses, thermometers, perambulators, subtense bars, mathematical books and computation forms, slide rules, note

books and a plentiful supply of pencils in addition to their camping equipment.

[271] IOR/L/PS/20/199 *A note on survey work in Persia, and survey instruments and equipment*, p.2

[272] Lorimer, J.G. *Gazetteer of the Persian Gulf. Vol.II. Geographical and Statistical*, p.233

[273] Ibid., p.116; p.1505

[274] Lord Curzon: His Resignation and Record, *The North American Review*, Vol. 181 (1905), pp.568–569

[275] Lorimer, J.G. to Assistant Secretary, Foreign Department, letter of 31 March 1905

Chapter 6 - The Sands of Time

[276] From 14 December 1904 to 20 June 1905, nearly twelve hundred rupees in cash had been handed over to seventy-nine individuals in return for information. The smallest payment was one rupee, the largest (which required a short statement to justify the amount) was one hundred and thirty-nine rupees. Enclosure 2, Pro. No118, Foreign Department External-B, Proceedings January 1906, Nos. 114–121

[277] Lorimer, J.G. *Gazetteer of the Persian Gulf. Vol.II. Geographical and Statistical*, p.ii

[278] Ibid., p.116

[279] Ibid., p.458; p.297

[280] Ibid., p.719; p.494

[281] Ibid., p.1171

[282] Ibid., p.910; p.350

[283] Ibid., p.519

[284] Ibid., p.209; p.1563; p.116 & 1563

[285] Ibid., p.116

[286] Ibid., p.1383 & 1426; p.1004; p.433, 941, 1441, 1825 & 1947; p.260 & 264; p.931

[287] Ibid., p.59; p.944; p.1425 & 1444; p.1426

[288] Ibid., p.1455

[289] Ibid., p.1203; p.1455

[290] Ibid., p.588; p.116

[291] Ibid., p.1383; p.443

[292] Ibid., p.747; p.1086; p.629

[293] Ibid., p.1703; p.1699

[294] Ibid., p.1016; p.267; p.1548; p.1455

[295] Ibid., p.1699

[296] As this was a new agency location, Lock was unusually given the responsibility of deciding where in Arabistan to base himself. He chose Ahvaz as this was where the sheikh of Muhammerah spent the winter months. He was responsible forArabistan, Pusht-i-Kuh and Luristan as well as maintaining communications with the tribal chiefs in Bakhtiari. Ibid., p.1772; p.45

[297] Lock joined Ambala (Umballa) on 9 March 1903 and Hazara on 22 October1903. He departed for Ahwaz on his birthday 24 December, arriving in Ahwaz on 16 January 1904.

[298] IOR/R/15/1/710 *Administration Reports 1905–1910*, 1905–06 report, p.4

[299] Ibid., p.483; IOR/L/PS/10/62 Douglas, to Grant-Duff, letter of 14 November 1904

[300] Lorimer, J.G. '*Gazetteer of the Persian Gulf. Vol.II. Geographical and Statistical*', p.1110

[301] Ibid., Douglas, to Grant-Duff, letter of 8 November 1904

[302] Ibid., Foreign Office letter of 10 February 1905

[303] Lorimer, J.G. *Gazetteer of the Persian Gulf. Vol.II. Geographical and Statistical*, p.118; p.1820; p.118

[304] Although referenced many times in the gazetteer, Isfahan does not have its own entry, suggesting that it was outside the gazetteer's geographical reach.

[305] Ibid., p.1574

[306] IOR/R/15/1/710 *Administration Reports 1905–1910*, p.20; Lorimer, J.G. *Gazetteer of the Persian Gulf. Vol.II. Geographical and Statistical*, p.1170; p.146

[307] IOR/L/PS/10/69 File 339/1905 *Koweit – PoliticalAgency. Expenditure, Steam Launch*, Cox, P.Z. to St J. Brodwick, W. Letter of 5 January 1905

[308] IOR/L/PS/18/B166 *Memorandum respecting British interests in the Persian Gulf*, p.7 & 19

[309] Mss Eur F112/450 *Memoranda Regarding Other External Affairs 1905 Volume II*, p.5; IOR/L/PS/10/25 *Muscat Arbitration. (1904–08)* P. 1 733/1904, p.166

[310] Cox, P. to Fraser, S. 16 July 1905

[311] 5 miles in depth.

[312] Lorimer, J.G. note of 29August 1905, Foreign Department, General-B, Progs October 1905, Nos. 200–202. The Foreign Department had originally asked if Lorimer could carry out the review from 16August to 15 September, but he was already overwhelmed with additional work falling out of the Transliteration Committee and having to write Curzon's Persian Gulf Administration Summary.

[313] Ibid.

[314] Grey, E., letter of 21 June 1906 to O'Conor

[315] Lorimer, J.G. note of 6 November 1906, Government of India, Foreign Department, Proceedings, January1907, Nos. 392–406

[316] Foreign Secretary draft letter to Cox, P. December 1906

[317] IOR/R/15/2/45 *File F/1 Criminal Intelligence, Circular Memoranda: Pan-Islamism*, Lorimer, J.G letter to Cox, P. 26 August 1906

[318] *Memorandum on military policy in the event of war with Turkey*, July 1906, WO 106/42

[319] Ibid., p.15

[320] IOR/R/15/1/710 *Administration Reports 1905–1910*, p.3

[321] IOR/R/15/5/67 *XXII/17 Boundary between Koweit & Katif Territory*, Cox, P. to Foreign Secretary, Telegram No. 1727 of 12 August 1912

[322] Somers-Cocks, C. Government of India, Foreign Department, Proceedings, September 1907 Nos. 334–361, 27 July 1906, p.8; Dane, L. Government of India, Foreign Department, Proceedings, September 1907 Nos. 334–361, 27 August 1906, p.12

[323] IOR/R/1/4/1052FileConEstA1919

[324] Goudie, A.S. George Nathaniel Curzon: Superior Geographer, *The Geographical Journal*, Vol. 146 (1980), pp.203–204

[325] Dane, L. to O'Conor, Constantinople, letter No 1682 EB of 25 April 1906

[326] O'Conor to Dane, L. Simla, letter of 24 May 1906

[327] Dane, L. to Minister, Tehran, No 1683 EB of 25 April 1906

[328] Dane, L. to O'Conor, Constantinople, No 1990 EB of 16 May 1906, Clemaw's substantial return was received in Simla on 19 June 1906

[329] Dane, L. to Minister, Tehran, No 1991 EB of 16 May 1906

[330] Dane, L. to O'Conor, Constantinople and Minister, Tehran, Nos. 2296 EB and 2297 EB of 4 June 1906

[331] Holland, R.to Tucker, A. No 2298 EB of 4 June 1906

[332] Holland, R. to Deane, H. No 2299 EB of 4 June 1906

[333] Dane, L. to Grant-Duff, E. Tehran No 2669 EB of 25 June 1906

[334] Dane, L. to O'Conor, No 2768 EB of 30 June 1906

[335] Lorimer, J.G. Government of India, Foreign Department, Proceedings, September 1907 Nos. 334–361, 27 July 1906, p.8

[336] Which in addition to his salary now included a winter fuel allowance of one hundred and fifty rupees to keep his office warm during the winter months.

[337] Lorimer, J.G.*Gazetteer of the Persian Gulf. Vol.I. Historical, Pt.2*, pp.2377–2378

[338] Lorimer, J.G. Memorandum of 10 September 1906, Foreign Department, Secret-E, Proceedings, March1907, Nos. 729–738

[339] Ibid.

[340] Which included working every Sunday and public holiday, using his privilege leave and forgoing his afternoon exercise, all of which took him away from his young family. Dane, L.W. note of 17

September 1906, Foreign Department, Secret-E, Proceedings, March 1907, Nos. 729–738

[341] Lorimer, J.G. to Clarke, E.H.S. letter of 18 March 1907, Foreign Department, Secret-E, October 1907, Nos. 195–205

[342] The exact number was four thousand, seven hundred and fifty-two. Ibid.

[343] Ibid.

[344] Lorimer, J.G. to Foreign Department, note of 14 May 1907, Finance Department, Salaries, Establishments, etc-A, Proceedings, September 1907, Nos. 142–148

[345] Lorimer, J.G. to Clarke, E.H.S. letter of 18 March 1907, Foreign Department, Secret-E, October 1907, Nos. 195–205. Lorimer, J.G. letter of 14 May 1907, Ibid.

[346] Ibid.

[347] Ibid

[348] Ibid., Dobbs, H. to Finance Department, memorandum No.1885E of 29 May 1907

[349] Lorimer's total salary for the three years and five months that he had been working on the gazetteer to March 1907 was eighty-eight thousand, five hundredrupees. The remainder had been spent employing local staff. The overall total was still less than to the expenditure incurred to produce the Rajputana and Baluchistan gazetteers during the same period, costing the Financial Department just over one hundred and twenty-two thousand, and two hundred and thirty-three thousand rupees respectively. Foreign Department, Secret-E, Proceedings, October 1907, Nos. 195–205

[350] Baker, N. note of 22 June 1907, Finance Department, *Salaries, Establishments, Etc-A*, Proceedings, September 1907, Nos. 142–148

[351] Ibid., Dobbs, H. to Wheeler, H. memorandum No. 2626 E-B of 17 July 1907; Dane, L.W. to Finance Department, letter of 17 May 1907

[352] Minto, G.J. to Morley, J. letter of 12 September 1907, Ibid.

[353] Morley, J. to Minto, G.J. letter of 1 November 1907, Foreign Department Notes, Secret-E, May 1908, Nos. 599–600

[354] Telegram No. S-283 of 7 June 1907

[355] Spring-Rice, E. to Foreign Secretary, 15 June 1907

[356] Deputy Secretary, Foreign Department. note of 22 April 1908, Foreign Department, General-B, Programmes May 1908, Nos. 367–369

[357] Lorimer, J.G. note of 23 April 1908, Ibid.

[358] Butler, H. to Lorimer, J.G. letter of 3 August 1908, Foreign Department *Deposit – Est* Programmes Jan 1909, No. 33

[359] Lorimer, J.G. to Butler, H. letter of 4 August 1908, Ibid.

[360] Butler, H. to Richie, R. India Office. letter of 24 September 1908, Ibid.

[361] Ritchie, R. to Butler, H. letter of 23 October 1908, Ibid.

[362] Butler, H. to Lorimer J.G. letter of 7 January 1909, Ibid.

[363] Foreign Department, General-B, Proceedings January 1909, Nos. 188–191

[364] Foreign Department, General-B, Proceedings January 1909, Nos. 183–184

[365] Pages 65–121, 1–12, 1–3 and 1–4 respectively. Years later, Lorimer would be temporarily struck by panic when his mother wrote to him, informing him that she had found some of his draft chapters. Although Lorimer admitted that he had shown his father some proofs, he was adamant that he had taken them away from him as 'one is not allowed to show Govt. secret works to anyone, even one's parents, one may not even have them oneself when one does not require them for one's work!' It was a reminder again about the sensitivity of the gazetteer's contents and if Reverend Robert was indeed the recipient of some of his son's gazetteer papers, it can be safely assumed that they were very quickly destroyed. Lorimer, J.G. to Lorimer, I.L. letter of 2 November 1913

[366] Lorimer, J.G. *Gazetteer of the Persian Gulf. Vol. II. Geographical and Statistical*, p.i

[367] Ibid., p.1; p.1952

Chapter 7 - Hunter's Map

[368] Tandy, C.O'H. to Foreign Department, letter of 22 June 1906, Foreign department, External-A, Proceedings, October 1907, Nos. 6- 49

[369] Malleson, W. to Lorimer, J.G. letter of 11 June 1906, Foreign Department, External-A, Proceedings October 1907, Nos. 6–49

[370] Longe, F.B. to department of Revenue and Agriculture, Note 870 of 1 November 1907, Department of Revenue and Agriculture, Land Surveys, February 1908, Proceedings Nos. 5–7

[371] Newton, D. '*Kipling's Canadian; Colonel Fraser Hunter, MPP, Maverick Soldier-Surveyor in "the Great Game"*', 2009

[372] Longe, F.B. to Fraser, F.F. letter of appointment, 7 August 1905

[373] Hunter, F.F. to Superintendent, Burma Surveys, letter of 4 September 1907, department of Revenue and Agriculture, Land Surveys, February 1908, A Proceedings Nos. 5–7

[374] IOR/L/PS/10/66 File 37/1905 '*Aden Frontier Delimitation*', Pt 4

[375] Hunter, F.F. Reminiscences of the Map of Arabia and the Persian Gulf, *The Geographical Journal*, Vol. 54 (1919), p.360

[376] Lorimer, J.G. Note of 14 May 1907, Finance Department '*Salaries, Establishments, Etc-A*', Proceedings, September 1907, Nos.142–148

[377] A New Map of Arabia, *Bulletin of the American Geographical Society*, Vol. 42 (1910), pp. 362–363

[378] Hunter, F.F. Reminiscences of the Map of Arabia and the Persian Gulf, *The Geographical Journal*, Vol. 54 (1919), p.356

[379] Buck, E, J. '*Simla Past and Present*', p. 20. Ibid., p.15

[380] Hunter, F, F. Reminiscences of the Map of Arabia and the Persian Gulf, *The Geographical Journal*, Vol. 54 (1919), p.356

[381] Hunter, F.F. to Burrard, S, Assistant Surveyor General, letter of 4 January 1906

[382] Hunter's guide was authored by Sir William Wilson Hunter as he was producing the first version of the Imperial Gazetteer of India. Hunter thought that Prideaux from Bahrain was also possibly part of

the committee, offering an anecdote that one day he was seen with a despatch box with Political Officer, Behrain painted on it. The next he was seen with a repainted box saying Bahrain instead after the committee had agreed on its respelling. As Prideaux was not an experienced Arabist, it is unlikely that he was a committee member, or if he was, that he contributed much. Hunter, F.F. Reminiscences of the Map of Arabia and the Persian Gulf, *The Geographical Journal*, Vol. 54 (1919), p.356

383 Hunter, F.F. to Dane, L. letter of 19 May 1906, Foreign Department Notes, External-A, October 1907, Nos. 6–49

384 At Longe and Lorimer's insistence, Hunter would eventually be given a twenty percent increase of pay/ allowance for the time he worked on the map as part of Number 19 party.

385 Lorimer, J.G. to Hunter, F.F. letter of 19 June 1906

386 Lorimer, J.G. Note of 26 June 1906, Foreign Department, External-A, Proceedings October 1907, Nos. 6–49

387 Lorimer, J.G. to Hunter, F.F. letter of 19 June 1906 (private collection)

388 Lorimer, J.G. note of 26 June 1906, Foreign Department, External-A, Proceedings October 1907, Nos. 6–49

389 Longe, F.B. to Foreign Department. letter of 12 March 1906, Foreign Department Notes, Secret-E, August 1906, Nos. 211–215

390 Tandy, C.O'H. note of 15 April 1906, Ibid. Lorimer, J.G. Note of 17 April 1906, Ibid.

391 Russell, L. Note of 25 June 1906, Ibid.

392 Lorimer, J.G. to Hunter, F.F. letter of 7 July 1906

393 IOR/R/20/G/182 '*Notes on the map of Arabia and the Persian Gulf*'

394 IOR/L/PS/20/199 '*A note on survey work in Persia, and survey instruments and equipment*'

395 In summer 1905, seven clerks were temporarily employed to work their way through the archives. Lorimer, J.G. to Foreign Department, letter of 24 October 1905, Foreign Department, External-B, Progs, March 1907, Nos. 164–167

396 Ibid., p.356

[397] The Gazetteer accredits 666 references but includes some duplication as it also records joint publications and translations.

[398] Hunter, F.F. Reminiscences of the Map of Arabia and the Persian Gulf, *The Geographical Journal*, Vol. 54 (1919), p.357

[399] In 1884 while travelling through Jeddah, Huber was robbed and murdered by his local guides.

[400] A New Map of Arabia, *Bulletin of the American Geographical Society*, Vol. 42 (1910), p.362

[401] Hunter, F.F. Reminiscences of the Map of Arabia and the Persian Gulf, *The Geographical Journal*, Vol. 54 (1919), p.357. St. John Philby who was also a critic of Palgrave, would later praise Hunter for his work and be able to confirm many of the features set in the map, Ibid., p.360

[402] Ibid.

[403] A British Orientalist who spent two years with Bedouin tribes in Arabia in the 1870s. Ibid., p.362

[404] Hunter, F.F. Reminiscences of the Map of Arabia and the Persian Gulf, *The Geographical Journal*, Vol. 54 (1919), p.361

[405] Tandy, C.O'H. to Hunter, F.F. letter of 15 June 1906

[406] Hunter, F.F. Reminiscences of the Map of Arabia and the Persian Gulf, *The Geographical Journal*, Vol. 54 (1919), p.361

[407] Hunter, F.F. to Lorimer, J.G. letter of 20 March 1908, Foreign Department, External-A, Proceedings, May 1908, Nos. 93–100

[408] IOR/R/15/5/14 File VI/3 I. '*Confidential Maps and Books'*, Haig, D. to Shakespear, W.H.I. letter of 1 June 1910

[409] IOR/R/20/G/182 '*Notes on the map of Arabia and the Persian Gulf*'

[410] Descriptions included a hill, district, village, anchorage, mountain, railway station, halting place or water course, Ibid.

[411] Lorimer, J.G. '*Gazetteer of the Persian Gulf. Vol. II. Geographical and Statistical*', p.405 & 1313; Lorimer was of the view that when Curzon had initially commissioned the gazetteer, he had assumed that maps that covered the whole of the Arabian Peninsula already existed and that all was needed was for them to be scaled and combined on to one map when in reality, much was unmapped.

Lorimer, J.G. letter of 2 July 1907, Foreign Department, Secret-E, Proceedings, October 1907, Nos. 195–205

[412] Lorimer, J.G. note of 26 November 1907, Department of Revenue and Agriculture, Land Surveys, February A Proceedings, Nos. 5–7. Although Hunter's map is a credible representation of the Arabian Peninsula, part of Qatar's coastline is inaccurate.

[413] Longe, F.B. to department of Revenue and Agriculture, note 870 of 1 November 1907, Department of Revenue and Agriculture '*Land Surveys*', February 1908, Proceedings Nos. 5–7

[414] Hunter, F.F. Reminiscences of the Map of Arabia and the Persian Gulf, *The Geographical Journal*, Vol. 54 (1919), p.356

[415] Note of 22 August 1908, Foreign Department, General-B, Progs. October 1908, No. 56

[416] Had the expedition gone ahead, Hunter was to be accompanied by Reverend Samual Zwemer, an American explorer and missionary who had visited the region several times and had even penetrated part of the Rub Al Khali.

[417] A New Map of Arabia, *Bulletin of the American Geographical Society*, Vol. 42 (1910), p.363

[418] Hunter, F, F. Reminiscences of the Map of Arabia and the Persian Gulf, *The Geographical Journal*, Vol. 54 (1919), p.363

[419] In 1913, Lieutenant-Colonel Francis Maunsell, former military attaché in Constantinople and leading military intelligence and topographical expert worked the Royal Geographical Society to produce a map of Arabia that also looked to plot Leachman's travels, using Hunter's map as a major point of reference despite its classification. IOR/R/15/1/504 File 53/32 III (D 53) '*Kowait – Miscellaneous*', Maunsell, F.R. to Cox, P. letter of 17 October 1913; Dillon, A.S. '*Captain Shakespear*', p.53

[420] IOR/R/15/6/126 File 3/8 '*Books etc: Transliteration of vernacular names and places*', Cox, P. to Political Agent, Muscat, letter of 31 August 1910. In Cox's initial draft, he was 'requested' to remedy the evil but it was struck-through and replaced with 'desired'.

[421] Ibid., Cox, P. to Political Agent, Muscat, letter of 25 March 1913

Chapter 8 - Double-Hatted in Baghdad

422 Bell, G. to Bell, F. letter of 14 April 1909

423 Wilson, A. '*S.W. Persia A Political Officer's Diary 1907–1914*', p.107

424 *Comet*'s top speed was nine knots. Elwell-Sutton, A.S. The Tigris above Baghdad, *The Geographical Journal*, Vol. 60 (1922), pp.20–40; Cheeseman, R.E. A History of Steamboat Navigation on the Upper Tigris, *The Geographical Journal*, 1923, Vol. 61 (1923), pp.27–34. *Comet* compromised of one officer, four warrant officers and thirty-five petty officers and men.

425 Reported in Wilson's diary as being 'a most pleasant wife'. Wilson, A. '*S.W. Persia A Political Officer's Diary 1907–1914'*, p.107

426 MSS Eur D922/1, Lorimer, E.O. to Lorimer, R. letter of 4 November 1913

427 The War Office had also got into the habit of encouraging the appointment of military intelligence officers into Levant Consular Service billets to increase their intelligence-gathering capability but still faced difficulties in securing a constant and credible feed of information. See Fisher, J. '*On the Baghdad Road: On the Trail of W J Childs; A study in Near East Intelligence and Historical Analysis, c1900–1930*'

428 The network and Foreign Department were not always supportive of the War Office's exploits. In 1905, Captain Edward Mahon was ordered by the Committee of Imperial Defence to carry out a secret reconnaissance of potential locations for the Gulf terminus for the ongoing Baghdad railway. His tradecraft was wanting, having travelled by ship to Kuwait using his own name on the passenger manifest, he arrived in disguise as a shipping agent carrying baggage with his real name and corps painted on it. Percy Cox, the then Political Resident was completely unaware of Mahon's mission and was only informed of his presence in Kuwait when a Dutch merchant on the same ship recognised Mahon and reached out to Cox. As Cox had been unable to inform Al Sabah of Mahon's presence, it risked his own credibility with the sheikh. This was

not helped by the fact that he had only seen Al Sabah just a few weeks before Mahon's arrival. His letter of complaint to Whitehall naturally found sympathy from within the Foreign Office. Hamm, G. '*British Intelligence and Turkish Arabia: Strategy, Diplomacy and Empire, 1898–1918'*

429 Although Lorimer was not disciplined for entertaining him, both Shakespear in Kuwait and brother Lock in Bahrain were chastised by the viceroy on orders from the Foreign Office for allegedly supporting the Dane's mission.

430 IOR/R/15/5/25 File X/2 '*Bin Saood, Koweit [Kuwait] & Ibn Rashid*'

431 It had always been a challenge to offer a credible estimate of the number of Ottoman troops garrisoned in the region as there was a general aversion to parades and ceremonies. Often, their presence was only ever confirmed when they were seen loitering in the local cafes. An estimation of thirty-two thousand troops in 1904 was obtained by Lorimer's predecessor but only after bribing a local Turkish official.

432 IOR/L/PS/20/61 Lorimer, J.G. '*Report on a Tour in Turkish Arabia and Kurdistan, April–May 1910*'

433 Ibid., p.7

434 IOL/L/MIL/17/16/3

435 Ibid., p.17

436 Lorimer was also responsible for submitting a report on Judaism in Baghdad. Drafted by one of his *dragomen* and annotated by Lorimer, it would later become a remarkable report, providing 'an inside view, intelligent and well-informed of this community at that point in its history. Lorimer, J.G. despatch 191/10 of 27 February 1910 quoted in Kedourie, E. The Jews of Baghdad in 1910, *Middle Eastern Studies*, Vol. 7 (1971), pp.355–361

437 In a letter to her step-mother written a day after her arrival in Baghdad, she explained that she had hoped to 'do two day's work in one' by sending her caravan straight to Baghdad whilst she rode on, hoping to photograph the Ctesiphon ruins. From there she hoped to cross the river and ride back up to Baghdad to meet

the rest of her party. Unfortunately, the river was too swollen and the ferry out of sight, forcing her to retrace her path back to from where she had begun. Bell, G. to Bell, F. letter of 12 March 1911

438 Ibid.

439 Bell, G. to Bell, H. letter of 18 March 1911

440 Ibid.

441 In January 1911, Lorimer passed his re-qualification in Arabic, continuing his language allowance which was a worthy addition given the level of entertaining that they were expected to provide.

442 Bell, G. to Bell, H. letter of 18 March 1911

443 Gaskin also accompanied them for part of the journey and was involved in a comedic incident on the boat transfer across the Tigris involving him being caught by a boathook and being thrown on top of Lorimer, pinning him down by his great weight. Gaskin was only stopped from falling into the fast-flowing river by Nesta who held on to him as he was about to fall over the gunnels. Lorimer, J.G. to Lorimer, R. letter of 18 May 1911

444 Nazim Pasha was assassinated on 23 January 1913 by a member of the CUP during the 1913 *coup d'état*.

445 Lorimer, J.G. to Lorimer, R. letter of 12 June 1911

446 Lorimer, J.G. to Lorimer, R. letters of 18 May 1911, 3 June 1911, and 14 June 1911

447 Cole, C. Controversial investments: trade and infrastructure in Ottoman-British relations in Iraq, 1861–1918, *Middle Eastern Studies*, 54:5 (2018), p.745

448 Ibid., p.746

449 IOR/L/PS/10/88/2 File 3531/1905 Pt 2, Euphrates and Tigris Steam Navigation Company to Foreign Office, Letter of 30 May 1910

450 With the aim of introducing electric tramways.

451 IOR/L/PS/10/188 File 3846/1910 '*Mesopotamia: Baghdad affairs. Miscellaneous*' Lorimer, J.G. to Lowther, G. telegram of 17 August 1910

[452] Lorimer's would later report that his German counterpart considered his own position with the Turkish authorities to be almost unbearable, convincing him that this was ultimately not an anti-British policy; IOR/L/PS/10/188 File 3846/1910 '*Mesopotamia: Baghdad affairs. Miscellaneous*', Lowther, G. to Grey, E. letter of 22 September 1911

[453] Lowther, G. to Grey, E. letter of 22 August 1910

[454] IOR/L/PS/10/188 File 3846/1910 '*Mesopotamia: Baghdad affairs. Miscellaneous*', Lorimer, J.G. to Government of India, telegram of 3 September 1910

[455] Duff, G. War Office minute of May 1906, WO 106/42, file C3/10

[456] Foreign Department, Secret – E, Proceedings, April 1912, Nos. 141–161

[457] O'Conor, N. to Grey, G. letter of 26 August 1906

[458] Lorimer, J.G. to Lowther, G. letter of 22 August 1910

[459] Wilson, H. War Office minute of 24 April 1911, WO 106/43, file C3/21

[460] Which would have used concrete rather than stone.

[461] Wilson, A.T. '*S.W. Persia A Political Officer's Diary 1907–1914*', p.132

[462] Lorimer, J.G. to Grant and Reynolds, letter of 8 January; Lorimer, J.G. to Reynolds, letter of 27 April 1913, Foreign, Section E, Nos. 807–825

[463] Money, R.I. The Hindiyya Barrage, Mesopotamia, *The Geographical Journal*, Vol. 50 (1917)

[464] Bell, G. to Bell, H. letter of 18 March 1911

[465] IOR/L/PS/10/112 File 619/1907 Pt 3 *'Arms Traffic:- Koweit Trade.'* Babington Smith, H. to Nicolson, A. report of 29 December 1910

[466] Ibid.; IOR/L/PS/10/188 File 3846/1910 '*Mesopotamia: Baghdad affairs. Miscellaneous*', Marling, C. to Grey, E. letter of 23 November 1910

[467] Ibid., Lorimer, J.G. to Lowther, G. letter of 17 July 1911

[468] Ahmad, F. Great Britain's Relations with the Young Turks 1908–1914, *Middle Eastern Studies*, Vol. 2 (1966), p.310

[469] Grey, E. to Lowther, G. letter of 31 July 1908, The Grey Papers, FO 800/78

[470] Lowther, G. to Foreign Office, letter of 25 January 1911, FO 424/226

[471] In Satia, P. '*Spies in Arabia. The Great War and the Cultural Foundations of Britain's Covert Empire in the Middle East*', p.26

[472] Ibid.

[473] Lorimer, J.G. to Lorimer, I.L. letter of 23 June 1913

[474] Ibid.

Chapter 9 - Between Bequests, Banquets and Coronations

[475] Aitchinson's Collections of Treaties, Engagements and Sanads, Vol. 2, pp.161–164

[476] Litvak, M. Money, Religion and Politics: The Oudh Bequest in Najaf and Karbala, 1850–1903, *International Journal of Middle Eastern Studies*,Vol. 33 (2010, pp.1–21)

[477] Litvak, M. A. Failed Manipulation: The British, the Oudh Bequest and the Shi'I Ulama of Najaf and Karbala, *British Journal of Middle Eastern Studies*, Vol. 27 (2000) pp.69–89

[478] IOR/L/PS/10/77 File 1290/1905 '*Mesopotamia: Oudh Bequest*'

[479] Ibid.

[480] Lansdowne to Hardinge, telegram No.60 of 11 June 1903, L/PS/3/399

[481] Ibid.

[482] IOR/L/PS/10/77 File 1290/1905 '*Mesopotamia: Oudh Bequest*', Lorimer, J.G. to McMahon, A.H. letter of 11 August 1911

[483] Ibid.

[484] Ibid.

[485] Ibid.

[486] Ibid.

[487] Foreign Secretary to Political Resident, telegram P, No.S–28 of 23 January 1912

[488] IOR/L/PS/10/77 File 1290/1905 '*Mesopotamia: Oudh Bequest, Events in Turkish Iraq, May 1912*'

[489] Lorimer, J.G. to Lorimer, I.L. letter of 22 March 1912

[490] Ibid.

[491] Ibid.

[492] IOR/L/PS/10/77 File 1290/1905 '*Mesopotamia: Oudh Bequest*'; Lorimer', J.G. to Wood, J.B. letter of 15 November 1913

[493] Lorimer, J.G. to Lorimer, I.L. letter of 22 March 1912

[494] Lorimer, J.G. to Lorimer, R. letter of 15 October 1911

[495] Who at his own expense, took his son Ali Khan who also worked as a *dragoman* at the residence.

[496] Over the course of the *durbar*, one hundred and fifty trains carried in excess of one hundred and fifty thousand officials, soldiers and civilians to the encampment.

[497] Appointed viceroy in November 1910

[498] Broaches were struck for qualifying women. Two hundred gold medals were also struck for senior figures.

[499] Hailey, W.M. letter of 2 September 1909, Foreign Department, Deposit-EST, Programmes January 1909, No. 33

[500] Lorimer, E.O. to Lorimer, R. letter of 18 January 1912, Mss Eur D922/1

[501] IOR/L/PS/10/212 File 211/1912 '*Turkish Arabia Summaries, Summary of events in Turkish Iraq for the month of January 1912*'

[502] Estimated to have been in the region of £700,000

[503] Tandy, C.O'H. note of 16 June 1911, Foreign Department Notes, Secret-G, October 1912, Nos. 18–32

[504] Ibid., Hirtzel, A. note of 20 March 1912

[505] Ibid., Lorimer, J.G. to McMahon, A.H. letter of 14 February 1912

[506] Ibid., Hirtzel, A. to McMahon, A.H. letter of 7 June 1912

507 Ibid., India Office to Viceroy, telegram of 12 July 1912

508 Lorimer, J.G. to Lorimer, R. letter of 17 October 1912

509 The accused would eventually be found guilty and sentenced to six years hard labour in Malta

510 Lorimer, J.G. to Lorimer I.L. letter of 15 March 1913

511 IOR/L/PS/10/144/2 Barclay, G. to Mallet, L. letter of 5 August 1909

512 Lorimer, J.G. to Lorimer, I.L. letter of 15 March 1909. Lorimer surmised that it might have been a disgruntled Customs Department employee.

513 Lorimer, J.G. to Lorimer, I.L. letter of 12 August 1911

514 Ibid.

515 Ibid.

516 Lorimer, J.G. to Lorimer, R. letter of 7 August 1911

517 Lorimer, J.G. to Lorimer, R. letter of 6 July 1913

518 Ibid.

519 Lorimer, J.G. to Lorimer, R. letter of 27 July 1913. Lorimer, J.G. to Lorimer, R. letter of 13 July 1913

520 Lorimer, J.G. to Lorimer, I.L. letter of 23 June 1913

521 Lorimer, J.G. to Lorimer, R. letter of 13 July 1913

522 Lorimer, E.O. to Lorimer, R. letter of 18 December 1913, Mss Eur D922/1

523 Ibid.

524 Lorimer, J.G. to Lorimer, I.L. letter of 2 November 1913

525 Lorimer, J.G. to Lorimer, R. letter of 12 October 1913

526 Lorimer, E.O. to Lorimer, R. letter of 18 December 1913, Mss Eur D922/1

527 Ibid.

528 War Office to Foreign Office, minute of 18 June 1912, FO 371/1485/2064/26379; Foreign Office to India Office minute of 2 Feb 1911, L/P and S/3, Vol. 276, No. 1910/2961-2

529 Lorimer, J.G. to Marling, letter of 4 August 1913, FO 371/1485/42138/42138

530 Ibid.

Chapter 10 – Life at the Colony

[531] Lorimer, J.G. to Lorimer, R. letter of 3 December 1913

[532] IOR/L/MIL/17/16/3 '*Routes in Arabia*'

[533] Ibid.

[534] Lorimer, J.G. to Lorimer, R. letter of 3 December 1913

[535] Lorimer, J.G. '*Gazetteer of the Persian Gulf. Vol.II. Geographical and Statistical*', p.339

[536] Lorimer wrote that his vice consul was from Europe. Lorimer, J.G. to Lorimer, R. letter of 14 December 1913

[537] Lorimer, J.G. to Lorimer, R. letter of 16 January 1914; Lorimer, E.O. to Lorimer, R. letter of 15 October 1914, MSS Eur D922/1

[538] Lorimer, M.A, to Lorimer I.L. letter of 25 January 1914

[539] Lorimer, J.G. to Lorimer, R. letter of 21 December 1913

[540] Lorimer, M.A. to Lorimer I.L. letter of 25 January 1914

[541] Ibid., p.173

[542] Ibid., p.266

[543] Ibid., p.280

[544] Lorimer, J.G. to Lorimer, R. letter of 16 January 1914

[545] Lorimer, M.A. to Lorimer I.L. letter of 25 January 1914

[546] Lorimer, J.G. to Lorimer, R. letter of 16 January 1914

[547] Lorimer, J.G. to Robertson, C. letter of 9 January 1914, MSS Eur D922/1

[548] Lorimer, J.G. to Lorimer, R. letter of 12 October 1913

[549] Lorimer, E.O. to Lorimer, R. letter of 10 January 1914, MSS D922/1

[550] IOR/L/PS/18/B164 '*British Relations with the Wahabees*'

[551] Dillon, A.S. '*Captain Shakespear, Desert Exploration, Turkish Intrigue and the Rise of Ibn Sa'ud*'

[552] Ibid.

[553] IOR/L/PS/10/385 Lorimer, J.G. to Foreign Department, letter of 12 January 1914

[554] Ibid.

[555] '*Memorandum Showing The Papers Transmitted To The India Office With The Foreign Secretary's Weekly Letter*'No 4-M of 2 January 1914, Foreign and Political Department – External Proceedings September 1914, Nos. 1–204

[556] Reynolds, I.W. letter of 26 July 1913, Foreign Department Proceedings-External, Proceedings November 1913, Nos. 36–147

[557] Lorimer, J.G. to Lorimer, R. letter of 16 January 1914

[558] Ibid.

[559] Lorimer, M.A. to Lorimer, R. letter of 4 January 1914

[560] Lorimer, J.G. to Lorimer, R. letter of 12 August 1911; Lorimer, J.G. to Lorimer, R. letter of 1 March 1912

[561] Lorimer, J.G. to Wood, J.B. letter of 13 October 1910, Foreign Department Notes, General-B, July 1911, Nos. 28–31. The rifle was probably manufactured at the Rifle Factory Ishapore in India. In addition, a request was made for two stirrup irons and two lance buckets.

[562] Imperial War Museum, FIR 3681

[563] Lawrence, T.E. '*Seven Pillars of Wisdom*', p.304

[564] Birdwood, R.L. to Wood, J.B. letter of 14 February 1914, Foreign and Political Department, General – A, Proceedings May 1914, Nos. 17–25

[565] Birdwood, R.L. to Foreign Department, telegram of 8 February 1914, Ibid.

[566] Hunt, S. '*Residency Surgeon's report*' 10 February 1914, Ibid.

[567] Ibid.

[568] Ibid.

[569] IOR/R/15/5/3 '*Establishment. No. I/12 Appointments and Changes in the Political Residents & Agents in the Persian Gulf, and Secretaries, Bushire, & of the Govt. of India. and Others*' Note of 4 March 1914

[570] Ibid.

Chapter 11 – Lamenting a Legacy

[571] *The Times of India*, 28 February 1914. Lorimer, M.A. to Lorimer, R. letter of 26 February 1914

[572] IOR/L/PS/10/827 & IOR/R/15/5/3 '*Political Residency monthly report*', Birdwood, R.L. February 1914

[573] Ibid.

[574] Lorimer left just over seven thousand Pounds in his will with another fifteen hundred pounds of estates and effects estimated to be overseas in 'Persia, India and elsewhere abroad', Lorimer, J.G. Will and Testament, Edinburgh Sheriff Court, SC70/1/551

[575] Lorimer, E.O. to Lorimer, R. and I, letter of 2 April 1914, Mss Eur D922/1

[576] Ibid.

[577] Ibid., Lorimer, R. to United Free Church, letter of 22 February 1914

[578] Ibid., Holland, R.E. and Grant A.H. Home Department telegram of 25 February 1914; Wheeler, H. Foreign and Political Department telegram of 27 February 1914; and Craddock, R.H. telegram of 27 February 1914, Foreign and Political Department, General-A, Proceedings, May 1914, Nos. 17–25

[579] Grant, A.H. note of 1 March 1914

[580] Ibid., Curzon, G.N. to Lorimer, M.A. letter of 21 May 1914

[581] Winstone, H.V.F. '*Gertrude Bell*'

[582] Ibid., p.180

[583] Winstone, H.V.F. '*Gertrude Bell*', 2004 p.204

[584] Birdwood, R.L. telegram P, 8 February 1914, Foreign and Political Department, General-A, Proceedings, May 1914, Nos. 17–25

[585] Ibid., Birdwood, R.L. telegram P, 8 February 1914

[586] Ibid., Birdwood, R.L. telegram R, No.185 of 10 February 1914. Birdwood was so distraught by events that when registering Lorimer's death, he wrote date of birth rather than date of death, requiring Delhi to correct his error.

[587] IOR/R/15/1/711'*Administration Report of the Persian Gulf Political Residency for the Years 1911–1914*', 1913, p.12

[588] Ibid., 1914, p.5

[589] Lorimer, J.G. '*Gazetteer of the Persian Gulf. Vol. I. Historical*', p.i

[590] It is not known who received volume one serial number 1. Volume one serial number 102, the highest recorded serial number known to the author was issued to the Political Agency in Meshad.

[591] Busch, B.C. '*Britain, India and the Arabs 1914–1921*'; Moberley, F.J. '*The campaign in Mesopotamia, 1914–1918*'; and Cohen, S. 'Mesopotamia in British Strategy, 1903–1914, *International Journal of Middle East Studies*, Vol. 9 (1978)

[592] *'Report of the Commission Appointed by Act of Parliament to Enquire into the Operations of War in Mesopotamia*', p.111

[593] Ibid., p.97

[594] Ibid., p.20

[595] Herbert, A. '*Mons, Anzac and Kut*', p.161

[596] Wilson, A.T. '*Loyalties: Mesopotamia 1914–1917*', pp.22 and 80

[597] Cohen, S. Mesopotamia in British Strategy, 1903–1914, *International Journal of Middle East Studies,* Vol. 9 (1978)

[598] Undersecretary of State for Foreign Affairs to Undersecretary of State for Colonial Affairs, letter of 26 August 1921, CO 727/2

[599] Ibid., Marshall, G. to Army Department, letter of 27 July 1921

[600] Ibid., Marshall, G. to India Office, Military Department, letter of 27 July 1921

[601] Ibid., Undersecretary of State for Colonial Affairs to Undersecretary of State for Foreign Affairs, letter of 5 September 1921

[602] Noel, E.W.C. to Gaisford, P. letter of 24 January 1929, Foreign and Political Department, File No. 401-G/29

[603] Letters No.419-S of 28 November 1921, No.75-S of 19 January 1922 and No.91-S of 21 January 1922

[604] Having also served in Muscat, Arabistan and Muhammerah.

[605] Haworth, L. to Foreign Department, telegram R No.143 of 25

September 1928, File No.348-E, 1928

[606] Ibid., Messrs. Law and Skrine and Majors Noel and Wickham. Major Daly was also initially considered but judged to be junior to the others.

[607] Ibid., Foreign Department to Johnston, F.W. telegram R, No 2061-S of 12 October 1928

[608] Foreign Department, note of 22 December 1928, File No. 30-E/29 1929

[609] Which would be extended until 9 June 1929.

[610] Noel, E.W.C. to Gaisford, P. letter of 24 January 1929, File No.401-G/29

[611] Ibid., Higgs, E. to Noel, E.W.C. letter of 20 March 1929

[612] Political Residency, Bushire to Foreign Department, letter of 27 January 1929, File No.20(7)-E, 1929

[613] The successor to the Military Department.

[614] Telegram of 12 July 1930, Foreign and Political Department General Branch, File No. 258-G/30

Chapter 12 - Finis Coronet Opus

[615] Somers Cocks, S. note of 26 June 1906, Foreign Department, Secret-E, Proceedings, September 1907, Nos. 334–361

[616] Ibid., Dane, L. note of 26 June 1906; Minto, note of 10 August 1906

[617] Who was considering writing a history of Iraq. Chancery to Foreign and Political Department, letter of 16 November 1933, File No. 218, General of 1933

[618] Ibid.

[619] Ibid., Foreign and Political Department note of 19 December 1933

[620] Ibid., Foreign Office telegram R No.3110 of 15 December 1933

[621] IOR/R/15/2/179 '*Cyphers and Secret Documents: Safe Custody Reports and Handing Over Certificates for Secret Documents*', Dayal, H. to Prior, C.G. letter of 26 June 1944

[622] Ibid.

[623] Political Agent, Bahrain to Prior, C.G. letter of 29 November 1944, Ibid. In 1928, the political agency in Ahwaz received volume two serial number 123 which had inadvertently been shipped back to the UK by T.W. Jackson, formerly a lieutenant in the Indian Army's 37th Lancers who was stationed there. Foreign and Political Department, File No.229, 1928

[624] Despite being specifically referenced in the communication, the RGS no longer has a registered copy of the gazetteer in its library or archives. IOR/L/PS/12/1404 Pol Ext 7649/49 'Access to Volumes of Lorimer's Gazetteer', Molyneux, J.A. to Foreign Office Library, letter of 2 August 1949

[625] He also requested access to the reports that he had written when serving in Kermanshah and as the political resident in Bushire.

[626] Ibid.

[627] Ibid., Passant, E.J. to Haworth, L. letter of 16 August 1949

[628] Roholl, M. Preparing for Victory. The U.S. Office of War Information Overseas Branch's illustrated magazines in the Netherlands and the foundations for the American Century, 1944–1945, *European Journal of American Studies*, 7-2 (2012)

[629] Facey, W. '*George Rentz and the Birth of Wahhabism in Saudi Arabia'*

[630] Walmsley, A.R. to Roberts, J. letter of 4 December 1958, FO 371/132618

[631] Ibid.

[632] Ibid., Walmsley, A.R. to Roberts, J. letter of 21 January 1959

[633] Ibid., Walmsley, A.R. to Roberts, J. letter of 4 December 1958

[634] Ibid.

[635] Sarell, R.F.G. note of 1 April 1952, FO 371/98832

[636] Ibid., Cranston, W.P. note of 25 April 1952

[637] Although exact boundaries remained vague.

[638] Ibid.

[639] Ibid.

[640] Ibid.

[641] Ibid.

[642] With the understanding that they would negotiate Qatar's boundaries separately.

[643] Ibid., Cranston, W.P. memorandum of 4 September 1952

[644] Lorimer, J.G. '*Gazetteer of the Persian Gulf. Vol. I. Historical*', p.1063

[645] Haller, A.N. Selective Recognition as an Imperial Instrument: Britain and the Trucial States, 1820–1952, *Journal of Arabian Studies*, Vol 8:2, p.280

[646] Morton, M.Q. '*Buraimi: The struggle for power, Influence and Oil in Arabia*', p.104

[647] Jones, K.H. '*The Buraimi Arbitration'*, 10 October 1960, FO 371/148961

[648] Ibid.

[649] *Hansard*, 30 July 1959, Vol. 610, cc 686

[650] Walmsley, A.R. minute of 3 March 1960, FO 371/ 148961

[651] Simpson, J.L. minute of 5 March 1959, FO 371/140121

[652] Lane, D.N. minute of 9 January 1953, FO 371/104318. Although initially not prepared to sell Gwadur to the Pakistanis, the sultan was willing to consider leasing it to the British to sub-lease to the Pakistani government.

[653] Ibid., Bowker, J. minute of 12 January 1953

[654] Ibid., Lane, D.M. to Miles, F.S. letter of 16 June 1953

[655] Ibid., Ross, A.D.M. minute of 18 June 1953

[656] Ibid., Oxley, H.L.M. minute of 16 June 1953

[657] Ibid., Fitzmaurice, F.F. to McPetrie, letter of 10 August 1953

[658] BHC Karachi telegram 23 of 7 January 1956, FO 371/ 120596

[659] Ibid., BHC Karachi telegram 112 of 17 January 1956

[660] Subsequently denied by the sultan.

[661] Ibid., BHC Karachi telegram 119 of 24 January 1956

[662] Molyneux, J.A. to Golds, A.A. letter of 8 May 1956, FO 371/120597

663 '*Memorandum of Agreement on the Transfer of Gwadur*', FO 371/ 132793

664 An improved derivative of the Vampire used to patrol the skies in Buraimi.

665 Telegram 146 of 29 August 1958, FO 371/132793

666 Egerton, S.L. to Arabian Department, letter of 14 November 1969

667 The survey's findings would be enshrined in UNSCR 278. Although the shah of Iran accepted the outcome and renounced any claim to Iran, this was itself renounced after the 1979 revolution.

668 Egerton, S.L. to Arabian Department, letter of 14 November 1969.

669 Lorimer, J.G. '*Gazetteer of the Persian Gulf. Vol.I. Historical*', p.423.Lorimer, J.G. Personal papers shared with author.

670 Al Arayed, J.S. to Schwebel, S.M. Letter of 25 September 1997

671 Al Muslemani, A.A. to Valencia-Ospina, E. letter of 1 February 1999

672 In their 1992 and 1996 memorials, the Qataris quoted Lorimer or the gazetteer 39 times, increasing to 56 in 1997 and 70 times in 1999. The Bahrainis in turn quoted Lorimer 6 times in 1992, 49 in 1996, 35 in 1997 and 24 in 1999.

673 '*Maritime Delimitation And Territorial Questions Between Qatar and Bahrain (Merits)*', ICJ judgement of 116 March 2001. Hawar Islands andAl-Jaradah 12 votes to 5 and unanimouslyfor Zubarah in favour of Bahrain and Janan Island, and Al Dibal votes 13 to 4 in favour of Qatar.

674 Prior, C.G. to Peel R.T. letter of 26 October 1941,Government of India External Affairs Department, File 50-N/41 1941

675 Ibid.

676 Ibid., Caroe, O.K. to Peel, R. T. letter of 19 November 1941

677 Bidwell, R.A British Official Guide to the Gulf; Review, *The Geographical Journal*, Vol. 138 (1972) pp.233–235

678 Ibid.

679 Ibid.

680 Al Qasimi, M. '*The Myth of Arab Piracy*', p.i

[681] Fuccaro, N. '*Knowledge at the Service of the British Empire*', p.18; Rich, P. 'Creating the Arabian Gulf', p.98

[682] Mostern, R. and Johnson, I. From named place to naming event: creating gazetteers for history, *International Journal of Geographic Information Science*, Vol.22 (2008), p.1092

[683] Rentz, G. '*The Imamate of Oman*', p.273 FO1016/313

[684] In Scoville, S. A Historiography on 'The Gazetteer of Arabia', Vol. I, *Proceedings of the Seminar for Arabian Studies*, Vol.12 (1982), pp.73–78. She acknowledged the challenge in trying to update the Gazetteer of Arabia.

[685] Winstone, H.V.F. '*Leachman, OC Desert*', Quartet Books, pp.217–219. Leachman travelled around Mesopotamia in a Light Armoured Motorcar Battery (LAMB), influencing and mediating as much by the threat of force and diplomacy and tact.

[686] *The Geographical Journal* Vol.70 (1927), pp.17–21

Bibliography

Miscellaneous Publications

Frontier and Overseas Expeditions From India, Vol.2, Government Monotype Press, Simla 1908

Gazetteer of the Peshawar District, Punjab Government, 1898

General Sir Alexander John Godley Papers, King's College London, Liddell Hart Military Archives

Hansard, HL Deb 7 March 1898, The North-West Frontier of India debate, Vol.54

Hansard, HL Deb 05 May 1903, Vol.121 cc1329-54

Hansard, 30 July 1959, Vol.610, cc 686

Mesopotamia Commission. Report of the Commission Appointed by Act of Parliament to Enquire into the Operations of War in Mesopotamia, London, HMSO, 1917

Sir Percy Cox papers, Middle East Centre Archives, St. Antony's College, University of Oxford

Tochi Valley Administration Report for 1898–99, Punjab Frontier Administration Report for 1898–99

Books and Periodicals

Ahmad, D. and Mohyuddin, A. 'Role of Malik in Pukhtoon Tribal Areas', *Journal of Studies in Social Sciences*, Vol. 5 No. 2 (2013), pp.239–253

Aitchinson, C.U. '*Collections of Treaties, Engagements and Sanads*', Vol.2, Government of India Central Printing Office, Calcutta, 1892

Al Qasimi, M. '*The Myth of Arab Piracy*', Routledge, London, 2020

Ali, G., Ali H., Hussain, I. and Zhiban, H. 'A Comprehensive Analysis of R.I. Bruce Maliki System: A Case Study of Mahsud Tribe 1888–1896', *PSAKU International Journal of Interdisciplinary* Vol. 9 No. 1 (2020), pp.1–9

Alston, R, and Laing, S. '*Unshook Till The End Of Time*', Gilgamesh Publishing, 2012

Baha, L. '*The Administration of the North West Frontier Province 1901–1919*', PhD thesis, SOAS, 1948

Bhattacharya, S. The Men Who Ruled India, 1899-1901 (A sketch by Lord Curzon), *Proceedings of the Indian History Congress*, Vol. 18 (1955), pp.209–216

British Journal of Middle Eastern Studies, Vol. 43 No. 1 (2016), '*Arabian Travellers, 1800–1950 An analytical bibliography*', pp.71–93

Buck, E.J. '*Simla Past and Present',* Government of India Central Printing Office, Calcutta, 1904

Bulletin of the American Geographical Society, Vol. 42 No. 5 (1910) '*A New Map of Arabia'*, pp.362–363

Busch, B.C. '*Britain, India and the Arabs 1914–1921',* Berkeley 1971

Cetinsaya, G. '*Ottoman Administration of Iraq: 1890–1908*', Routledge, 2006

Cock, A. and D. Forsdyke, D. '*Treasure Your Exceptions: The Science and Life of William Bateson'*, Berlin, 2008

Curzon, G.N. '*British Government in India*', Cassell and Company Ltd, London, 1925, Vol. II

Curzon, G.N. '*Persia And The Persian Question'*, Longmans, Green and Co., London, 1892, Volume I

Curzon, G.N. '*Persia And The Persian Question*', Longmans, Green and Co., London, 1892, Volume II

Dickson, H.R.P. '*The Arab of the Desert: A Glimpse into Badawin Life in Kuwait and Sau'di Arabia*', London: George Allen & Unwin Ltd, 1949

Dillon, A.S. '*Captain Shakespear, Desert Exploration, Turkish Intrigue and the Rise of Ibn Sa'ud*', Medina Publishing, 2019

Facey, W. '*The Birth of the Islamic Reform Movement in Saudi Arabia: Muhammad Ibn Abd al-Wahhab (1703/4–1792) and the Beginnings of Unitarian Empire in Arabia*', Arabian Publishing, 2004

Foster, J. '*Oxford men & their colleges. Illustrated with portraits &*

views. Together with the matriculation register, 1880–1892', James Parker and Co., Oxford, 1893

Fuccaro, N. '*Knowledge at the Service of the British Empire*', SOAS, 2015

Goldberg, J. '*The Foreign Policy of Saudi Arabia; The Formative Years, 1902–1918*', Harvard University Press, London, 1986

Gordon, J. '*The New Statistical Account of Scotland / by the ministers of the respective parishes, under the superintendence of a committee of the Society for the Benefit of the Sons and Daughters of the Clergy. Mains and Strathmartine, Forfar*', Vol. 11, Edinburgh, Blackwoods and Sons, 1845

Hamm, G. '*British Intelligence and Turkish Arabia: Strategy, Diplomacy and Empire, 1898–1918*', University of Toronto, 2012

Herbert, A. '*Mons, Anzac and Kut*', edited by Melotte, E. Pen and Sword, 2009

History and Anthropology, Vol. 17, No. 3 (2006) '*Shaikhly Authority in the Pre-Oil Gulf: An Historical-Anthropological Study*', pp.189–208

Howell, E. *Mizh: A Monograph on Government's Relations with the Mahsud Tribe*, Oxford University Press, 1979

Indian History Congress, Vol. 67 (2006–7) '*Curzon and British Strategy for the Persian Gulf*', pp.880–7

International Journal of Geographic Information Science, Vol. 22 No. 10 (2008), '*From named place to naming event: creating gazetteers for history*', pp.1091–1108

International Journal of Middle East Studies, Vol.9 No.2 (1978) '*Mesopotamia in British Strategy 1903–14*', pp.171–181

International Journal of Middle Eastern Studies, Vol. 33 No. 1 (2010), '*Money, Religion and Politics: The Oudh Bequest in Najaf and Karbala, 1850–1903*', pp.1–21

Journal of Arabian Studies, Vol. 8 No. 2 (2019) '*Selective Recognition as an Imperial Instrument: Britain and the Trucial States 1820–1952*', pp.275–297

Journal of the Royal Asiatic Society, 1998, Vol. 8 No. 2 (1998) '*Stein's Recording Angel: Miss F M G Lorimer*', pp.207–228

Journal of the Royal Society of Arts, Vol. 56 (1908) '*The Imperial Gazetteer of India*', pp.364–373

Kemball, G.V. '*Operation of the Tochi Field Force in 1897–98*', Government Central Printing Office, Simla, 1900

Kidd, C. and Rose, J. '*Political Advice, Past, Present and Future*', I.B.Tauris, 2021

Lawrence, T.E. '*Seven Pillars of Wisdom*', Jonathan Cape, London, 1935

Lorimer, J.G. '*Grammar and Vocabulary of Waziri Pashtu*', Government of India Central Printing Office, Calcutta, 1902

Middle Eastern Studies, Vol. 17 No. 3 (1981) '*Family and Faction in the Great Game in Asia: The struggle over the Persian Mission, 1828–1835*', pp.291–309

Middle Eastern Studies, Vol. 2 No. 4 (1966) '*Great Britain's Relations with the Young Turks 1908–1914*' pp.302–329

Middle Eastern Studies, Vol. 24 No. 2 (1988) '*The Persian Army, 1880– 1907*', pp.206–229

Middle Eastern Studies, Vol. 54 No. 5 (2018) '*Controversial investments: trade and infrastructure in Ottoman-British relations in Iraq, 1861–1918*', pp.744–768

Middle Eastern Studies, Vol. 7 No. 3 (1971) '*The Jews of Baghdad in 1910*', pp.355–361

Moberley, F.J. '*The campaign in Mesopotamia, 1914–1918*', London, 1923–1927

Morton, M.Q. '*Buraimi: The struggle for power, Influence and Oil in Arabia*', I.B Tauris, 2013

Newton, D. '*Kipling's Canadian; Colonel Fraser Hunter, MPP, Maverick Soldier-Surveyor in "the Great Game"*', Trafford Publishing, 2009

Onley, J. '*The Arabian Frontier of the British Raj; Merchants, Rulers, and the British in the Nineteenth-Century Gulf*', Oxford University Press, 2007

Philby, H. '*The Heart of Arabia: A Record of Travel and Exploration*', Constable and Co., London, 1922

Rich, P. '*Creating The Arabian Gulf; The British Raj and the invasions of the Gulf*', Lexington Books, 2009

Roberts, A. '*Salisbury: Victorian Titan*', Weidenfeld, 1999 Ronaldshay, Earl of. '*The Life of Lord Curzon*', Ernest Benn Ltd, 1927

Satia, P. '*Spies in Arabia. The Great War and the Cultural Foundations of Britain's Covert Empire in the Middle East*', Oxford University Press, 2008

The Cambridge Classical Journal, 2005, Vol. 51 (2005) '*Greek, Latin and the Indian Civil Service*', pp.35–71

The English Historical Review, Vol. 117, No. 472 (2002), *'Not Quite a Gentleman': The Desk Diaries of the Assistant Private Secretary (Appointments) to the Secretary of State for the Colonies, 1899–1915*', pp.622–633

The Geographical Journal, 1980, Vol. 146, No. 2 (1980) '*George Nathaniel Curzon – Superior* Geographer', pp.203–9

The Geographical Journal, Vol. 138, No. 2 (1972) '*A British Official Guide to The Gulf: review*', pp.233–235

The Geographical Journal, Vol. 146, No. 2 (1980) '*George Nathaniel Curzon: Superior Geographer*', pp.203–209

The Geographical Journal, Vol. 46, No. 6 (1915) '*Obituary: Barclay Raunkiaer*', p.479

The Geographical Journal, Vol. 50, No. 3 (1917) '*The Hindiya Barrage, Mesopotamia*', pp.217–222

The Geographical Journal, Vol. 54, No. 6 (1919) '*Reminiscences of the Map of Arabia and the Persian Gulf*', pp.355–362

The Geographical Journal, Vol. 60, No. 1 (1922) '*The Tigris Above Baghdad*', pp.20–40

The Geographical Journal, Vol. 61, No. 1 (1923) '*A History of Steamboat Navigation on the Upper Tigris*', pp.27–34

The Geographical Journal, Vol. 70, No. 1 (1927) '*Gertrude Bell's Journey to Hayil*', pp.17–21

The Indian History Congress Vol. 29, Pt II (1967), '*Lord Curzon's visit to the Persian Gulf "politics of pageantry"*', pp.230–233

The Journal of Arabian Studies, Vol. 8, No. 2 (2018) '*Selective Recognition as an Imperial Instrument: Britain and the Trucial States, 1820–1952*', pp.275–297

The Journal of Asian Studies, Feb 1971, Vol. 30, No. 2 (1971) '*The Problem with Recruitment for the Indian Civil Service During the Late Nineteenth Century*', pp.341–360

The Journal of Historical Association, Vol. 47, No. 159 (1962), '*Splendid Isolation*', pp.32–41

The Journal of Middle Eastern Studies, Vol. 27, No. 1 (2000), '*A Failed Manipulation: The British, the Oudh Bequest and the Shi'i 'Ulama' of Najaf and Karbala*', pp.69–89

The Journal of the British Records Association, Vol. 24, No. 101 (1999) '*On the Baghdad Road: On the Trail of W J Childs; A study in Near East Intelligence and Historical Analysis, c1900-1930*', pp.53–70

The North American Review, Vol. 181, No. 587 (1905) '*Lord Curzon: His Resignation and Record*', pp.568–77

The Royal Geographical Society, Vol. 9, No. 5 (1864–1865), '*Address to The Royal Geographical Society*', pp.195–274

The Royal Geographical Society, Vol. 9, No. 6 (1864–1865) '*A visit to the Wahabee Capital, Central Arabia*', pp.293–296

The school of Oriental and African Studies, University of London, Vol. 28, No. 1 (1965) '*British Policy in Persia, 1892–1903*', pp.4–60

The Seminar for Arabian Studies, Vol. 12 (1982) '*Historiography On "The Gazetteer Of Arabia"*', pp.73–78

Wilson, A.T. '*S.W. 'Persia A Political Officer's Diary 1907–1914*', Oxford University Press, 1941

Wilson, A.T. '*Loyalties: Mesopotamia 1914–1917*', Oxford University Press, 1930

Winstone, H.V.F. '*Gertrude Bell*', Quartet Books, New York 1978
Winstone, H.V.F. '*Gertrude Bell*', Stacey International, 2004 Winstone, H.V.F. '*Leachman, OC Desert*', Quartet Books, 1982

Zeitschrift der Gesullschaft fur Erdkunde zu Berlin (1916) '*Der Krieg und das Studium der Geographie*', pp.158–222

Documents and Other Material Held at the National Archives, British Library London (India Office Records and Private Papers) and National Archives of India

Cabinet Office Folio 727/2

Cabinet Office Folio 727/6

Civil Service of India Open Competition, Regulations, Examination Paper, Table of Marks, And Statistics

Civil Service Regulations Article 291

Department of Revenue and Agriculture, Land Surveys, Proceedings, February 1908, Nos 5–7

Eur F111/359/1 'Persia – especially Seistan'

External Affairs Department, File 50-N/41 1941

Finance Department, Salaries, Establishments, etc-A, Proceedings, September 1907, Nos 142–148

Foreign Department, Deposit-E, Programmes, January 1909, No. 33

Foreign Department, Deposits-G, Programmes January 1910, No. 11

Foreign Department, External-A, Proceedings, October 1907, Nos 6–49

Foreign Department, External-A, Proceedings, May 1908, Nos 93–100

Foreign Department, External-B, Programmes, April 1905, Nos 63–65

Foreign Department, External-B, Programmes, March 1907, Nos 164–167

Foreign Department, External-B, Proceedings, November 1904, Nos 19–21

Foreign Department, External-B, Proceedings, January 1905, Nos 84– 88

Foreign Department, External-B, Proceedings, December 1905, Nos 143–146

Foreign Department, External-B, Proceedings, January 1906, Nos 114– 121

Foreign Department, External-B, Proceedings, November 1913, Nos 36–147

Foreign Department, Frontier-B, October 1900

Foreign Department, General-A, Proceedings, July 1904, Nos 1–14

Foreign Department, General-B, Proceedings, December 1904, Nos 64–73

Foreign Department, General-B, Proceedings, January 1909, Nos 183– 184

Foreign Department, General-B, Proceedings, January 1909, Nos 188– 191

Foreign Department, General-B, Proceedings, July 1911, Nos 28–31

Foreign Department, General-B, Programmes, October 1904, Nos 66– 68

Foreign Department, General-B, Programmes, November 1904, Nos 259–261

Foreign Department, General-B, Programmes, November 1904, Nos 291–292

Foreign Department, General-B, Programmes, December 1904, Nos 155–157

Foreign Department, General-B, Programmes, October 1905, Nos 200-–202

Foreign Department, General-B, Programmes, May 1908, Nos 367–369

Foreign Department, General-B, Programmes, October 1908, No. 56

Foreign Department, Internal-A, Proceedings, January 1904, Nos 30– 31

Foreign Department, Secret-E, Proceedings, May 1903, Nos 64–87

Foreign Department, Secret-E, Proceedings, February 1904, Nos 33– 127

Foreign Department, Secret-E, Proceedings, August 1906, Nos 211–215

Foreign Department, Secret-E, Proceedings, January 1907, Nos 392– 406

Foreign Department, Secret-E, Proceedings, March 1907, Nos 729–738

Foreign Department, Secret-E, Proceedings, September 1907, Nos 334– 361

Foreign Department, Secret-E, Proceedings, October 1907, Nos 195–205

Foreign Department, Secret-E, Proceedings, May 1908, Nos 599–600

Foreign Department, Secret-E, Proceedings, April 1912, Nos 141–161

Foreign Department, Secret-G, Proceedings, October 1912, Nos 18–32

Foreign and Political Department, External, Proceedings, September 1914, Nos 1–204

Foreign and Political Department, General-A, Proceedings, May 1914, Nos 17–25

Foreign and Political Department, General, 1928, File No.401-G/29

Foreign and Political Department, General, 1929, File No.20 (7)-E

Foreign and Political Department, General, 1929, File No.30-E/29

Foreign and Political Department, General, 1929, File No.229

Foreign and Political Department, General, 1930, File No.258-G/30

Foreign and Political Department, General, 1933, File No.218

Foreign Office Confidential Print, Vol. 17

Foreign Office Folio 78/5354

Foreign Office Folio 317/154/29027

Foreign Office Folio 371/148961

Foreign Office Folio 371/104318

Foreign Office Folio 371/120596

Foreign Office Folio 371/120597

Foreign Office Folio 371/132618

Foreign Office Folio 371/132793

Foreign Office Folio 371/140121

Foreign Office Folio 371/1485/2064/26379

Foreign Office Folio 371/1485/42138/42138

Foreign Office Folio 371/148961

Foreign Office Folio 371/98832

Foreign Office Folio 424/226

Foreign Office Folio 800/78

Foreign Office Folio 1016/313

IOR: L/MIL/17/16/3 'Routes in Arabia'

IOR: L/PJ/6/304 Files 1312, 1356, 1418, 1446, 1459

IOR: L/PJ/6/308, File 1874

IOR: L/PJ/6/309, File 1885

IOR: L/PS/3/399

IOR: L/PS/3/1910/2961

IOR: L/PS/3/1910/2962

IOR: L/PS/10/25 'Muscat Arbitration (1904-08)' Pt.1

IOR: L/PS/10/47 File 1855/1904 Pt 1 'Koweit:- H.M. Govt and Political Agentat Koweit. (Representations from Turkish Govt & temporary withdrawal of Agent'

IOR: L/PS/10/62

IOR: L/PS/10/66 File 37/1905 'Aden Frontier Delimitation', Pt.4

IOR: L/PS/10/69 File 339/1905 'Koweit – Political Agency. Expenditure, Steam Launch'

IOR: L/PS/10/77 File 1290/1905 'Mesopotamia: Oudh Bequest'

IOR: L/PS/10/87 File 3131/1905 'Mesopotamia:- Irrigation'

IOR: L/PS/10/112 File 619/1907 Pt3'Arms Traffic:- KoweitTrade'

IOR: L/PS/10/88/2 File 3531/1905 'Euphrates and Tigris Steam Navigation Company to Foreign Office' Pt.2

IOR: L/PS/10/144/2

IOR: L/PS/10/188 File 3846/1910 'Mesopotamia: Baghdad affairs. Miscellaneous'

IOR: L/PS/10/212 File 211/1912 'Turkish Arabia Summaries'

IOR: L/PS/10/259 File 1202/1912 'Arabia:- Travellers. Capt. F.F Hunter. Herr Runkiar (Danish Expedition). Capt Shakespear'

IOR: L/PS/10/385

IOR: L/PS/10/827 'Political Residency monthly report'

IOR: L/PS/12/1404 Pol Ext 7649/49 'Access to Volumes of Lorimer's Gazetteer'

IOR: L/PS/18/B164 'British Relations with the Wahabees'

IOR: L/PS/18/B166 'Memorandum respecting British interests in the Persian Gulf'

IOR: L/PS/20/61 'Report on a Tour in Turkish Arabia and Kurdistan, April–May 1910'

IOR: L/PS/20/199 'A note on survey work in Persia, and survey instruments and equipment'

IOR: L/PS/20/C91/1 '*Gazetteer of the Persian Gulf. Vol I. Historical. Part IA & IB*'

IOR: L/PS/20/C91/2 '*Gazetteer of the Persian Gulf. Vol I. Historical. Part II*'

IOR: L/PS/20/C91/3 '*Enclosure to Part III of Volume I of the Persian Gulf Gazetteer: Geneaological Tables*'

IOR: L/PS/20/C91/4 '*Gazetteer of the Persian Gulf. Vol. II. Geographical and Statistical*'

IOR: L/PS/20/C237 '*Persian Gulf gazetteer. Part 1. Historical and political materials. Précis on arms trade in the Persian Gulf*'

IOR: L/PS/20/C247 '*Précis of correspondence on international rivalry and British policy in the Persian Gulf, 1872–1905*'

IOR: R/1/4/1052, File Con Est. A 1919 Lorimer, J. G. Personal File

IOR: R/15/1/330 File 19/118 (C 7) 'Bahrain'

IOR: R/1/4/1337 Lorimer, D, L, R. Personal File

IOR: R/15/1/476 File 53/7 C (D 6) 'Koweit Affairs, 1903–1904'

IOR: R/15/1/504 File 53/32 III (D 53) 'Kowait – Miscellaneous'

IOR: R/15/1/553 File 59/15 C (A 15) 'Muscat Miscellaneous'

IOR: R/15/1/709 'Persian Gulf Administration Reports 1904/05'

IOR: R/15/1/710 'Administration Reports 1905–1910'

IOR: R/15/1/711 'Administration Report of the Persian Gulf Political Residency for the Years 1911–1914'

IOR: R/15/1/722 'Persian Gulf Gazetteer, Part 1, Historical and Political Materials, Precis of Bahrain Affairs 1854–1904'

IOR: R/15/2/45 File F/1 'Pan-Islamism'

IOR: R/15/2/51 File II/I 'Appointment of Political Agents'

IOR: R/15/2/179 'Cyphers and Secret Documents: Safe Custody Reports and Handing Over Certificates for Secret Documents'

IOR: R/15/5/3 'Establishment. No. I/12 Appointments and Changes in the Political Residents & Agents in the Persian Gulf, and Secretaries, Bushire, & of the Govt. of India. and Others'

IOR: R/15/5/14 File VI/3 I 'Confidential- Maps + Books'

IOR: R/15/5/25 File X/2 'Bin Saood, Koweit [Kuwait] & Ibn Rashid'

IOR: R/15/5/67 File XXII/17 'Boundary between Koweit & Katif Territory'

IOR: R/15/6/29 File XXIII/5 'Travels in Oman. Intending Travellers'

IOR: R/15/6/126 File 3/8 'Books etc: Transliteration of vernacular names and places'

IOR: R/20/G/182 'Notes on the map of Arabia and the Persian Gulf', Superintendent Government Printing, Calcutta

Military Department, Arms-A, Proceedings, March 1901, Nos 1835–1843

Military Department, Disturbances-B, Proceedings, April 1900, Nos 1294–1295 'Arrangements under which the Khyber Pass is being held and enquiry as to the responsibility of the Lieutenant-General Commanding the Forces, Punjab in the event of an uprising'

Military Department, Disturbances-B, Proceedings, March 1900, Nos 1208–1211 'Proposed Establishment of New Posts on the Afridi Border near Peshawar to be garrisoned by the Khyber Rifles. Instructions as to the conduct of Political Business in the Khyber'

Military Department, Notes No.180 'Future garrison and management of the section of the frontier between Kohat and the Gomal Valley – Report of the Committee assembled to report on the organisation of the tribal militia in Waziristan'

Military Department, Proceedings, August 1902 No. 972, 'Despatches Regarding the Mahsud Blockade operations'

Mss Eur D922/1 'An account of a journey in Kashmir 1898–99'

Mss Eur F111/358 'Notes Prepared for Reference during Curzon's Tour of the Persian Gulf, and Other Papers on Persia and the Persian Gulf'

Mss Eur F111/531 'Persia And The Persian Gulf' volume IV

Mss Eur F112/450 'Memoranda Regarding Other External Affairs 1905', Volume IIp

WO 106/42 File C3/10 'Memorandum on military policy in the event of war with Turkey'

WO 106/43 File C3/21

Gazetteer Index

All entries follow the format used in Volume II.

* identifies entries not uniquely referenced in Volume II.

The index is not exhaustive. The reader is also encouraged to consult pages v - cxxx of either Volume I Historical pt 1a or pt.2 Historical's Table of Chapters, Annexures, Appendices and Genealogical Trees

Index

Page numbers in **bold** refer to maps.